PERFORMANCE TESTING
MICROSOFT®
.NET
WEB APPLICATIONS

Microsoft®
.net™

Microsoft Application Consulting
and Engineering (ACE) Team

PUBLISHED BY
Microsoft Press
A Division of Microsoft Corporation
One Microsoft Way
Redmond, Washington 98052-6399

Library of Congress Cataloging-in-Publication Data
Performance Testing Microsoft .NET Web applications / Microsoft ACE Team.
    p. cm.
  Includes index.
  ISBN 0-7356-1538-1
   1. Application software--Testing. 2. Microsoft .NET. 3. Web site development. I.
Microsoft ACE Team.

  QA76.76.T48 P457   2002
  005.2'76--dc21   2002026545

Printed and bound in the United States of America.

1 2 3 4 5 6 7 8 9   QWT   7 6 5 4 3 2

Distributed in Canada by H.B. Fenn and Company Ltd.

A CIP catalogue record for this book is available from the British Library.

Microsoft Press books are available through booksellers and distributors worldwide. For further information about international editions, contact your local Microsoft Corporation office or contact Microsoft Press International directly at fax (425) 936-7329. Visit our Web site at www.microsoft.com/mspress. Send comments to *mspinput@microsoft.com*.

Acquisitions Editor: Juliana Aldous
Project Editor: Lynn Finnel

Body Part No. X08-73309

*To the team spirit at Microsoft, which gave the ACE Team
the opportunity to develop and write this book.*

Contents at a Glance

Table of Contents

Acknowledgements

The Microsoft Application and Consulting Engineering (ACE) Team would like to acknowledge a number of people for their help and support throughout this project. First, we want to thank our managers, Mike Adams and Tracy Shell, for trusting us to get our regular work done while we were writing this book. Next, a number of technical editors ensured the accuracy of the material presented in the book. Starting with Chapter 3, we want to thank Matt Odhner for reviewing and offering insightful feedback on the ACT material. Chapter 5 was tech-edited by Jim Pierson. Thanks go out to Fabio Yeon and Mitica Manu for tech-editing Chapter 6. We express our gratitude to Eric Rachner, Chad Dellinger, and Mitica Manu for their contributions to Chapter 7. Julius Chen and Ken Henderson reviewed Chapter 8, while Chapter 9 was reviewed by one of the patent holders of the Transaction Cost Analysis (TCA), David Guimbellot. Others involved with Chapter 9 include Perry Clarke, also a patent holder for TCA, and Chris Lawson, a fine intern who was kind enough to run the TCA verification tests. In addition, we express our gratitude to the MSN Enterprise Tools team, specifically to Jonathan Hardwick and Stathis Papaefstathiou, who contributed a great deal of time and energy to Chapter 10. We also want to acknowledge Robert Dillingham, program manager on the ACE Team, for his help with the editing process. In addition, we thank Juliana Aldous and Lynn Finnel of Microsoft Press for their patience through the writing process. Lastly, we are very grateful to Mahesh Prakriya of the .NET Framework team for helping steer the book in the right direction.

Introduction

This book was written by members of the Microsoft Application Consulting and Engineering (ACE) Team, which provides performance analysis services for some of the most heavily utilized Web applications and sites at Microsoft. Our responsibilities include, but are not limited to, providing throughput or response time numbers, identifying bottlenecks, and optimizing and tuning Web applications in an enterprise environment to achieve required application performance.

Our mission is to drive performance improvements into Microsoft's production Web applications. We do this by providing performance analysis leadership and world-class tuning services. This book outlines and details our experiences and the methodology we've developed while working in the dynamic and challenging environment of Microsoft's corporate intranet and extranet infrastructure.

Who This Book is For

Because Web performance analysis is a relatively new field (compared to software development and its traditional developer, test, and IT roles) it's difficult to name a specific group of professionals for whom this book is intended, except to say that anyone who needs to ensure that a Web application running on Microsoft technologies can perform adequately will find this book valuable. For test teams, this book offers a full spectrum of "how to" techniques to analyze applications for performance. For managers who are responsible for Web application performance planning, this book offers help with how to include performance analysis in the development life cycle, estimate hardware capacity needs, and budget for future infrastructure needs.

About the Companion CD-ROM

The CD-ROM included with this book contains the following items:

■ An AutoRun menu for linking to the resources on the CD

■ Sample files for the book

■ Information on ASP Timers

■ System Monitor templates

■ A setup program to install the sample files

■ A Microsoft PowerPoint presentation of Compuware's Application Expert

■ An electronic version of the book (eBook)

Using the Companion CD-ROM

The StartCD program provides a graphical interface to the content on the CD-ROM. If you have AutoRun enabled, this program will open by default when you insert the CD into your CD-ROM drive. To use the companion CD, insert it into your CD-ROM drive. If AutoRun is not enabled on your computer, run StartCD.exe in the root of the CD to display the Start menu. The menu provides access to all the resources on the CD, including links for installing the software you will need to view the files contained on the CD and to access the Microsoft Press product support Web site.

Sample Files

ACT test scripts for the test runs discussed in the book are included on the CD-ROM in the Sample Files folder. To copy all the sample files to your hard disk, run Setup.exe in the Setup folder and follow the instructions that appear on the screen. The samples require about 5 MB of hard disk space. To uninstall the sample files, open the Control Panel, choose Add or Remove Programs, and make the appropriate selection.

ASP Timers

A Microsoft Word document that describes how to create an ASP Timer using Microsoft Visual Basic Scripting Edition (VBScript) or JScript can be found in the Chapter05 folder on the CD-ROM.

System Monitor Templates

System Monitor templates with pre-defined performance counters are also included on this CD-ROM. These templates allow you to easily start monitoring the performance of your Internet Information Services (IIS) or SQL server. The templates can be found in the Chapter04 folder.

PowerPoint Presentation: Compuware Application Expert

Compuware's Application Expert is covered in Chapter 5 of the book. The PowerPoint presentation included in the Chapter05 folder on the CD-ROM illustrates some of the common features of Application Expert.

EBook

The complete text of the printed book is contained on the CD-ROM in a fully searchable electronic version. To install the eBook, run Autorun.exe in the eBook folder. Microsoft Internet Explorer 5.01 or later and the proper HTML Help components are required to view the eBook. If your computer does not have Internet Explorer 5.01 or later, the setup program will offer to install Internet Explorer 5.5 for you. The setup program has been configured to install the minimum files necessary to view the eBook, and it will not change your current settings or associations. If your computer runs on Microsoft Windows NT 4.0, Microsoft Windows 2000, or Microsoft Windows XP, you will need administrative privileges to install the eBook. If you do not have administrative privileges and your system has Internet Explorer 5.01 or later, you can view the eBook by opening the perftest.CHM file in the \eBook\Is_001 folder.

CD-ROM Requirements

- Microsoft Windows XP or Windows 2000

- Microsoft Visual Studio .NET, Enterprise Developer or Enterprise Architect Editions

   The following are the requirements to run Visual Studio .NET

- **Computer/Processor**   PC with a Pentium II-class processor, 450 MHz

- **Memory**   96 MB for Windows 2000 Professional; 160 MB for Windows XP Professional

- **Hard Disk**   2.5 GB of hard disk space including a minimum of 500 MB on the system drive

- **Drive**   CD-ROM or DVD-ROM

- **Display**   Super VGA (800 x 600) or higher resolution monitor with 256 colors

- **Operating System**   Windows 2000 or Windows XP

- **Peripherals**   Microsoft Mouse or compatible pointing device

Chapter Overviews

The book is divided into four parts to address the differing phases of the performance testing process, as shown in the following table.

Table I-1   Phases of Performance Testing

For this content	See these chapters
Planning	1, 2
Execution	3, 4
Analysis	5, 6, 7, 8
Modeling	9, 10

Following is a brief overview of each chapter. For those of you in a hurry to skip some chapters, we give you an idea of the concepts covered in each.

Chapter 1: Laying the Performance Analysis Ground Work   Chapter 1 details where performance testing resides in the software development life cycle and why performance testing is as important as functional testing of the application. It describes how the results from a performance test provide a more realistic application deployment scenario and a substantial cost savings for the project. Additionally, it provides a background of the performance testing methodology used in the book.

Chapter 2: Preparing and Planning for the Performance Test Before executing the performance test, you must compile specific information regarding the application being tested. Chapter 2 provides an overview of the information the tester is expected to gather and the sources where they can find this data. Sources include marketing forecasts, production IIS logs, performance logs, and functional specifications for the application.

Chapter 3: Stress Testing with Microsoft Application Center Test (ACT) Because the book discusses Web applications built solely using Microsoft software and technologies, the application stress tool discussed in the book is Microsoft Application Center Test (ACT). ACT is relatively new. Chapter 3 takes a detailed look at the tool, focusing on how to create test scripts using ACT and explaining the intricacies of scripting Web applications.

Chapter 4: Monitoring Application Performance with System Monitor The primary tool that you'll use when conducting Web application performance analysis is System Monitor. Chapter 4 introduces System Monitor and explains some of the most commonly used performance counters and how to use them when tracking down processor, disk, and memory bottlenecks.

Chapter 5: Application Network Analysis Chapter 5 provides an overview network performance analysis, which is targeted at identifying pages or functions that are taking the most time to load within an application. ACE provides tips on identifying slow pages or functions by capturing all traffic within your application using Network Monitor and then analyzing the captured data to extrapolate end user response times, bytes transferred, and network round trips.

Chapter 6: Analyzing and Performance Tuning the Web Tier Data collected at the IIS tier can reveal bottlenecks within the ASP.NET code, middle tier or SQL tier. The reader is instructed to interpret the IIS logs and performance monitor logs to find these bottlenecks. Recommendations are included in Chapter 6 on how to address bottlenecks at the IIS tier.

Chapter 7: Profiling Managed Code It is essential to understand how to analyze and profile managed code to successfully performance test Microsoft .NET Web applications. Chapter 7 details features of the .NET Framework that directly effect performance of your .NET Web application. This chapter also provides an overview of key .NET performance counters and two useful applications that can be used when profiling managed code performance.

Chapter 8: Analyzing the SQL Tier   Bottlenecks at the SQL tier can reduce the performance of Web-based applications by thousands of percent. Bottlenecks at the back end can also be extremely difficult to pinpoint and correct. It takes a high level of SQL expertise to correctly diagnose and correct problems at the Microsoft SQL server level. Chapter 8 shows the reader some of the more basic methods to profile SQL server activity, detect the bottleneck, and then correct the problem by optimizing SQL Server code and modifying the database architecture.

Chapter 9: Estimating IIS Tier Capacity with Transaction Cost Analysis   Chapter 9 explains in depth Microsoft's methodology for calculating the Transaction Cost Analysis (TCA) of a Web-based application. TCA numbers are used to measure a Web site's capacity to host users; they can also be a means to measure performance improvements made to the application.

Chapter 10: Performance Modeling: Tools for Predicting Performance   One goal of performance modeling is to be truly proactive in performance engineering— to examine a proposed system in its entirety, from hardware and network resources to code optimization, before completely building any one component. In Chapter 10, ACE covers scenarios in which performance modeling can replace other methods of performance assessment and engineering, different methods of modeling and when they are appropriate for use, a brief look at currently available performance modeling tools and a detailed look at the toolkit approach, represented by Microsoft's Indy project.

Support

Every effort has been made to ensure the accuracy of this book and the contents of the companion CD-ROM. Microsoft Press provides corrections for books through the World Wide Web at the following address:

http://www.microsoft.com/mspress/support/

To connect directly to the Microsoft Press Knowledge Base and enter a query regarding a question or issue that you may have, go to:

http://www.microsoft.com/mspress/support/search.asp

If you have comments, questions, or ideas regarding this book or the companion CD-ROM, please send them to Microsoft Press using either of the following methods:

Postal Mail:

Microsoft Press

Attn: *Performance Testing Microsoft .NET Web Applications* Editor

One Microsoft Way

Redmond, WA 98052-6399

E-mail:

MSPINPUT@MICROSOFT.COM

Please note that product support is not offered through the above mail addresses. For support information, please visit the Microsoft Product Support Web site at

http://support.microsoft.com

1

Laying the Performance Analysis Groundwork

Now that Microsoft's .NET strategy has made it possible for us to connect information, devices, and people in a unified way, Web-enabling traditional desktop applications are no longer an option but a requirement. Customers will expect to have access to their office productivity applications from any Web-capable device, be it the browser on their desktop, a Personal Digital Assistant (PDA) device, or a Wireless Application Protocol (WAP) enabled phone. This drive to bring applications to the Internet will push development teams and the software they build to their limits. The Web-enabled application will have to perform as well and be as reliable and extensible as its desktop counterpart. This paradigm shift away from stand-alone desktop applications will focus increased attention on performance testing and tuning throughout the application development life cycle as many more variables that could affect application performance are introduced.

Why Is Performance Testing and Tuning Important?

When designing an application that will be accessed over the Internet, development teams must keep in mind that hundreds of thousands of users could concurrently access the application. This concurrent user load could place tremendous stress upon a system, cause unexpected delays, and result in a poor user experience. However, if the application has been adequately tested and tuned for optimal performance under stress, managers and software developers will be confident that their code will perform at optimal levels and have the necessary data to plan site capacity needs. The following real world example demonstrates what can happen when adequate performance testing has not occurred.

Real World Example—Site Traffic Spikes

On September 11, 2001, news events of attacks on the World Trade Center and the Pentagon caused site traffic at a Microsoft Web news site to increase by threefold compared to pre-September 11 levels. In the days following the attack, the increased level of traffic persisted as the public demand for news persisted. This caused the page response times on this particular site to degrade to unacceptable levels, and the Web servers required rebooting every couple of hours as available memory became critically low. It was subsequently determined that there was an existing memory leak associated with this site, which was exacerbated by the sudden increase in traffic. The methodology presented in this book is designed to proactively test and subsequently prevent unacceptable Web site performance degradations, even in the face of unexpectedly large traffic spikes, which can be caused by extraordinary events such as those on September 11, 2001.

This example should lead to the question, "How does one approach the task of accurately performance testing and tuning a Web application?" Unfortunately, there isn't one correct answer to this question. Methodologies aimed at performance testing and tuning Web applications are constantly evolving, and new tools for obtaining a more accurate result set are quickly becoming available. In the case of a simple Web site, a set of static stress scripts might do the job; whereas, in the case of a complex e-commerce site, performance modeling tools and dynamic stress scripts would be required to better predict how the application would react under a particular user load. Because acceptable Web site performance is application dependent and Web site architecture can vary widely from site to site, Web site performance analysis can be viewed as more an art than a science. The goal of effective performance testing, however, is to ensure that the site will perform within acceptable performance levels, whatever those levels need to be.

Effects of Current and Emerging Architecture Technologies

While the focus of this book will be on performance testing applications built with the Microsoft .NET Framework, the methodology presented also offers a backward compatible approach for Windows Distributed interNet applications Architecture (DNA). Given that .NET will still be relatively early in the market adoption cycle by the time this book goes to print, many Microsoft customers will still be running traditional ASP-based Web applications. Therefore, we present the performance analysis methodology that can be effectively utilized by Microsoft customers running both .NET Web services as well as Windows DNA Web applications. Where appropriate, we have included specific "how to" methodology for Windows DNA applications. The methodology laid out in this book focuses on identifying performance metrics that are business critical, such as response times, throughput, and scalability. As illustrated below, setting performance goals in the planning phase drives critical performance testing breakpoints.

Real World Example—Site Performance Goals

For Microsoft's e-commerce Internet sites, we define maximum throughput for given user scenarios such as browsing products, adding products to a shopping basket, and checking out. We test the throughput for these scenarios both separately and while running in what is called a "mixed test." The former defines the maximum scalability for each scenario individually with nothing else running on the servers. The latter (a mixed test) more closely simulates what actually occurs on the live site with various percentages of activity associated with a number of transaction types. Defining the maximum throughput of Microsoft's e-commerce sites directly depends on what the minimum performance goals are. For example, all pages must load within 10 seconds, average CPU utilization on servers must be less than 70 percent, and available memory must remain stable throughout the period of the test, all while the site is maintaining 10 customer checkouts per second. When page response times degrade to 11 seconds at higher throughput rates, the site is considered to be performing unacceptably. At this point, it is time to figure out what is causing and contributing to the unacceptable response time. In this manner, performance goals set in the planning phase drive break points during the performance-testing phase.

When performance planning is completed, our methodology focus shifts to utilizing software load simulation tools for pushing Web applications to their performance breakpoints. The goal during the testing phase is to define the real-world performance limits for the Web application. Finally, the focus shifts to the methods of drilling down into each application layer through effective analysis techniques with the goal of identifying the bottlenecks and formulating performance-enhancing solutions.

What Is .NET?

As the purpose of this book is to explain how to performance test a .NET application, and many of the application samples used throughout this book were built using the .NET Framework, it is necessary to first understand what .NET is. In fact, experience has shown us that effective performance testing is difficult, if not impossible, without an in-depth understanding of the underlying technologies involved. The material presented here serves only as an introduction to Microsoft's .NET initiative. For a more detailed perspective of the .NET initiative please visit *http://www.microsoft.com/net*.

The .NET Platform

What is .NET? Or alternatively, what are the services that make up the .NET platform? The .NET platform is a set of developmental tools and operational systems used to build, expose, and consume XML Web services thereby enabling a personal, integrated Web delivered through smart devices while using open standards. The main .NET platform components are as follows:

- The .NET Framework is an environment for building, deploying, and running XML Web services and other applications. The .NET Framework has two parts: the common language runtime (CLR) and the class libraries, which include ASP.NET, Enterprise Services, ADO.NET, and Windows Forms.

- Visual Studio .NET provides a complete development environment for building on the Microsoft .NET platform.

- The Mobile Internet Toolkit is a set of programming interfaces that enable developers to target mobile devices like smart phones, PDAs, and server infrastructure.

- The .NET Enterprise Servers include Application Center 2000, BizTalk Server 2000, Commerce Server 2000, Exchange Server 2000,

Internet Security and Acceleration Server, Host Integration Server 2000, Mobile Information 2001 Server, and SQL Server 2000.

■   .NET services is the set of core XML Web services that will be supplied by Microsoft. However, XML Web services can be built by anyone.

Figure 1-1 illustrates how the core components of the .NET platform fit together to provide user experiences anywhere and on any device. Developers can use the .NET Framework to build XML Web services. The CLR is important because it is the engine at the core of managed code execution. With the runtime engine, developers creating Web services can integrate and execute their code in different languages. Web services that are created with the .NET Framework run on the .NET Enterprise servers and can be accessed anytime, anywhere, and on any device.

.NET Framework					
VB	C++	C#	Perl	Python	...
Web forms		Web services		Win Forms	
Mobile Internet Toolkit					
ASP.NET					
Class libraries (ADO.NET, ...)					
Base class libraries					
common language runtime					

.NET Enterprise Servers
Sql Server · SharePoint Portal Server · Mobile Information Server · ISA Server · Host Integration Server · Exchange Server · Content Management Server · Commerce Server · BizTalk Server · Application Center
Windows 2000 (Server, Advanced Server, Datacenter Server)

Experiences and solutions anywhere on any device			
mobile phone	PDA	PC	...

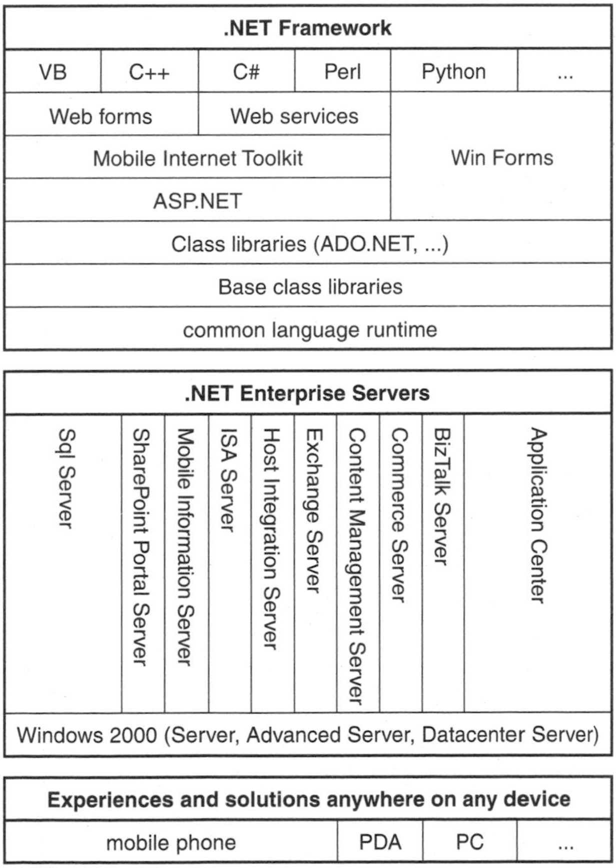

Figure 1-1   Core components of the .NET platform

Real World Example—.Net Cross Company Calendaring Service

Let's say you are flying home and need to schedule a meeting with vendors the next morning. Traditionally, because your vendors are not on your company calendar system, you cannot see their schedules to deliver a meeting request. In addition, the only way you can efficiently connect to the Internet during this flight is through a cell phone or wireless PDA. However, if both companies had calendaring systems built using XML Web services and the programming interfaces included with the Mobile Internet Toolkit, not only would you be able to view your suppliers' calendar, you would be able to send the meeting request using a wireless PDA or phone utilizing the various programming interfaces for mobile devices. .NET makes this possible because the two calendaring systems are now compatible (that is, they integrate through various programming interfaces), and XML calendaring Web services allow you to schedule the meeting using any device. Features like this exist today on many Web sites, but each site has its own solution, and these solutions do not always allow sharing information among sites.

Standard .NET Protocols

The fact that .NET is built on open Internet-based standards makes the .NET Framework extensible and enables it to easily communicate with other Web and non-Web-based solutions. The predominant standards that .NET employs to make Web services possible are:

- Extensible Markup Language (XML)
- Simple Object Access Protocol (SOAP)
- Hypertext Transfer Protocol (HTTP)

XML, a text-based language much like the ubiquitous HTML, is a specification that allows for custom HTML-like tags that describe both the document (metadata) and the content (data). The .NET vision needs XML because of the inherent problems with HTML. There are conflicting standards with HTML, which cause different browsers to handle standard tags in different ways. This means that Web designers need to create different versions of the same HTML document for different browsers. To date, efforts to create international HTML standards have not materialized. In addition, HTML has an inadequate linking system. HTML links are hard coded into documents and must be searched and changed for each link that changes. XML allows you to associate links to any element and to link to multiple locations, effectively solving these HTML limitations.

Web Service Description Language (WSDL)

.NET also employs a newer XML standard formerly known as the Service Description Language (SDL), and now known as Web Services Description Language (WSDL). As the name implies, WSDL is a language designed for describing a Web service. It is used to create or generate a .wsdl file that other services can use to determine the exposed functionality a Web service offers. Simple Object Access Protocol (SOAP) is used as the basic wire format for communicating between objects and solutions. Very much like Remote Procedure Calls (RPC) in functionality, SOAP uses XML to describe its contents. XML makes it simple, humanly interpretable, open, and extensible.

Universal Description, Discovery, and Integration (UDDI)

.NET also takes advantage of the new Universal Description, Discovery, and Integration (UDDI) specification that is aimed at creating Web service registries. These registries will enable companies to register information about their Web service solutions, as well as other data, so that those who wish to use them can easily find them. Internet Native Integration Methodology (INIM) allows for XML interaction between systems and an open set of standards. INIM works with any operating system, programming model, or network and can expose existing code as XML Web services, giving different systems the ability to communicate. UDDI specifications define a standard to publish and discover information about Web services.

What Is an XML Web Service?

Today's Internet services are mostly portals that offer services that cannot be used anywhere else. One inconvenient result of this service is that companies cannot easily share information. For example, even contact and other personal information has to be entered for each site. XML Web services are units of application logic providing data and services to other applications and users. An example of a Web service is the authentication functionality provided by Microsoft .NET Passport service. Applications access XML Web services via standard Web protocols and data formats (i.e. HTTP, XML, and SOAP) independent of how each XML Web service is implemented. XML Web services combine the benefits of component-based development and the Web, and are a cornerstone of the Microsoft .NET programming model. XML Web services transform read-only Web sites into computing sites that can both expose methods and read other XML Web services. The use of XML allows for the sharing of data between any operating system and network via XML and SOAP services which act to connect formerly incompatible or disparate systems (i.e. accessing an application running on a Macintosh, a Unix, or a Linux via a Windows CE device).

Web Services are software solutions delivered via the Internet to *any* Web-enabled device. Today, this device is the Web browser on your computers, but the device-agnostic design of .NET will eliminate this limitation. XML is an industry standard, and XML support is currently offered in all Microsoft products, including the latest generation of servers. The .NET Framework is built into all the .NET products such as Microsoft Visual Basic .NET, Microsoft Visual C++, and Microsoft Visual C#.

Real World Example—Microsoft .NET Passport

Some potential Web services that can be created with the .NET platform include yellow pages, a dictionary, or an encyclopedia. An example of a Web service is Microsoft .NET Passport. Passport is one of the ten largest Web sites in the world with more than 160 million active accounts, and it is increasing at a rate of more than 10 million accounts per month. Though .NET Passport receives more than 1.5 billion authentications each month, the Web site itself seldom receives visitors because it is an XML Web service.

Devices Drive Demand for Web Services

Web-enabled devices are driving the need for services provided by the .NET platform. There is a plethora of new devices available today. These devices are mobile, small, and smart, and all require different interconnectivity depending on the desires of their users. Meanwhile, businesses want information from a multitude of sources, and they want it immediately. Applications that supply information any time and from any location need to run across multiple client platforms with widely diverse capabilities. The following example illustrates what is possible with the .NET XML-centric programming model.

Real World Example—Pre-Heat Your Jacuzzi

Imagine that you are returning home on a long flight, and you want the water in your Jacuzzi to be hot when you get home. With .NET Web services, this futuristic scenario could happen automatically, provided that your Jacuzzi has a thermostat that uses XML Web services. Through pre-programmed algorithms, the XML Web services component could check your flight arrival time and your travel time from the airport based on existing traffic conditions to calculate heating time for the Jacuzzi to pre-set temperatures based on all the timing variables. With .NET this scenario is possible because your home network can potentially read the airlines' current flight arrival information in real time made compatible through XML. A refrigerator already exists that has a built-in smart device component, which includes a bar code reader. This smart device can keep the refrigerator stocked by automatically ordering grocery items at intervals, which are set by the user. Traditional platforms and development environments with "bolted-on" solutions cannot keep pace with this type of phenomenon.

Web Services Will Increase Importance of Web Performance Testing

This paradigm shift in the way information is delivered to devices will require new ways to test and tune applications for performance. Just as traditional platforms cannot keep pace with this shift in technology, traditional functional testing methodologies cannot adequately define application performance and identify bottlenecks associated with these new .NET applications. A new way of approaching the traditional software development life cycle, which includes effective performance testing throughout, is required for the .NET world. Presenting these new requirements is the driving force behind this book.

Performance Goals

Given this general understanding of Web services based on .NET, what becomes obvious is that the expeditious delivery of these services to devices any time and anywhere is critical. There are many aspects to performance but the most important from the ACE team perspective is increasing performance by reducing end user response time bottlenecks. Optimizing user response times is our top goal because the response time is the only performance metric to which the users are directly exposed. Scalability and availability are important inputs to optimal response times and these will be discussed in detail. Just because the user does not "see" them, does not diminish their importance. Without adequate scalability and availability, the application response times will obviously suffer. Ultimately though, application responsiveness is the critical component that will determine success or failure with the customer in the performance game.

Computer Interaction Behavioral Patterns

Despite the relatively recent rise in Internet usage during the last decade, computer interaction response time studies have been around since the advent of the computer. Research indicates that users interact with a computer to perform a task. According to an article titled *"Response Time In Man-Computer Conversational Transactions,"* written in 1968 by R.B. Miller for the AFIPS Fall Joint Computer Conference, Vol. 33, 267-277, the computer user will react to response time performance in predictable behavioral patterns similar to those listed here:

■ **0.1 second** is the limit for having the user feel that the system is reacting instantaneously, meaning that no special feedback is necessary except to display the result.

■ **1.0 second** is the limit for the user's flow of thought to stay uninterrupted, even though the user will notice the delay. Normally, no special feedback is necessary during delays of more than 0.1 but less than 1.0 second, but the user does lose the feeling of operating directly on the data.

■ **10 seconds** is the limit for keeping user attention focused on the screen dialogue. For longer delays, users will want to perform other tasks while waiting for the computer to finish, so they should be given feedback indicating when the computer is likely to be done. Feedback during the delay is especially important if the response time is likely to be highly variable, since users will then not know what to expect.

When measuring response times, it might become apparent that the root cause for the high response times could be beyond your control, making it impossible to attain one-tenth of a second times. For example, there really is not a lot that can be done about Internet congestion or a slow client dial-up connection. Nevertheless, it is still necessary to understand the root cause of the high response times, to make an impact wherever possible. The goal of this book is to lay out a reliable methodology for identifying this cause, otherwise known as the bottleneck, and subsequently addressing that bottleneck in such a manner that it results in improved application performance. This book will hopefully serve as proof that proper performance testing and tuning methodologies integrated into the software development life cycle can result in sub-second response times for the resultant .NET application.

Performance Testing Your Application

With an increased movement toward the use of Web services driving an ever-increasing amount of traffic, the key challenge that emerges is one of ensuring optimal application performance. This book will offer the solutions to meet this challenge by presenting an in-depth approach for determining the following key performance-related factors:

- Calculating maximum scalability

- Quantifying average client response times under load

- Identifying bottlenecks that prevent performance gains

- Addressing these bottlenecks to tune for optimum performance

Additionally, this book will present alternative approaches for estimating Web application capacity with a methodology developed by Microsoft. This methodology has been dubbed Transaction Cost Analysis (TCA). The TCA methodology assists with estimating capacity planning needs for Web applications by associating server resource costs such as CPU to typical user operational costs. In this manner, one can estimate and prepare for site capacity needs prior to large traffic spikes that can occur as a direct result of large marketing or news events.

At the 10,000-foot level, the performance testing life cycle presented in this book consist of:

- Planning Performance Analysis

- Creating Effective Stress Scripts

- Executing Stress Tests

- Analyzing performance data to identify and address performance bottlenecks

Each of these steps will be discussed in the chapters that follow. To reiterate, performance analysis requires an extremely in-depth approach, coupled with experience and knowledge regarding the technologies utilized.

Figure 1-2 shows the performance analysis methodology this book will discuss.

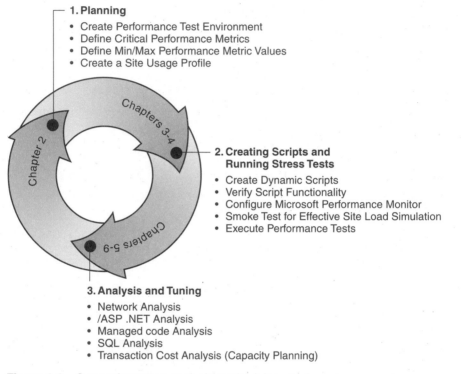

1. Planning
- Create Performance Test Environment
- Define Critical Performance Metrics
- Define Min/Max Performance Metric Values
- Create a Site Usage Profile

Chapter 2

Chapters 3-4

Chapters 5-9

2. Creating Scripts and Running Stress Tests
- Create Dynamic Scripts
- Verify Script Functionality
- Configure Microsoft Performance Monitor
- Smoke Test for Effective Site Load Simulation
- Execute Performance Tests

3. Analysis and Tuning
- Network Analysis
- /ASP .NET Analysis
- Managed code Analysis
- SQL Analysis
- Transaction Cost Analysis (Capacity Planning)

Figure 1-2   Our performance analysis methodology cycle

Planning Performance Analysis

This step involves gathering key preliminary information that will structure and focus the testing approach. Data collected in the planning phase should, at a minimum, provide two things: 1) the details necessary to duplicate the production application environment as closely as possible, and 2) an understanding of how the application is used, including indicators of critical performance issues. Useful performance information sources can include marketing forecasts, production IIS logs, production performance logs, and functional specifications for the application. The quality of the performance data collected in advance of the actual performance testing is critical. It will help determine the requirements for the test environment and will be used in all phases of the analysis from staging the environment to deciphering performance test results. We present a detailed approach to planning in Chapter 2.

Creating Effective Stress Scripts

After gathering the required information and preparing your test environment, the next step is to create stress scripts that accurately simulate the expected production traffic. This is most effectively accomplished using historical data from the production site that is combined with expected data from the marketing or business analysts. Creating bulletproof stress scripts using Microsoft's Application Center Test (ACT) tool will be detailed in Chapter 3.

Executing Stress Tests

After bulletproof scripts have been created to simulate peak client load, stress testing begins. At this point, it is critical to have verified script functionality to ensure the scripts simulate production site traffic as closely as possible as the quality of the stress test is directly tied to the quality of the scripts. In addition, using a methodology dubbed "smoke testing," the optimal load should be identified prior to running the actual stress tests, which generate the performance data that will aid in pinpointing the bottlenecks. Details for executing stress tests, including key focal elements while smoke testing, are presented in Chapter 3.

Analyzing Performance Results

After the stress tests have been run and data generated, the analysis phase begins. The first concern is to verify that the stress test ran through the simulation successfully because the quality of the data is only as good as the quality of the test. The analysis phase is the most technically in-depth step in effective performance analysis methodology, so starting with high quality data is critical to deriving high quality results and conclusions. The majority of time budgeted for performance analysis should be concentrated in this phase. It is for this reason that three chapters of this book are dedicated to analysis concepts. Chapter 6 offers an in-depth approach to analyzing the Web tier. Chapter 7 offers an in-depth approach to profiling managed code. And finally, Chapter 8 offers an in-depth approach to identifying bottlenecks on the data or SQL tier. Experience has shown that the SQL tier can be a common place for bottlenecks if the code at this tier is not designed and tuned properly. Bottlenecks on the SQL tier are pivotal because it is more difficult to scale out databases through clustering versus the available options for scaling out the Web tier. Of course, there are entire books written on these technologies alone. The testing methodology in this book will focus on efficiently identifying performance bottlenecks and strategically offering tuning approaches aimed at achieving better performance.

Identifying Performance Bottlenecks

Bottlenecks that can affect end user response times include application and server throughput, end-to-end Internet connection speed, and Internet congestion. Server throughput (the rate at which the server can process client requests) should not be a problem given that high performance hardware is a readily available commodity that is relatively inexpensive when compared with site development costs. Like server hardware, network bandwidth is a readily available commodity, and with adequate network saturation monitoring, network capacity can easily be purchased prior to growth in traffic. In the same sense, the user connection to the Internet is a commodity; however, average connection speeds remain very low for the majority of the user community and will stay that way until prices for broadband connections become more affordable.

Despite the fact that bandwidth, servers and Internet connectivity are commodities, it only makes good business sense to apply these commodities efficiently and effectively after improving application code performance not as a prelude to or substitute for performance testing and tuning. Only after the application has been fully tuned to utilize these existing commodity resources in the most optimal fashion, does it make sense to invest more money in hardware and bandwidth.

Given the criteria of optimizing prior to expanding resource usage, where in the application can the greatest performance gains be achieved using proper performance testing and tuning techniques? The greatest impact is derived from improving the performance of the application code itself. Why? The initial costs of the development team, managers, and testers are significant enough to mandate the most efficient usage of this resource time. Creating optimal, efficient code is most effectively achieved through budgeting time and resources for performance testing and tuning during the traditional development life cycle rather than upgrading hardware and software after release to react to production problems. Building the code correctly the first time can save hard dollars in support costs and soft dollars in user acceptance given an unexpected spike in traffic. In the .NET world, the focus centers on the ability of an application to quickly process a client request and return the results while simultaneously processing millions of other requests. Here is the key area where attention to adequate application performance can make the most impact on end-user response times, regardless of the hardware platform and available bandwidth. With adequate performance testing techniques, application throughput can be accurately predicted allowing site administrators to prepare for the worst-case scenarios.

Verifying Performance Tuning Results

The final step to a performance/stress analysis is to clearly communicate your stress results to the application stakeholders. This should be done in a manner that effectively enables them to understand and improve performance based on the information presented in the analysis. Proof-of-concept testing (re-running the stress tests after analysis and tuning and comparing the performance results side by side) is the most effective way to communicate performance improvement results. It is not sufficient to speculate that your tuning efforts have improved performance; it has to be objectively and conclusively proven! Have response times decreased, and scalability increased? Have server resources required to serve the same level of client requests decreased significantly? These are the questions that a thorough performance analysis will address.

Conclusion

Now that you understand the groundwork for .NET and our analysis methodology, we will present an in depth approach to performance analysis planning in Chapter 2. We will detail how to analyze site traffic in order to characterize the site average and peak loads. This will offer the foundation for setting reasonable and attainable performance targets in the analysis phase.

2

Preparing and Planning for the Performance Test

Often Web applications fail to meet their customers' needs and expectations. When a Web application generates errors, has poor response times, or is unavailable, customers can easily become frustrated. If your performance test procedure or methodology is not well thought out and properly planned, the odds of a successful Web application launch are significantly reduced. This chapter identifies the key processes and planning required before you execute a single performance test. By following these steps you will enhance your odds of executing an effective Web application performance test. These steps include identifying performance goals, creating a user activity profile, and defining the key metrics to monitor and analyze when creating a performance test plan.

> **Note** We have found that many performance test projects fail because testing begins too late in the Web application development cycle or have requirements that are too complex to complete in the allotted time. Focus on the key elements of your Web application and on user scenarios that will occur most often. If time permits, you can always go back and execute a performance test on the other features that are rarely used.

Identifying Performance Goals

High-level performance goals are critical to ensure your Web application meets or exceeds current or future projected requirements. The best approach is to use historical data or extensive marketing research. Examples of poor planning are e-commerce Web applications that can't handle the peak holiday shopping rush. Every year the media publicizes Web applications that cannot procure all their orders, suffer from slow user response times, Web server error messages, or system downtime. This costs not only in terms of lost sales, but in bad press as well.

High-level performance requirements can be broken down into the following three basic categories:

■   Response time acceptability

■   Throughput and concurrent user goals

■   Future performance growth requirements

Response Time Acceptability Goals and Targets

By researching how and where your users will connect to your Web application, you can build a table similar to Table 2-1 to show the connection speeds and latency of your potential customers. This can help you determine an acceptable amount of time it can take to load each page of your Web application.

Table 2-1   Predicted Connection Speeds

User	Worst Connection	Average Connection	Best Connection
Line Speed	28.8-kbps modem	256-kbps DSL	1.5-mbps T1
Latency	1000 milliseconds	100 milliseconds	50 milliseconds

Once you have identified how your user base will access your Web application, you can determine your response time acceptability targets. These targets define how long it can acceptably take for user scenarios or content to load on various connections. For example, with all things being equal, a 70-kilobyte page will obviously load faster on a 256-kbps DSL connection than on a

28.8-kbps modem connection. The response time acceptability for your 28.8-kbps modem might be 15 seconds, while the 256-kbps DSL connection might be significantly less, at 5 seconds. Response time acceptability targets are useful when you perform an application network analysis, which is discussed in detail in Chapter 5. The purpose of conducting the application network analysis is to perform response time predictions at various connection speeds and latencies, determine the amount of data transferred between each tier, and determine how many network round trips occur with each step of a user scenario. If you do not have historical data or projections for potential customer connection speeds and latencies we recommend using worst-case estimates. The data in Table 2-1 represents worst, average, and best connections of typical end-user Internet connection speeds.

Throughput Goals and Concurrent User Targets

Answering the following questions will help to determine throughput goals and concurrent user targets:

- How many concurrent users do we currently sustain or expect in a given time period?

- What actions does a typical user perform on our Web application and which pages receive the most page views in a given time period?

- How many user scenarios will my Web application process in a given time period?

The best place to gather this information is from historical data, which can be found in Web server log files, System Monitor data, and by monitoring database activity. If you are launching a new Web application, you may need to perform marketing research analysis for anticipated throughput and concurrent user targets. Historical production data or marketing research is useful to ensure you execute the performance tests using the right concurrent user levels. If, after you complete your performance tests, your Web application meets your throughput and concurrent usage requirements, you can continue adding load until your Web application either reaches a bottleneck or achieves maximum throughput. Table 2-2 shows predicted throughput goals and concurrent user profile expectation for the IBuySpy sample Web application. Using the information in this table, a performance test script can be created to mimic anticipated load on the Web application. The ratio column represents the percentage that this particular user operation is executed with respect to all the user operations. The anticipated load per hour is taken from historical data, which will be illustrated in the next section of this chapter and represents how many times per hour this particular user operation typically occurs.

Table 2-2 Throughput and Concurrent User Targets

User Operations	Ratio	Anticipated Load per hour
Basic Search	14%	1,400
Browse for Product	62%	6,200
Add to Cart	10%	1,000
Login and Checkout	7%	700
Register and Checkout	7%	700
Total	100%	10,000

Performance Growth Analysis

A performance growth analysis is required if your Web application user base is expected to grow over a given time period. You need to account for user growth when performance testing. Performance testing and tuning your Web application after your development cycle is complete will cost more in time and money, when compared to fixing your performance problems during the software development life cycle (SDLC). In the real world example in Chapter 1, expenses incurred by finding and fixing their Web application performance issues after the SDLC included: lost marketing revenues due to bad press, lost users who are not patient enough to wait for slow page views, and test and development labor costs spent troubleshooting and fixing the issue. Taking a little extra time during the performance test cycle to populate your database with additional data to see how it will perform when it is larger will save you money in the long run. Also, execute the stress test with more load and with higher levels of concurrent users to predict future bottlenecks. By fixing these issues ahead of your growth curve, you will reduce your performance testing and tuning needs in the immediate future and ultimately provide your users with a better experience.

> **Tip**   One tip for preloading your database with extra orders, baskets, and so on is to run your performance test script for a sustained period of time (possibly a few days) before executing your actual performance analysis. Your Web application UI will ensure data is accurately added to your system. The fastest way to pre-populate your database is to have the database developer create and test data via SQL scripts. However, one common mistake when pre-populating a database with SQL scripts is to miss certain tables that are updated through the UI of a Web application. The point is to ensure that you populate your database accurately; otherwise, it will adversely affect your performance test results.

The easiest way to determine the growth capacity of your Web application is to calculate the increase in volume you are currently experiencing over a specific period of time. For example, assume your user base is growing at a rate of 10 percent per month. Table 2-3 illustrates an anticipated growth plan that can be used when performing your stress tests. This assumes your Web application is currently seeing 10,000 users per day and will grow at a rate of 10 percent per month. When determining your growth rate, don't forget to account for special promotions that may increase traffic to your Web application.

Table 2-3 Future Growth Profile

Time Period	Users Per Day
Current	10,000 per day
Three months out	13,310 per day
Six months out	16,104 per day
Nine months out	21,434 per day
Twelve months out	28,529 per day

User Activity Profile

We use IIS logs to create user activity profiles. The IIS logs are text files that contain information about each request and can be viewed directly with a simple text editor or imported into a log analysis program. We recommend using a set of IIS logs covering at least a week's worth of user activity from your Web application to obtain realistic averages. Using more log files creates more reliable usage profiles and weightings. To illustrate the process of creating a user activity profile, we imported a month of IIS log data from a recent performance analysis on a typical e-commerce Web application into a commercial log file analyzer. These IIS log files are comprised of shopper page views related to Homepage, Search, Browse for Product, Add to Basket, and Checkout operations performed on the Web application. The logfile analyzer enabled us to generate Table 2-4. Many commercial log file analyzers that fit all budgets are available. These log analyzers can accurately import, parse, and report on Web application traffic patterns.

Table 2-4   User Activity Profile

User Operation/ Page Name(s)	Number of Page Views	Ratio
Homepage	720,000	40%
default.aspx	720,000	40%
Search	90,000	5%
search.aspx	90,000	5%
Browse	450,000	25%
productfeatures.aspx	216,000	12%
productoverview.aspx	234,000	13%
Add to Basket	360,000	20%
basket.aspx	360,000	20%
Checkout	180,000	10%
checkout.aspx	90,000	5%
checkoutsubmit.aspx	54,000	3%
confirmation.aspx	36,000	2%
Totals	1,800,000	100%

There is a distinction between a hit and a page view. A *hit* is defined as a request for any individual object or file that is on a Web application, while a *page view* or request is defined as the request to retrieve an HTML, ASP or ASP.NET page from a Web application and the transmittal of the requested page, which can contain references to many additional page elements. The page is basically what you see after the transfer and can consist of many other files. Page views do not include hits to images, component pages of a frame, or other non-HTML files.

> **Tip**   To simplify constructing your user profile, leave Web application traffic such as image and miscellaneous requests out of the user profile. Also, leave out activity from monitoring tools that ping or access various pages to verify the Web application is functioning properly.

Backend Activity Profile

A *backend activity profile* is used to identify user activity and performance bottlenecks at the database tier of an existing Web application. This information can be useful to ensure your performance test is accurate.

Identifying a Web Application's User Activity

Existing databases contain concrete information concerning what your users are doing with your Web application. Examples of this type of information for a typical e-commerce application include how many baskets are being created, how many orders are processed, how many logins occur, how many searches are taking place, and so on. This information can be gathered using simple queries to extract the data from your existing database. This data can assist you in creating user scenarios, user scenarios ratios, or other marketing information that can help you make decisions from the business side. For example, you can compare the number of baskets created to the number of checkouts to find the abandoned basket rate. This information can be important to designing your stress test to execute in the correct ratio. If you find that 50 percent of the baskets created turn into actual orders processed, you can mimic this ratio when executing your performance test.

Identifying a Web Application's Backend Performance Bottlenecks

If you are performance testing an existing Web application you can identify current performance bottlenecks by interrogating the database server for queries that take a long time to process, cause deadlocks, and result in high server resource utilization. This data collection process occurs during the planning phase of the performance testing methodology, and involves capturing SQL trace data using SQL Profiler, and Performance Monitor logs that are comprised of Windows and SQL Server objects in a typical Web application. In other words, the timeframe for the captured SQL trace should be when application performance goes from acceptable to poor performance. The captured information will give you a clearer picture of where the bottleneck is occurring. Chapter 8 walks you through the process of determining the source of the SQL performance issue. These possible causes include: blocking, locks, deadlocks, problematic queries, or stored procedures with long execution times.

Key Performance Metrics Criteria

As a performance analyst, tester, or developer, you must produce a blueprint on how to performance test the Web application to ensure the high-level performance goals are met. If you don't create a performance test plan, you may find out about requirements too late in the SDLC to properly test for them. Using the performance requirements criteria in the section above, you now need to identify key metrics that will be monitored and analyzed during the actual performance test.

> **Tip**   The breakpoint of your Web application can be defined in various ways. Examples include a server that exceeds predefined resource utilization targets, too many server errors, or unacceptable response times due to processing delays.

Key metrics for the performance test include the following:

- **Server errors acceptability**   This may seem like a moot point, and no server errors are acceptable because they result in a bad user experience. However, during stress testing you will probably come across these errors, so you should be prepared to understand why they are occurring and decide whether they will happen in your live production environment, with real users hitting your Web application. For example, often when a stress test first begins and then again when it shuts down, errors are caused by too much load occurring too quickly, or by uncompleted page requests. These errors are caused by your stress test, so you can ignore them because they are unlikely to reoccur in the production environment.

- **Server utilization acceptability**   This is an important aspect of performance testing. By identifying this up front, you will be able to determine the maximum allowable level your servers should endure. When performance testing, this will be a key element in determining the maximum load to apply to your Web application. This metric can differ for each Web application and should be documented for support, development, test, and management teams to agree on. For example, you might ramp the Web tier up until we reach 75 percent CPU utilization. At this level we are serving approximately 2,000 users per server, which meets the concurrent user targets identified by our performance requirements. With documentation of these metrics, the support team can monitor the production Web servers looking for spikes that meet or exceed the performance requirement. The support team can begin to scale the Web application up or out to support the increased traffic.

- **Memory leaks or other stability issues**   These issues often arise when running extended performance tests. For example, if you execute a stress test for a short period of time you may not find the memory leak or other stability issues that only occur after an extended period of heavy activity. Many times multiple tests can be executed to accomplish different goals. You may want to run a quick one-hour test to determine your Web application's maximum throughput, and then run a weekend-long extended stress test to determine if your Web application can sustain this maximum load.

- **Processing delays**   These will occur in almost every Web application where complex business logic requires coding. The key is to minimize process delays to an acceptable amount of time. It's a good idea to know what's acceptable before performance testing, so you don't waste time escalating an issue to your development team that does not require fixing because it meets performance goals. Examples of processing delay acceptability are shown in Table 2-5 and include stored procedures taking more than 500 milliseconds and any Web page duration (measured by the time taken field in your Web tier logs) taking more than one second to process. Table 2-5 shows an example of a performance metric acceptability table. Your requirements may be different; the key point is to come up with a set of requirements that make sense for your Web application.

Table 2-5   Performance Metrics and Acceptable Levels

Metric	Location	Acceptable Level
CPU utilization	Performance Monitor	< 75%
Memory—available MB	Performance Monitor	> 128 MB
Memory—pages/second	Performance Monitor	< 2
ASP execution time	Performance Monitor	< 1 second
DB processing delays	SQL Profiler	< 500 milliseconds
Web tier processing delays	Time Taken field of Web logs	< 1 second

Mirroring the Production Environment

The performance test environment should be as close to the production environment as possible. This includes the server capacity and configuration, network environment, the Web tier load balancing scheme, and your backend database. By mirroring your production environment you ensure that your throughput numbers will be more accurate.

Tip   If production equivalent hardware is not feasible for your performance-testing environment, you can still uncover many bottlenecks in the code and architecture. Even though a production equivalent environment is optimal, performance testing is possible in almost any environment you can scrape together.

Putting It Together in a Performance Test Plan

The performance test plan is a strategy or formal approach to allow everyone involved in a Web application, from the development team, test team, and management team, to understand exactly how, why, and what part of the application is being performance tested. The following sections are found in a performance test plan:

- **Application overview**   This gives a brief description of the business purpose of the Web application. This may include some marketing data stating estimates or historical revenue produced by the Web application.

- **Architecture overview**   This depicts the hardware and software used for the performance test environment, and will include any deviations from the production environment. For example, document it if you have a Web cluster of four Web servers in the production environment, but only two Web servers in your performance test environment.

- **High-level goals**   This section illustrates what you are trying to accomplish by performance testing your Web application. Examples include identifying what throughput and concurrent usage levels you will be striving for as well as the maximum acceptable response times.

- **Performance test process**   This will include a description of your user scenarios, tools you use to stress test, and any intricacies you will put in your stress scripts. This section will also explain what ratios and sleep times or user think times you will include in your test script.

- **Performance test scripts**   The scripts are unlikely to be completed until after your performance analysis cycle has finished. But it is important to include these in the test plan to make them available in the next release or phase of the Web application test cycle. Because stress test scripts take time and effort to create, having test scripts available as a reference for future testing can save time.

Conclusion

Performance testing is a critical phase of any Web application's development cycle and needs to be the critical path for release to production. By planning properly before you start, you can ensure a successful performance test that will improve your odds of having a high-performing Web application when your customers begin to use it.

3

Stress Testing with Microsoft Application Center Test (ACT)

The purpose of stress testing is to identify and isolate Web application performance bottlenecks under load. Decreasing or eliminating these bottlenecks allows you to meet or exceed anticipated traffic requirements. After you have identified bottlenecks, you can tune the Web application and server to help minimize end user response times and ultimately provide a better user experience. *Stress testing* involves testing an application under load to determine maximum throughput. *Throughput* refers to the number of client requests processed within a fixed amount of time. Stress testing is also commonly referred to as load testing, performance testing, soak testing, spike testing, and Web server testing. It is important to note that performance requirements will vary for each application.

Getting Started

Load simulation against a Web application is usually implemented through a combination of hardware- and software-based emulation of users executing real-world transaction scenarios against an application. The hardware method usually requires several dedicated test clients and represents one user per client. This method can be quite expensive and time consuming to maintain, given the required hardware resources for heavy stress testing. The hardware method is neither the most effective nor the most efficient method of stress testing, but due to the nature of a given application, hardware-based stress testing maybe the only choice. With the software method, user transaction scenarios are typically recorded or captured by a software tool and converted to test scripts during a walkthrough of the application. When playing back or executing a test script, one machine typically acts as a controller to distribute the test script across multiple client machines. As the test runs, the controller produces load in unison to simulate many virtual users, and when the test is complete, it summarizes the test data from all of the clients. These virtual users create load on the backend servers and help to determine the stability and responsiveness of the Web application.

There are many software-based stress testing tools. While the purpose of these tools is to produce load by simulating many users, the syntax used for creating stress scripts and the load engine varies per tool. The stress tool discussed throughout this book is Microsoft Application Center Test (ACT). The goal of this chapter is not necessarily to make you an expert at using ACT but to give you a brief overview of the product and discuss the core concepts and features we frequently use. We will also demonstrate and explain how to create and verify dynamic test scripts using ACT to accurately simulate load against a .NET Web application

What is ACT?

ACT is a software-based stress testing tool that applies load to Web servers, so that you can capture performance metrics, analyze and diagnose performance problems, and make capacity decisions about your Web applications. You apply load to a Web application using ACT by recording or manually creating a *test script*, which simulates many simultaneous browser connections requesting pages defined by a user scenario.

Installing Microsoft ACT

ACT is included with Visual Studio .NET Enterprise and Architect editions. Many different components comprise Visual Studio .NET, but for this book, we will only select the components necessary to run ACT as a stand-alone client.

The installation process is broken down into three major steps. Step 1 is shown in Figure 3-1.

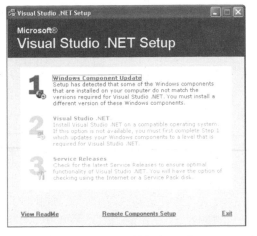

Figure 3-1   The Install Windows Component Update dialog box

Select Step 1: The Install Windows Component Update dialog box to update the system components. This option is available in the Installation dialog box if the update is required for your system. If a component update is not required, this option is not available.

> **Note**   If you are running an anti-virus program during setup, warnings may be displayed as setup runs scripts that access the file system object.

After updating the system components, the Installation dialog box enables Step 2: Install Visual Studio .NET. Select Step 2 to install Visual Studio .NET. Our installation will be very slim because we are only installing the components required to run ACT. If you require the flexibility of creating and running projects and test scripts directly from the integrated Visual Studio IDE, you must add additional components. Application Center Test is located under Enterprise Development Tools in the Select Items to Install list, as shown in Figure 3-2, and should be checked by default.

Figure 3-2 Selecting options for installation

Selecting Step 3: Service Releases Check is optional but highly recommended to ensure that you have all of the latest patches or fixes.

Core Concepts of ACT

The purpose of this section is to explain the core details related to ACT and provide a few tips and share experiences we have encountered to help minimize your learning curve.

Dynamic Tests

The *dynamic test* is a very powerful feature of ACT, which gives you the ability to record or manually create a list of HTTP requests that are sent to the Web server concurrently. Also, you can modify request header information such as referrer, user-agent, and query string. Dynamic test scripts can be created using Visual Basic Script (VBScript), Jscript, PERL, or any other COM-enabled scripting language. ACT only supports VBScript for recording a test script.

Concurrent Users and ACT Simultaneous Browser Connections

A concurrent connection to the Web application making a single request or a series of requests contained in a ACT test script is measured in simultaneous browser connections (SBCs). Other stress tools use terms such as "stress threads" or "virtual users," which are synonymous with the ACT SBC (load level). We are often asked "How do SBCs relate to concurrent users?" Equating SBCs with concurrent users is difficult, because we do not always know the rate at which customers will be requesting pages from the Web application. Test scripts played back with no *sleep time* (the user's think time during transaction execution) often produce a faster rate of execution and greater load against the Web server than would be produced by the user walking through the application from a Web browser. Therefore, you may need to include random sleep times comparable to actual user think time in your scripts to slow the request arrival rate on the Web server, allowing you to more closely relate one SBC to one user connection and to better simulate real-world Web traffic arrival rates.

User Sleep Times

When creating test scripts, you will have the option of inserting user sleep times. These sleep times help simulate realistic usage of the application as they introduce user think times. For example, by inserting a 5-second sleep time in a script that simulates a user filling out an online form, you simulate a typical user's actions more accurately by taking into account the think time needed for the user to fill out the form. In ACT, *Sleep* is a method of the *Test* object. When an ACT test script is recorded, the following code will be inserted:

```
fEnableDelays = False
If fEnableDelays = True then Test.Sleep (0)
```

By default, at the top of a recorded test script the *fEnableDelays* variable is set to false. To use a 5-second delay, or 5,000 milliseconds, you will need to change the following code in the ACT test script:

```
fEnableDelays = True
If fEnableDelays = True then Test.Sleep (5000)
```

If needed, a random sleep function can be used by inserting the following snippet of code into a test script and then calling this function between each request:

```
Function RandomSleep()
   Dim lMinSleep, lMaxSleep, lSleep
   lMaxSleep = 5000 ' 5 seconds
   lMinSleep = 1000  ' 1 second
   ' create a random int within our range
   Call Randomize()
   lSleep = Int((lMaxSleep - lMinSleep + 1) * Rnd(1) + lMinSleep)
   Call Test.Sleep(lSleep)
   ' return the delay time
   RandomSleep = lSleep
End Function
```

One negative aspect of sleep times is that they can decrease the amount of load a given client can produce. This could prevent you from identifying the true maximum concurrent usage. Also, if there is insufficient client capacity, you will have a much more difficult task detecting performance bottlenecks, because bottlenecks appear when maximum load is applied to the system. A test script with no sleep times simulates the transaction as if users had a pre-filled form which is being submitted immediately. Utilizing sleep times more accurately simulates production traffic and allows you to more precisely estimate concurrent usage numbers. When random sleep times are used, the argument can be made that one SBC equals one real-world user.

Users and Groups

Users are handled in ACT dynamically by providing a single unique user and password for each entry located in the default user group. There is a one-to-one relationship between SBCs and users. For example, if you set the SBC level to 25 you will need a minimum of 25 users to run the test. If your Web application uses anonymous authentication, by default ACT automatically generates the users required. If your Web application requires Basic or Windows NT LAN Manager (NTLM) authentication, you must have predefined usernames and passwords. ACT provides the ability to customize users either by manually generating user data (from the user interface) or by importing data from a separate input file. When executing your test, each SBC will have a unique username and password. This data is exposed in your script by using the *ACT Test Object*. The following code is an example of the *Test.GetCurrentUser*, which can be used to retrieve the username and password:

```
Dim oUser, sUserName, sPassword
Set oUser = Test.GetCurrentUser
sUserName = oUser.Name
sPassword = oUser.Password
```

Cookies

For most Web applications, allowing ACT to control your HTTP cookies is the optimal method for handling cookies. However, cookies can be set up initially when the test starts and handled automatically by ACT thereafter. For any request that includes an HTTP header named "Cookie," ACT will show the exact response generated by the Web server, and it will be commented out by default when a test is recorded. The next line of code within your script will show the same request with the value "(Automatic)." The ACT help file covers the syntax for reading and modifying cookie information in more detail.

Headers

Headers are handled automatically, but they can be changed in your test script to modify information such as referrer, user-agent, host, HTTP version, and other information passed in the header.

> **Note** If you create a test script that only contains the following syntax:
>
> ```
> "Test.SendRequest("http://localhost/samples/browser.asp")"
> ```
>
> ACT adds a set of default headers using "Mozilla/4.0 (compatible; MSIE 5.01; Windows NT 5.0)" as the user agent.

For example, if your application contains logic that is dependent on multiple user-agents (different Web Browsers), you can modify the HTTP header of a request to dynamically change and pass a mix of user-agents:

```
Dim sUserAgent, sArray(3), sSeed
sArray(1) = "Mozilla/4.0 (compatible; MSIE 6.0; Windows NT 5.1)"
sArray(2) = "Mozilla/4.0(compatible;MSIE 4.0;Mac PowerPC)"
sArray(3) = "Mozilla/5.0 (Windows; U; Win98; en-US; m18) Gecko/
20001108 Netscape6/6.0"
Randomize()
sSeed = Int((3 * Rnd ) + 1)
sUserAgent = sArray(mySeed)
```

Authentication and Encryption

ACT supports the most common authentication models and encryption methods that applications use during test execution. This includes Windows NT LAN Manager (NTLM) challenge-response Integrated Windows Authentication, Basic Authentication, Anonymous Access, Digest Authentication, and Passport Authentication. However, the ACT recorder does not record all of these technologies. There are workarounds for Integrated and Passport Authentication, which are discussed in their related sections. The following table provides a quick checklist of supported Authentication methods by ACT Test Recorder and Test Execution:

Table 3-1   Supported Authentication Methods

Authentication Method	Test Recorder	Test Execution
Anonymous Authentication	YES	YES
Basic	YES	YES
Integrated Windows	NO	YES
Passport	NO	YES
Digest	YES	YES

Integrated Windows Authentication

ACT supports the playback of Integrated Windows Authentication; however, you cannot record a Web application that has the Integrated Authentication option enabled within the IIS configuration. Some Web applications may still be functional with IIS set to accept Anonymous or Basic Authentication. For such Web applications, you can use the following workaround to record a test script with ACT:

1. Enable Basic Authentication in addition to Integrated Windows Authentication. This will enable ACT to record while other users browsing your Web application automatically use integrated authentication.

2. Record the ACT test script. You will be prompted to fill out the appropriate domain\username and password for your Web application.

3. Change the configuration for the Web application back to Integrated Windows Authentication.

4. Modify the ACT test script by commenting out the line of each request:

    ```
    oHeaders.Add "Authorization", "Basic XXXXX"
    ```

5. Set up the ACT users with the proper domain\username and password that you want to simulate.

6. Execute the ACT test script.

Basic and Digest Authentication

ACT supports the recording and execution of your script with applications using both Basic and Digest Authentication. ACT will automatically include the following code in your script to specify the use of Basic or Digest Authentication:

Basic and Digest Authentication.cs

```
'Basic Authentication Code
oHeaders.Add "Authorization", "Basic xxxxx="
'Digest Authentication Code
oHeaders.Add "Authorization", "Digest username="+chr(34)+"domain\username"+_
    chr(34)+", realm="+chr(34)+"IBUYSPY"+chr(34)+", qop="+chr(34)+"auth"+_
    chr(34)+", algorithm="+chr(34)+"MD5"+chr(34)+", uri="+chr(34)+_
    "/storevbvs/"+chr(34)+", nonce="+chr(34)+"xxxxxxxx"+chr(34)+",_
    nc=00000001, cnonce="+chr(34)+"xxxxxxx"+chr(34)+", response="_
    +chr(34)+"xxxxxx"+chr(34)
```

Anonymous Authentication

The most common authentication method for Web applications is anonymous. ACT fully and automatically supports anonymous authentication for both the recording and the execution of your test script.

Passport Authentication

Microsoft .NET Passport is a suite of Web-based services that makes using the Internet and purchasing online easier and faster by providing users with single sign-in and fast purchasing capability. The single username or sign-in service is designed to provide a centralized, secure, and convenient service with which end users can complete transactions. Because Passport Web applications use SSL, the ACT Recorder cannot record when using this authentication scheme. You have to build the login portion of the ACT test script manually or remove Passport from the testing phase. Additionally, Passport applications may be implemented in a variety of ways, so test scripts can vary from application to application. When new builds of Passport launch, you might need to modify your test scripts accordingly. We provide a sample Passport Authentication test script written by the ACT Development Team on the companion CD included with this book.

Secure Sockets Layer (SSL)

ACT fully supports the execution of test scripts which request 40-bit or 128-bit SSL encrypted elements. However, recording an ACT test script with an SSL-enabled Web application is not supported, because ACT records through a proxy, and the data is already encrypted when it reaches the proxy. The workaround for this issue is to disable SSL during the record phase. Change the *Test.CreateConnection* method within your test script to use port 443 instead of port 80 and re-enable SSL on your Web server. The following code shows the syntax for the *Test.CreateConnection* method and a sample of the *Test.Create-Connection* method using port 80 and port 443:

Syntax	oConnect = Test.CreateConnection(strServer, lPort, bUseSSL)
Without SSL	oConnect = Test.CreateConnection("YourServerName", 80, False)
With SSL	oConnect = Test.CreateConnection("YourServerName", 443, True)

If it is not possible to disable SSL for your Web application, you can manually add the reference to encrypted pages of the site using the syntax above.

Using SOAP with ACT

SOAP is a slim XML-based protocol for information sharing in a decentralized distributed architecture. For more information on SOAP, visit *http://msdn.microsoft.com/vstudio/*. ACT does not include native support for SOAP requests, but a workaround is available that involves wrapping the SOAP body in concatenated quotes. The following code shows an example of this approach:

SOAP Workaround Code Sample

```
set con = Test.CreateConnection(YourServerName, 80, false)
set req = Test.CreateRequest
set headers = req.Headers
req.Path = "/Logon.asmx"
req.Verb = "POST"
req.HTTPVersion = "HTTP/1.1"
headers.RemoveAll
headers.Add "Host", "(automatic)"
```

```
headers.Add "SOAPAction", chr(QUOTE) & _
    "http://YourServerName/LogonUser" & chr(QUOTE)
headers.Add "Content-Type", "text/xml; charset=utf-8"
headers.Add "Content-Length", "(automatic)"
body = "<?xml version="& chr(QUOTE) & "1.0" & chr(QUOTE) & " encoding="_
    & chr(QUOTE) & "utf-8" & chr(QUOTE) &"?>"
body = body & "<soap:Envelope xmlns:xsi="&chr(QUOTE)&_
    "http://www.w3.org/2001/XMLSchema-instance" &chr(QUOTE)& "_
    xmlns:xsd=" &chr(QUOTE)& "http://www.w3.org/2001/
XMLSchema" &chr(QUOTE)& "_
    xmlns:soap=" &chr(QUOTE)& "http://schemas.xmlsoap.org/soap/envelope/"_
    &chr(QUOTE)&">"
body = body & "<soap:Header>"
body = body &  "<CorrelationHeader xmlns="&chr(QUOTE)&"http://YourServerName/"_
    &chr(QUOTE)&">"
body = body &  "<Contents>string</Contents>"
body = body & "   </CorrelationHeader>"
body = body & "  </soap:Header>"
body = body & "  <soap:Body>"
body = body & "    <LogonUser xmlns="&chr(QUOTE)&"http://YourServerName/"&_
    chr(QUOTE)&">"
body = body & "       <licenseeAccount>Microsoft</licenseeAccount>"
body = body & "       <userName>testact</userName>"
body = body & "       <userPassword>testact123</userPassword>"
body = body & "    </LogonUser>"
body = body & "  </soap:Body>"
body = body & "</soap:Envelope>"
req.Body = body
set res = con.Send(req)
```

Parsing *Viewstate* within ACT

Viewstate is a feature of ASP.NET implemented to maintain state by using hidden form elements within your pages. ACT does not include native support for ASP.NET viewstate. However, the following example shows a workaround for this by parsing and manually encoding the viewstate:

Do *Viewstate*.cs

```
'Do VIEWSTATE parsing
If InStr(oResponse.Body, "__VIEWSTATE") Then
    Pos1 = InStr(InStr(oResponse.Body, "__VIEWSTATE"),_
        oResponse.Body, "value=")
    Pos2 = InStr(Pos1, oResponse.Body, ">")
    res = Mid(oResponse.Body, Pos1 + 7, Pos2 - Pos1 - 8)
    viewst = res
End If
```

(continued)

```
' Manually encode viewstates:
' Replace all occurrences of "+" with "%2B"
    viewst = Replace(viewst, "+", "%2B")
' Replace all occurrences of "=" with "%3D"
    viewst = Replace(viewst, "=", "%3D")
```

Manual encoding viewstates (or Post data in general) can be avoided by setting the following property: `oRequest.EncodeBody = True`

Protecting your Web Site from Inadvertent Stress Testing

ACT supports the Robots Exclusion Standard method used by developers of automated user-agents ("robots") and Web site administrators to determine areas of a Web application that are accessible to particular user-agents. To prevent ACT from sending requests to a Web server, you can create or edit a file named "robots.txt" in the server's root directory and add the following lines to the file:

```
# Stress Agent is the user-
agent string ACT sends when identifying itself
User-agent: Stress-Agent
# / excludes ACT from all parts of the Web site
Disallow: /
```

When a test is run against a Web site that is protected by a robots.txt file, ACT will appear to be running but no requests will be generated. However, the status pane will state that "Robots.txt denied access to Web server."

> **Note** There are scenarios where checking this exclusionary protocol will prevent you from running a test, such as when testing Passport. So, ACT allows you to disable this check in the project Properties dialog box. (Right-click the project name and choose Properties).

Running ACT

This section provides you with a starting point from which to gain familiarity with the ACT stress testing tool. A brief description of the user interface is provided with a discussion on how to create test scripts. Examples are provided for recording a test script from scratch and for leveraging ACT to create a test harness that will directly stress the SQL tier. Finally, this section concludes by providing guidelines on how to run a stress test using ACT. Other topics discussed include the optimal number of scripts to create, the appropriate number of clients to use, and the optimal amount of load to produce (measured in SBCs).

Overview of the ACT User Interface

The ACT user interface is straightforward. After launching ACT, you will see the screen shown in Figure 3-3.

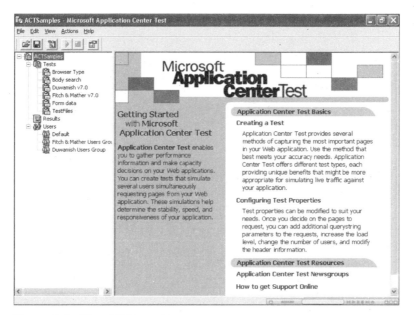

Figure 3-3   The ACT launch screen

The window is divided into two sections—a left and right pane. The left pane is used for navigation and the right pane is used to display details. In the left pane, the tree control displays a root node named ACTSamples, which represents an ACT project. Only one ACT project can be open at a time. By default, this project is stored in a folder with the same name as the project under C:\Documents and Settings*<user>*\My Documents\ACT Projects. The project file with the extension .act is located in this folder and contains pointers to all items referenced by the project such as tests and reports.

> **Note** If you use a share to store My Documents, the ACTUser account must have read and write permissions to this share—otherwise ACT will not be able to run tests. It will state that "ACTUser does not have permissions to the folder" in the status pane.

At the next level, there are three nodes: *Tests*, *Results*, and *Users*; these are described below:

Tests

This node enumerates all test scripts created by a user. Selecting a test script under this node displays the code in the right pane, where modifications can be made. Every test script has properties, such as duration, that control how a test script will run. To see the properties of a particular test, you simply right-click a test and choose Properties. A properties page will appear, as shown in Figure 3-4:

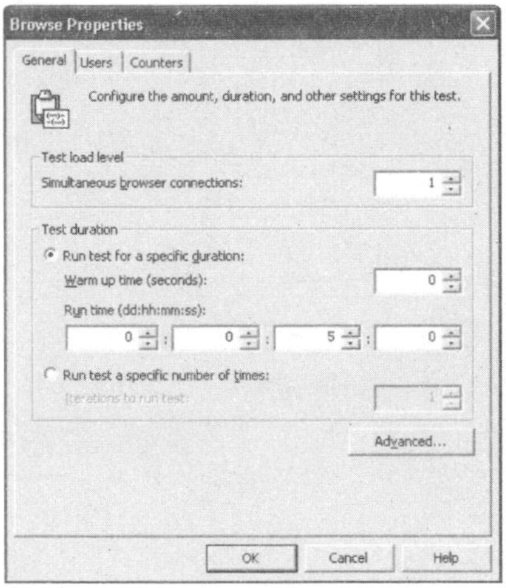

Figure 3-4 Viewing the properties of a test

You can create new test scripts by right-clicking the *Tests* node and choosing *New Test* from the context menu. You can also start and stop tests through the context menu of a particular test. A single ACT client can run only one test at any given time.

Results

This node displays the results of each test run of every scenario on the right hand pane. Clicking the *Results* node will display the screen shown in Figure 3-5.

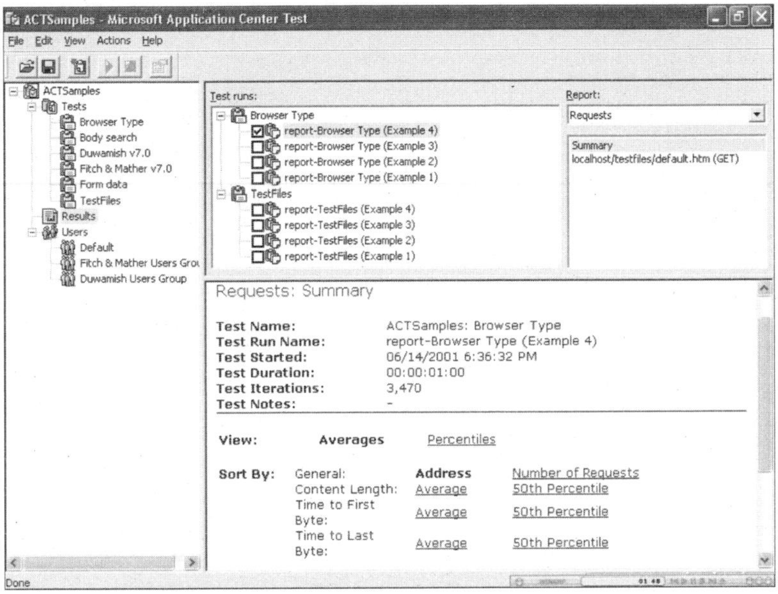

Figure 3-5   Reviewing test results

The right side of the screen is divided into three regions. The top left region lists all tests that previously ran. Under each test is a collection of results for every test run, listed in descending order by timestamp. To view the test results, you simply select a particular test run, select the type of report from the dropdown list under Report, and select the category from the list. All of the report details will be listed in the lower region of the right pane on the screen.

ACT provides different categories of reports such as Overview, Graphs, and Requests. You can view information such as requests per second (RPS), Time To Last Byte (TTLB), details on page view statistics and even performance counters through this reporting feature. All of this information is stored on the file system as XML documents. Please consult the ACT help file for further details.

Users

This node lists user groups that can be accessed by tests. Clicking on a user group displays the individual users within the group in the right-hand pane. Usernames and corresponding passwords can be added by simply selecting a blank line in the right-hand pane and typing a value. These values can also be deleted by highlighting lines and pressing the Delete key. Another useful feature that ACT supports is importing username/password combinations from a comma delimited text file. You can use this feature by selecting a user group and then choosing Import Users from the Actions menu.

Every browser connection initiated by ACT needs a username and password combination to log into a Web application. If the Web application being accessed requires Basic or NTLM authentication, this is where the users (or usernames) can be created.

> **Note**   From the perspective of manageability among different test runs, you should create a user group and then create the required number of users within the user group. The number of users created within a user group has to be greater than or equal to the number of SBCs. Alternatively, if the Web application is set for Anonymous connections, you can let ACT generate users automatically through the properties page (Users tab).

Creating a Test Script

To demonstrate ACT as a stress tool, we have created some test scripts that exercise the search and browse features of the IBuySpy sample site. IBuySpy is an online store application that is intended to showcase the .NET platform and technologies. We refer to the IBuySpy sample .NET application throughout this book. A copy of this application is available for viewing at *http://www.ibuyspy.com/store*. You can also download and install the application from *http://www.ibuyspy.com/downloads.htm*.

For better manageability of the test scripts, we advise you to create a new project for each testing initiative. By creating a separate project in its own folder, you can archive the entire folder at the end of the testing cycle and know that all test scripts and data related to the testing effort have been saved. To create a project, choose New Project from the File menu. In the New Project dialog box, specify a name for the project. For simplicity we have named the project IBuySpy, and the location has also been changed to C:\Project\. This action causes a folder called IBuySpy to be created under C:\Project. The folder is empty until you save the project, at which time a file by the name of IBuySpy.act is created along with some other files which comprise the project. ACT will create separate files for reports from each test run including test properties, project properties, user groups and client groups, all of which are formatted in XML.

Recording a Test Script

A simple way to create a test script is by recording a walkthrough of a user scenario. To start a recording session, right-click the *Tests* node and select New Test from the context menu to bring up the New Test Wizard. Click Next and then select Record A New Test from the wizard. Proceed by clicking Next, and then click the Start Recording button. The default browser will launch at this point and you can walk through the following search user scenario.

1.   Browse to *http://<**YourServerName**>/*

2.   Enter **boat** in the Search text box located at the top right of the Web page.

3.   Click Go to execute the search.

After completing the scenario, click the Stop Recording button. All of the requests captured during the session are visible in the list box but cannot be modified at this point. Click Next and specify a name for the script. Click Next one more time and then click Finish. The newly recorded test should appear in the tree control on the left panel of the screen.

Below is an excerpt of a script that exercises the search feature of IBuySpy:

Search.vbs

```
Option Explicit
Dim fEnableDelays
fEnableDelays = False

Sub SendRequest1()
    Dim oConnection, oRequest, oResponse, oHeaders, strStatusCode
    If fEnableDelays = True then Test.Sleep (0)
    Set oConnection = Test.CreateConnection("YourServerName", 80, false)
```

(continued)

```
            If (oConnection is Nothing) Then
                Test.Trace "Error: Unable to create connection to YourServerName"
            Else
                Set oRequest = Test.CreateRequest
                oRequest.Path = "/StoreVBVS/default.aspx"
                oRequest.Verb = "GET"
                oRequest.HTTPVersion = "HTTP/1.0"
                set oHeaders = oRequest.Headers
                oHeaders.RemoveAll
                oHeaders.Add "Accept", "image/gif, image/x-xbitmap, image/jpeg,_
                    image/pjpeg, application/vnd.ms-excel,_
                    application/vnd.ms-powerpoint, application/msword, */*"
                oHeaders.Add "Accept-Language", "en-us"
                oHeaders.Add "User-Agent", "Mozilla/4.0 (compatible; MSIE 6.0;_
                    Windows NT 5.1)"
                'oHeaders.Add "Host", "YourServerName"
                oHeaders.Add "Host", "(automatic)"
                oHeaders.Add "Cookie", "(automatic)"
                Set oResponse = oConnection.Send(oRequest)
                If (oResponse is Nothing) Then
                    Test.Trace "Error: Failed to receive response for URL to " + _
                        "/StoreVBVS/default.aspx"
                Else
                    strStatusCode = oResponse.ResultCode
                End If
                oConnection.Close
            End If
    End Sub

    Sub SendRequest2()
        Dim oConnection, oRequest, oResponse, oHeaders, strStatusCode
        If fEnableDelays = True then Test.Sleep (130)
        Set oConnection = Test.CreateConnection("YourServerName", 80, false)
        If (oConnection is Nothing) Then
            Test.Trace "Error: Unable to create connection to YourServerName"
        Else
            Set oRequest = Test.CreateRequest
            oRequest.Path = "/StoreVBVS/IBuySpy.css"
            oRequest.Verb = "GET"
            oRequest.HTTPVersion = "HTTP/1.0"
            set oHeaders = oRequest.Headers
            oHeaders.RemoveAll
            oHeaders.Add "Accept", "*/*"
            oHeaders.Add "Referer", "http://YourServerName/StoreVBVS/default.aspx"
            oHeaders.Add "Accept-Language", "en-us"
            oHeaders.Add "User-Agent", "Mozilla/4.0 (compatible; MSIE 6.0;_
                Windows NT 5.1)"
```

```
    'oHeaders.Add "Host", "YourServerName"
    oHeaders.Add "Host", "(automatic)"
    oHeaders.Add "Cookie", "(automatic)"
    Set oResponse = oConnection.Send(oRequest)
    If (oResponse is Nothing) Then
        Test.Trace "Error: Failed to receive response for URL to " + _
            "/StoreVBVS/IBuySpy.css"
    Else
        strStatusCode = oResponse.ResultCode
    End If
    oConnection.Close
    End If
End Sub


Sub SendRequest3()
    Dim oConnection, oRequest, oResponse, oHeaders, strStatusCode
    If fEnableDelays = True then Test.Sleep (20)
    Set oConnection = Test.CreateConnection("YourServerName", 80, false)
    If (oConnection is Nothing) Then
        Test.Trace "Error: Unable to create connection to YourServerName"
    Else
        Set oRequest = Test.CreateRequest
        oRequest.Path = "/StoreVBVS/images/sitebkgrdnogray.gif"
        oRequest.Verb = "GET"
        oRequest.HTTPVersion = "HTTP/1.0"
        set oHeaders = oRequest.Headers
        oHeaders.RemoveAll
        oHeaders.Add "Accept", "*/*"
        oHeaders.Add "Referer", "http://YourServerName/StoreVBVS/default.aspx"
        oHeaders.Add "Accept-Language", "en-us"
        oHeaders.Add "User-Agent", "Mozilla/4.0 (compatible; MSIE 6.0;_
            Windows NT 5.1)"
        'oHeaders.Add "Host", "YourServerName"
        oHeaders.Add "Host", "(automatic)"
        oHeaders.Add "Cookie", "(automatic)"
        Set oResponse = oConnection.Send(oRequest)
        If (oResponse is Nothing) Then
            Test.Trace "Error: Failed to receive response for URL to " + _
                "/StoreVBVS/images/sitebkgrdnogray.gif"
        Else
            strStatusCode = oResponse.ResultCode
        End If
        oConnection.Close
    End If
End Sub

    ⋮
```

(continued)

```
Sub SendRequest17()
    Dim oConnection, oRequest, oResponse, oHeaders, strStatusCode
    If fEnableDelays = True then Test.Sleep (6910)
    Set oConnection = Test.CreateConnection("YourServerName", 80, false)
    If (oConnection is Nothing) Then
        Test.Trace "Error: Unable to create connection to YourServerName"
    Else
        Set oRequest = Test.CreateRequest
        oRequest.Path = "/StoreVBVS/SearchResults.aspx"
        oRequest.Verb = "POST"
        oRequest.HTTPVersion = "HTTP/1.0"
        oRequest.EncodeBody = False
        set oHeaders = oRequest.Headers
        oHeaders.RemoveAll
        oHeaders.Add "Accept", "image/gif, image/x-xbitmap, _
            image/jpeg, image/pjpeg, application/vnd.ms-excel,_
            application/vnd.ms-powerpoint, application/msword, */*"
        oHeaders.Add "Referer", "http://YourServerName/StoreVBVS/default.aspx"
        oHeaders.Add "Accept-Language", "en-us"
        oHeaders.Add "Content-Type", "application/x-www-form-urlencoded"
        oHeaders.Add "User-Agent", _
            "Mozilla/4.0 (compatible; MSIE 6.0; Windows NT 5.1)"
        'oHeaders.Add "Host", "YourServerName"
        oHeaders.Add "Host", "(automatic)"
        oHeaders.Add "Pragma", "no-cache"
        oHeaders.Add "Cookie", "(automatic)"
        oHeaders.Add "Content-Length", "(automatic)"
        oRequest.Body = "txtSearch=boat&image1.x=13&image1.y=11"
        Set oResponse = oConnection.Send(oRequest)
        If (oResponse is Nothing) Then
            Test.Trace "Error: Failed to receive response for URL to " + _
                "/StoreVBVS/SearchResults.aspx"
        Else
            strStatusCode = oResponse.ResultCode
        End If
        oConnection.Close
    End If
End Sub

Sub Main()
    call SendRequest1()
    call SendRequest2()
    call SendRequest3()
    ⋮
    call SendRequest17()
End Sub
Main
```

Analyzing a Recorded Test Script

At a high level, you can see that each request is encapsulated in a subroutine labeled *SendRequest#()* where # is an ordered sequence. All calls to these subroutines are then encapsulated within a *Main()* subroutine. The starting point of execution is at the top of the test script where variables are declared and initialized. At this point, execution jumps to the last line where *Main()* is called. Within the *Main()* subroutine, each request is called and then the script ends. Subsequent iterations repeat all the steps described above.

The code makes use of ACT objects that facilitate connecting to a Web server and sending requests. These objects fall into what is known as the Test Object Model. At the root of this object model is the *Test Object*. This particular test script uses the *Test*, *Headers*, and *Request* objects. ACT also supports an Application Model that can be utilized to run tests programmatically. More details on the two object models can be found in the help file installed with ACT.

The search test script that we recorded demonstrates how to issue GETs (*subroutine SendRequest1*) and POSTs (*SendRequest17*). Additionally, you can see how to specify request headers. For example, to get ACT to handle cookies automatically during script playback, you can add the following line of code as illustrated in the previous recorded test script:

```
oHeaders.Add "Cookie", "(automatic)"
```

To send content in the request body, as is the case with POST requests, ACT will automatically determine the content length using the following line of code as also illustrated in the previous recorded test script:

```
oHeaders.Add "Content-Length", "(automatic)"
```

By examining the search test script and test scripts included in the *ACTSamples* project, which is part of Visual Studio .Net, you can gain familiarity with the object model, which will enable you to create and modify tests effectively.

Creating a Test Script Manually

Step 2 of the New Test Wizard allows for an empty test to be created. A walkthrough with the wizard produces the following single line script:

```
Test.SendRequest("http://localhost")
```

The argument in the above line can be changed to exercise the task of hitting the default page for the IBuySpy application. The line below illustrates this:

```
Test.SendRequest("http://YourServerName/StoreVBVS")
```

The left side of the default page of the IBuySpy application contains links for each of the product categories. Moving the mouse over the product category links displays the URLs in the status bar. By adding more lines to the test script, similar to the one to access the default page, a test script can be created to simulate browsing through the product categories. Additional logic can be added to randomize the selection of links between test script iterations. An example of such a test script follows.

Browse.vbs

```
Option Explicit

'////////////////////////////////////////////////////////
' Description: Browse different products in random order.
' Summary:
'         Below is a sample ACT test script that simulates
'         browsing through different product categories in
'         random order.
'////////////////////////////////////////////////////////

Dim i, sParams, sServerName, oUser

'////////////////////////////////////////////////////////
' TODO: -Enable Integrated security only, via the Security
'       -tab in IIS
'       -Replace these sample values with your site values
'       -Set the username (domain\username" and password
sServerName = "YourServerName"

'Get a reference to the current ACT generated user
Set oUser = Test.GetCurrentUser

oUser.Name = sServerName & "\USERNAME"
oUser.Password = "UserPassword1"
'////////////////////////////////////////////////////////

'Generate a new seed for random numbers
Randomize()

'Generate a random number between 0 and 6
i = Cint(7 * Rnd())

'Output the random number to the trace file
Test.Trace "i = " & cstr(i)
```

```
Select Case i
  Case 0
    sParams = "CategoryID=14&selection=0"

  Case 1
    sParams = "CategoryID=15&selection=1"

  Case 2
    sParams = "CategoryID=20&selection=2"

  Case 3
    sParams = "CategoryID=18&selection=3"

  Case 4
    sParams = "CategoryID=17&selection=4"

  Case 5
    sParams = "CategoryID=19&selection=5"

  Case 6
    sParams = "CategoryID=16&selection=6"

End Select

'Request the default page
Test.SendRequest("http://" & sServerName  & "/storevbvs/Default.aspx")

'Request a product category
Test.SendRequest("http://" & sServerName  & _
    "/StoreVBVS/productslist.aspx?" & sParams)

'This Request has been added to mark the end of a user scenario
Test.SendRequest("http://" & sServerName  & _
    "/storevbvs/Default.aspx?test=count")
```

This test script was set to generate users automatically, and the Web application was configured to require integrated security. To allow a successful login by the test script, a reference to the user object generated by ACT is obtained and then a username and password are specified through the properties of the *User Object*. You would have to create this username as a local account on the Web server prior to running the ACT test script.

> **Note**   The last request in the test script demonstrates how to add a marker to the IIS log (W3SVC format). We choose "test=count" in our example since it is not interpreted by the Web application logic. You can use this to count completed user scenarios (transactions) after the test run. Another instance where this technique is useful would be in identifying throughput for Web applications in which you have different parameters representing different transactions which are passed to the same page.

Creating a test script to Stress the SQL Tier

ACT can also be used to make SQL calls through ActiveX Data Objects (ADOs). This is useful since ACT supports the creation of multiple threads and can thus simulate multiple concurrent connections to the database. Another reason for using this method would be if you are at a point in the development life cycle where the Web and data tiers are not ready to be integrated.

> **Note**   You should ensure that the SQL Server User Options (that is, the Transaction Isolation level) for the SQL connection created by the test script and those for a connection created by the application are the same.

By starting with an empty test script, you can connect to a SQL server and execute a stored procedure or any dynamic SQL statements. For example, the search functionality of the IBuySpy application calls the following stored procedure:

```
ProductSearch @Search = N'search string'
```

The test script that follows demonstrates connecting to a SQL server directly using the Scripting Library and ADO and exercising the database component of the search functionality exposed by IBuySpy. This script also shows how to retrieve input data from an external file.

Search_SQL.vbs

```
Option Explicit

'//////////////////////////////////////////////////////////
' Description: Directly Stress SQL Tier via ADO calls
' Summary:
'         Below is a sample ACT test script that be used to
'         make SQL calls via ADO. This script passes
'         parameters from a text file to execute a search
'         stored procedure.
'//////////////////////////////////////////////////////////

Dim oFso, oCsvFile, oSQLConn, sConnStr, sSearchStr, sServerName
Dim sUserName, sPassword, sPath

'//////////////////////////////////////////////////////////
' TODO: - Set the Server Name
'       - Create a SQL server account with dbo privileges
'         to the Store database
'       - Verify path to the input file search.txt
sServerName = "juaceeval5"
sUserName = "USERNAME"
sPassword = "UserPassword1"
sPath = "D:\Chapter_3\ACT_Project\search.txt"
'//////////////////////////////////////////////////////////

'Create an ADO Connection object
Set oSQLConn = CreateObject("ADODB.Connection")
sConnStr = "driver={SQL Server};Server=" & sServerName & "_
    ;Database=Store;uid=" & sUserName & ";pwd=" & sPassword
oSQLConn.Open sConnStr

'//////////////////////////////////////////////////////////
' Open a text file containing search sConnStrings
Set oFso = CreateObject("Scripting.FileSystemObject")
Set oCsvFile = oFso.OpenTextFile(sPath ,1)
'//////////////////////////////////////////////////////////

'Repeat until end of file is reached
Do While oCsvFile.AtEndOfStream <> True

  'Read a sSearchString from the text file
  sSearchStr = oCsvFile.ReadLine
```

(continued)

```
'Output the search sConnString to the ACT log file
Test.Trace  sSearchStr

'////////////////////////////////////////////////////////
' Execute the ProductSearch stored procedure

oSQLConn.execute "exec ProductSearch @Search = N'" &_
    trim(sSearchStr) & "'"


'////////////////////////////////////////////////////////

Loop

'Close the text file
oCsvFile.Close
Set oCsvFile = Nothing
Set oFso = Nothing

'Close the database connection
oSQLConn.Close
Set oSQLConn    = Nothing
```

Setting Test Properties Prior to Script Playback

Before running a test, there are certain test properties that must be set to override the default settings. These properties can be set via the test property page. The following properties can be set:

- **Test load level** (General tab). This is achieved by setting a value for simultaneous browser connections. One browser connection can be thought of as virtual users accessing the application. For example, if you want to simulate 10 concurrent connections to the Web application, set this to 10. ACT will spawn 10 SBCs, each of which will execute the test script.

- **Test Duration** (General tab). There are two choices here; either a time can be set or a specified number of iterations can be set. It should be noted that the number of iterations is the total number of iterations across all connections. If the simultaneous browser connections setting is 10 and the number of iterations setting is 100, then each connection will execute the script such that the sum of all executions across the 10 connections does not exceed 100 iterations. For a stress test, we typically set the duration by specifying a time value which allows sufficient warm-up time for the load to reach a steady-state. This time value can be determined by observing the CPU utilization or requests per second for various sample runs of the test script against the server. ACT allows for this transient behavior to be eliminated in its reports by letting the user specify a warm-up time.

■ **Detailed Reporting**   (General tab). ACT can summarize the statistics for each request by page name, or it can simply aggregate the statistics across all requests. To get more detailed reporting, the check box Generate detailed test results located on the Advanced Settings dialog box should be checked. Clicking the Advanced button on the General tab of the test Properties dialog box brings up the Advanced Settings window.

> **Note**   To reduce the reports generation time and "out of memory" errors generated from long test runs, we recommend that this setting be turned off for tests that generate a large number of unique requests.

■ **Users**   (Users tab). ACT can generate users automatically, or you can specify a user group which has predefined users. For Web applications that require specific username/password combinations, users can be created in a user group and then the group can be selected through this tab from the properties page. The number of users defined in the group needs to be equal to or greater than the number of simultaneous browser connections. Note that all iterations of the script will use the same user unless the test script programmatically calls the *GetNextUser* method of the *Test* object. More details on the *Test* object's methods are discussed in the ACT help file.

ACT can speed up the creation of users by generating users for a test. You can invoke this feature by first creating a user group. Next, select the user group and choose Generate Users from the Action menu. This will bring up the Generate Users dialog box, where the number of users, username prefix, and password are specified. The newly created user group must also be associated with a given test for this user group to be used.

- **Counters** (Counters tab). The same counters that are captured through Performance Monitor are exposed on the Counters tab. You can set the sampling duration by specifying a value for the Counter interval. To add counters, click the Add button and then from the Browse Performance Counters dialog box select the target machine and the desired counters. Counters added will appear in the Performance Counters list box on the Counters tab of the test property page.

Script Modification—Avoiding "Record and Playback"

Web applications typically have dynamic content that is generated based on user input. These applications often have a data tier implemented using a database management system such as SQL Server. For this reason, a simple record and playback of a test script will not always accurately simulate real-world usage. To illustrate, a scenario may involve exercising the search functionality of an application. Recording such a scenario will only capture one search string that was entered during the recording session. Playing back such a script for multiple iterations will not create realistic traffic, because the search query and search results may be cached. In such a case, the test results will be skewed, and the test will not be representative of actual user interaction with unique search strings.

Recording is a quick and easy starting point in test script creation and can be used to capture most, if not all, of the Web requests, such as *GET* and *POST* methods. Once a recorded test script has been created, you may have to modify the code to allow for dynamically changing user data. For example, a Web application may have a scenario which involves user account registration as in an online store. Recording such a test script will embed data like the username that was used at record time. Playing back such a test script does not work since the user account will have already been created. This test script has to be modified to use a different value for the user account between successive iterations so the same account previously created will not be attempted more than once. One approach is to modify the test script to read user account data from a text file and supply this data as part of the Web request. You will have to create sufficient data so that the test script can run for a desired duration or complete a desired number of iterations.

> **Note**   To avoid having to create enormous amounts of data that can be used for successive test runs, you should backup your application's SQL databases before your test run and restore the database to its previous state before each subsequent test run. This method will allow you to use the same data file for repeated iterations of the test.

There may be scenarios that require data generated in one step to be used in subsequent steps, such as a GUID referencing an address. In such a case, the test script may have to be modified to parse through the response from a request obtaining the dynamic data which can then be assigned to a variable and subsequently used in the following steps. Fortunately, ACT exposes a *Response* object for such a situation to capture the Web response of a client request. For an example of using the *Response* object, see the code sample in the section "Parsing ViewState within ACT" on page 39.

Debugging ACT Test Scripts

ACT helps with modification and debugging of test scripts by supplying a log file which can capture messages generated during playback. The ACT log file is named ACTTrace.log by default and is located under Program Files\Microsoft ACT. Through the Project Property page (Debugging tab), you can change the location of this file, specify a maximum size for this file (after which it gets recycled) and enable or disable logging entirely. The *Test* object also allows for tracing to be controlled programmatically. Tracing levels can be set via the *TraceLevel* property and user defined messages can be output via the *Trace* method. You can also use the trace log file to uncover errors at runtime during test execution. The example code that follows demonstrates setting the trace level to log all messages and to write a custom message to the trace log file:

```
Test.TraceLevel = -1

' The tracelevel property can be set to one of the following values
' -1: log all information
' 0: disable logging
' 1: log internal program information only
' 2: log external information only, from the Test.Trace method.
'    This is the default setting.

Test.Trace("Trace level is set to  " & CStr(Test.TraceLevel))
```

> **Note** Note that unless the *TraceLevel* is set, no data will be written to the ACTTrace.log unless you specifically call *Test.Trace*.

Test Script Verification

Test scripts should always be verified for accuracy before engaging in an actual test run. Some scenarios may only read data from a database while others may insert, update or delete data. You should verify such data changes before a test script is considered complete. For example, scenarios that involve data insertion can be checked by counting rows of data within your database before and after a test run and comparing the numbers with a walkthrough of the scenario. The number of data insertions for a single user walkthrough and the number for a single test script execution should be the same for an accurate test script.

Another good technique to verify test script functionality is to look at the IIS log file. By comparing the IIS log of a walkthrough and the IIS log of a test run, you can ensure that all the right requests are being performed in the correct order. Occasionally, applications may perform some action via client-side script which does not get captured. By parsing through the IIS logs you can find such omissions.

> **Note** Note that this chapter specifically discusses Microsoft Internet Information Server; however, ACT can be used to apply stress against any Web server for performance testing.

Test script verification can include both capturing SQL calls through SQL Profiler for a walkthrough and comparing these calls to ensure that all the necessary calls are being generated in the correct sequence. SQL Profiler configuration is discussed in more detail in Chapter 8.

Scripts and Load Clients

ACT Developer Edition was not designed to run on multiple machines. It is only licensed to run on one client at a time. Depending on the application being tested, one client machine may be inadequate to generate sufficient load to effectively stress your Web application without the client machine itself becoming the bottleneck.

Note   Client bottlenecks can be identified when the resources such as CPU, Memory, and Network I/O are fully utilized. Another method to check a client bottleneck, if you suspect one, is to run a test to determine the throughput and then repeat the same test by dividing up the SBCs across additional clients. If the throughput is much greater when you add additional clients, then it is safe to assume that your client was a bottleneck.

Most Web applications that we test require multiple client machines to be used in generating sufficient load. With ACT, the only way to do this is to purchase and install additional copies of Visual Studio .NET for each required stress client. You then must recreate the tests, setting the properties and users individually on each machine. To aid in this task, you can simply copy the entire project folder to each client machine, modify input data files where necessary, open up the project and run a particular test.

Note   The maximum number of browser connections in ACT is limited to 2000. This should be more than sufficient for a single client machine. If for some reason you require more than 2000 browser connections for a single load client, you can modify the XML test properties directly, but you should not open the properties page in the user interface after making the change. Alternatively, you can double-up the connections per thread by adding another *CreateConnection* within your test script.

Another possible reason for using multiple stress clients is that ACT executes one test run per stress client at a given time. Most applications have more than one scenario and you can run multiple scenarios concurrently (a mixed test) by using at least one client machine per scenario.

This raises the question of how many test scripts need to be created. Should you use one large test script that exercises all of the scenarios, or should you use multiple test scripts, one for each scenario? We prefer to create multiple test scripts, because this facilitates separate test runs for each scenario and helps us identify bottlenecks in individual scenarios. Alternatively, you can execute multiple user scenarios with one large test script using the following logic:

```
Sub main()

    WhichScenarioToRun = Int(Rnd * 100)
    Randomize

    Select Case WhichScenarioToRun
        Case 0 To 75
            Call myTest1
        Case 76 To 87
            Call myTest2
        Case 87 To 100
            Call myTest3
    End Select

End Sub
```

For the IBuySpy sample application, we have created separate test scripts for Browsing, Searching, Registration, and Checkout which can be found on this book's companion CD.

Executing a Performance/Stress Test

Determining how much stress is sufficient depends on the goals outlined prior to testing. You have to define the criteria which indicate when appropriate stress levels are reached. To aid in this decision, some examples of possible test criteria are included:

- Stop increasing load when an excessive number of errors occur in the event or Web server logs.

- Increase load to a point where throughput diminishes.

- Set a threshold on CPU utilization (for example greater than 75 percent).

- Set a threshold on memory utilization.

- Set a threshold on page response time.

- Obtain a predefined number of requests per second or concurrent connections that the Web application must be able to handle, based on business requirements.

Once the test criteria have been defined, several test runs are required at different load levels (simultaneous browser connections). By starting off low and letting the test execute for a sufficient time to allow an adequate number of user scenarios to be completed, you can determine the throughput for a particular scenario within an application. While increasing load, you should also monitor the stress on the client machine to ensure that the stress client is not saturated. Additional clients can be used to ensure that individual client machines do not become a bottleneck or a source of errors during a stress test. During these preliminary tests, which we refer to as "smoke tests," you should monitor the application servers to ensure that all the performance criteria are being met. You can also generate a tabulation of application throughput. By repeating these tests, you will eventually reach a point where one or more of the threshold criteria are met. This is an indication that the appropriate level of load has been reached. At this point, you are ready to conduct a test run of longer duration with the appropriate load using only the necessary monitoring tools to minimize the server's resource utilization.

Depending on the scope of testing, you may have one or more test scripts. We recommend that separate tests be run for each scenario in addition to running all scenarios concurrently with a specified weighting. Running scenarios separately will aid in uncovering bottlenecks in the system or code that affect only that specific area of application logic. These isolated bottlenecks will help you in identifying later bottlenecks that are due to code interaction in the mixed scenario test run. The mixed scenario test run (where all scenarios are run concurrently) helps stress the application in a more realistic fashion, representative of actual application usage. This will help you reveal application bottlenecks, such as blocking and timeouts, that are due to the interaction of all scenarios.

Overall test duration is another important variable to define in the stress testing effort. This variable really depends on how fast an application can process requests and complete user transactions (scenarios). Other factors that can influence the length of a test are the length of time required to reach a steady state and the amount of available test data. Stress tests that are used to calculate throughput under load are typically run for at a minimum of 5 to 30 minutes.

> **Note**   Total Transactions = Total successful Page View/s or SQL Row Counts that indicate a completed scenario
> Transactions per minute = Total Transactions / Test time interval
> Transactions per second = Transactions per minute / 60 sec.

Extended tests can run for a minimum of eight hours under load or can last up to a week. However, the exact length of time really depends on the application being tested. Such tests are useful for determining the stability of the application, uncovering memory leaks and monitoring application through-put over a longer period of sustained stress.

Create a Controlled Environment

In addition to determining the adequate number of browser connections and the optimal number of stress client machines, we advise you to conduct testing in a controlled environment. *Controlled* implies that there should be machines designated as stress clients and others as servers which host applications. These machines should be as close as possible in hardware specifications to your pro-duction environment. All systems should be connected on a private network with adequate bandwidth. Test results are of little value if performance issues cannot be reproduced. A controlled environment helps ensure test reliability by eliminating non-test related network noise.

The absence of a controlled environment can potentially skew test results by introducing dependencies on external servers for DNS lookups, authentica-tion, and so on. Depending on the time of day that the tests are conducted, net-work delays can change based on network congestion, which could affect application throughput. If such dependencies on external servers do exist, the testing schedule can be affected due to problems with one or more of these servers, which delays the overall stress testing effort. With a controlled environ-ment, you can also be certain that the entire load generated on the application servers is solely due to the stress clients.

Conclusion

ACT is a powerful tool, and you can only expect its capabilities to expand with future releases as it changes to accommodate new technology. Given the importance of stress testing, it behooves you to become familiar with a stress tool such as ACT. The sooner you learn the tool, the sooner you will be able to put it to good use. We hope this chapter helped provide a quick start to becom-ing productive with ACT.

4

Monitoring Application Performance with System Monitor

The Microsoft Windows 2000 family of servers provides a graphical performance-monitoring tool called System Monitor, which is a Microsoft Management Console (MMC) snap-in. (It was called Performance Monitor, or Perfmon, in previous versions of Windows NT.) This snap-in assists you with monitoring the performance of your Web applications, database systems, and hardware resources on Windows-based servers. MMC has two parts: System Monitor, for monitoring your system in real time; and Performance Logs and Alerts, for monitoring your system in logging mode.

In this chapter we discuss how to use the MMC snap-in, which resources to monitor, and how to interpret some of the most common system counters. Performance objects and counters specific to the .NET Framework are discussed in Chapter 7, ASP.NET and IIS counters and objects are detailed in Chapter 6, and SQL Server–specific counters and objects in Chapter 8. Note that we refer to the Windows 2000 server family in this chapter, not Windows .NET Server, because at the time of this writing, Windows .NET Server is still in beta.

Using System Monitor

The units of measurement used to monitor hardware and software resources through System Monitor are called *counters*, which are then further grouped into categories called *objects*. In some cases, counters also have instances. For example, when monitoring the processor activity of a Web server, you monitor the *% Processor Time* counter, which is found under the *Processor* object. If there is more than one processor in the server, you can choose to monitor the total activity of all of the processors or instances for each individual processor.

A default set of System Monitor objects and counters are made available when you install Windows 2000 Server. If a specific application, such as SQL Server, is installed on the server, SQL Server–specific objects and counters are also made available. In this case System Monitor will use remote procedure calls to collect information from SQL Server.

System Monitor consumes a small amount of CPU and disk resources on the system it is monitoring, which you should keep in mind when measuring and determining the performance of systems and applications. If you are monitoring the machine remotely, System Monitor will also consume bandwidth from the network card. On highly utilized systems and applications hosted on the Windows 2000 platform, this overhead could be cause for concern, especially if you're monitoring production systems, but in most dedicated test environments it should not be a concern.

In addition to monitoring performance counters, System Monitor allows you to

- view selected system performance objects and counters in real time.

- log performance counter information for later analysis.

- monitor multiple Windows 2000 servers from one instance of System Monitor.

- create alerts to notify you when certain performance thresholds or conditions occur. For example, when the processor time goes above 90 percent, you can configure the alert to log an entry in the Event Viewer, send a network message, start a performance data log file, run a program when the condition occurs, or all of the above.

- trace events to record data when certain activities occur for processes, threads, disk I/O, network I/O, file details and page faults. Trace logs require a parsing tool to interpret the output. You can create such a tool using APIs provided at the following location: *http://msdn.microsoft.com/msdn-files*. Tracing is rarely used, except by Microsoft support providers.

This chapter looks at the first two methods in detail and also provides an overview of the fourth (creating notification alerts).

Viewing Real-Time Performance Data

In real-time mode you can view performance data in three different categories: chart, histogram, or report. Viewing data in real time is useful if you know what you are looking for or if you want to verify the existence of a particular bottleneck. When you have to run a stress test overnight for a bottleneck to appear, the best approach is to log the performance data. See the section "Logging and Viewing Logged Data" later in this chapter for more information on this topic.

Chart View

The real-time chart view is an excellent method for identifying trends in the data over time and comparing multiple instances of a counter such as *% Processor Time*. For the most part you will find yourself using chart view for your performance tests, so it's important to become familiar with this particular view to take full advantage of its rich feature set. There are two views available under chart view, graph view and histogram view. An example of the graph view is shown in Figure 4-1.

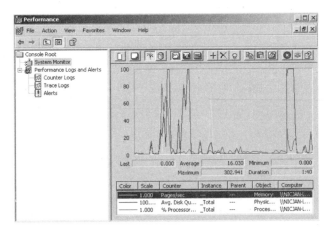

Figure 4-1   System Monitor graph view

Graph View

1.   Click Start, point to Programs, then Administrative Tools, and then click Performance.

2.   Click System Monitor in the console tree on the left to view System Monitor in the right pane.

      To explain the power of chart view for monitoring performance, we'll walk you through an example of using the graph and histogram views. So, let's say you want to monitor processor utilization of a multiprocessor system. First, launch System Monitor. The performance console that contains System Monitor opens as shown in Figure 4-2.

> **Tip** You can also launch System Monitor by typing **perfmon** in the Run command.

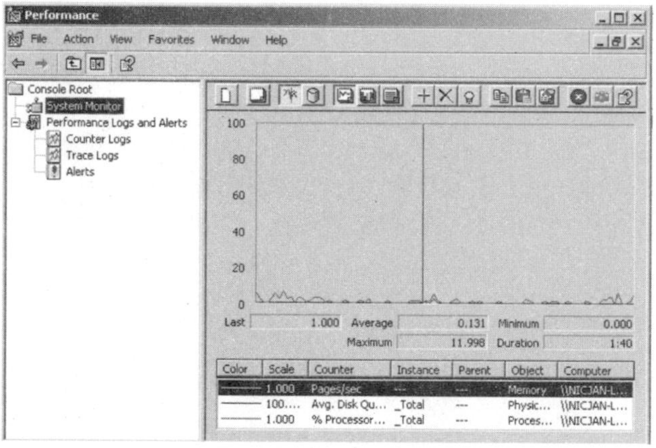

Figure 4-2 System Monitor console tree

3. If the monitor is not in chart view, click the View Chart button at the top of the right pane to switch to chart view.

Counter Color Now that you have a graph view containing processor utilization information, let's explore some of the features of System Monitor you can use to work with the performance data you are collecting. Some of the features are specific to chart view, while others can be used under the report and histogram views as well.

It is important to use the colors to distinguish the data you are monitoring. You can choose each color from a palette (in the Property Name list box of the System Monitor Properties dialog box) or you can base the colors on system colors defined using the Display icon in Control Panel. When using the palette, note the following:

- BackColorCtl refers to the area surrounding the chart.
- BackColor refers to the chart data-display area.
- ForeColor refers to the color of the text in the display and legend.

Counter Scale   Depending on the counter you are monitoring, there will be times when you'll need to adjust the counter's scale so the counter information displayed makes more sense. For instance, when monitoring memory-related counters, you will need to increase the scale of the counters that deal with bytes of information. The value of a counter scale can be changed exponentially from .0000001 to 1000000.

Counter Characteristics   When you're selecting counters for data collection, note the counter characteristics. Some counters are formulated as instantaneous and others are averages. Instantaneous counters display the most recent measurements, while averaging counters display the average of the last two measurements over the period between two samples. For the processor object counters on a multiprocessor server, each processor will be listed in the Instances selection box. System Monitor will list the instances from zero. For example, a four-processor server will be listed from instance 0 to 3, where the third instance represents the fourth processor.

It is important that you understand the implications of the counter on the data. For example, if *transaction/sec* is being monitored, be aware that the data is calculated as the number of transactions counted for the sample time selected. The number of transactions is divided by the number of seconds in the interval selected. Additionally, note how to interpret a spike when working with averaging counters. For example, when you first begin to monitor the *% Processor Time* counter you may see an initial spike in processor usage. For an accurate view of processor utilization, wait until the second or third reading for the average value for the counter.

Parent Instance Name   If you are monitoring threads of the Microsoft Windows Explorer process, track the Windows Explorer instance of the *Thread* object (Windows Explorer would be the parent instance), and then each thread running Windows Explorer (these threads are child instances). The instance index allows you to track these child instances. The instance index for the thread you want might be 0, 1, and so on, for each thread, preceded by the number sign (#). The operating system configures System Monitor properties to display duplicate instances by default. Instance index 0 is hidden; numbering of additional instances starts with 1. You cannot monitor multiple instances of the same process unless you display instance indexes.

Computer Name   Each object has counters that are used to measure various aspects of performance, such as transfer rates for disks or the amount of processor time consumed for processors.

Computer Name is the name of the computer that will be displayed at the bottom of the chart view. Be careful when collecting the same objects and counters from different servers; use the colors and different fonts to distinguish between instances on different servers.

Value Bar   The value bar under the chart contains statistical information for the currently selected counters. The value bar can be turned on or off by right-clicking anywhere in the chart and selecting Properties, selecting the General tab in the System Monitor Properties dialog box and deselecting Value Bar under Display Elements.

The values displayed in the value bar are as follows:

- **Last**   The last value displayed for the currently selected counter.

- **Average**   The average value of the currently selected counter.

- **Minimum**   The minimum value of the currently selected counter.

- **Maximum**   The maximum value of the currently selected counter.

- **Duration**   The total elapsed time displayed in the graph, this value is based on the interval value. The interval value you set determines how often counter data should be collected. For more information on the interval setting see the section "How Often Should You Collect Data?" later in this chapter

Histogram View

The histogram view is the preferred method of viewing data when monitoring multiple instances of the same counter. For example, you can compare the *% Disk Read Time* for all of the drives in your server to understand which drive is being taxed with read requests. You can switch to histogram view by clicking the Histogram button on the toolbar or typing Ctrl+B. Additionally, you can select Histogram on the General tab of the System Monitor Properties dialog box.

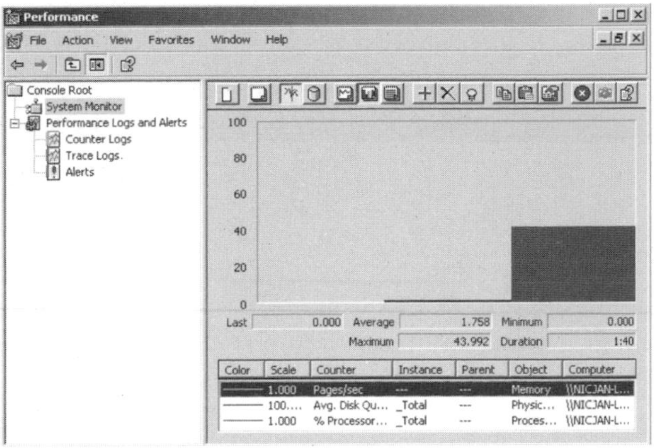

Figure 4-3   Histogram view

Report View

Report view is extremely useful when monitoring counters dealing with logical and physical I/O, such as disk or network I/O. For example, if you have to monitor all the processes running on your Web server concurrently, doing so under chart view would create an extremely hard-to-read graph or histogram. Instead, you can switch to report view for an easy-to-read view of the data.

To view real-time data as a report, you can click the Report tool on the toolbar or type Ctrl+R. Or, you can select Report on the General tab of the System Monitor Properties dialog box.

How Often Should You Collect Data?

For both real-time performance monitoring and data logging, you can set a specific interval for data collection. The interval you set for data collection will have a significant impact on your ability to capture potential performance bottlenecks. For the most part, the type of bottleneck you are investigating will determine the interval period you set. For instance, if you are monitoring a problem that manifests itself slowly, such as a memory leak, you should set a longer interval period. On the other hand, if the bottleneck tends to occur frequently, set a lower interval period. When you're not sure of the bottleneck or when it's occurring, setting the interval period to 15 minutes should be sufficient to start with.

Also consider the overall length of time you want to monitor when choosing this interval. Updating every 15 seconds is reasonable if you will be monitoring for no more than four hours. If you'll be monitoring a system for eight hours or more, do not set an interval shorter than 300 seconds (five minutes). Setting the update interval to a frequent rate (that is, a low value) can cause the system to generate a large amount of data, which can be difficult to work with especially if you're simultaneously monitoring a large number of counters.

Monitoring many objects and counters can also generate a large amount of data and consume disk space. Try to strike a balance between the number of objects you monitor and the sampling frequency to keep log file size within manageable limits.

If you prefer to maintain a long update interval when logging, you can still view data fluctuations that occur between those intervals. To do so, see the next section, "Logging and Viewing Logged Data" for information about manipulating time ranges within logs.

Logging and Viewing Logged Data

One of the most valuable features of System Monitor is its logging capability. Regular logging of performance data allows you to compare before and after a change to the system's hardware, software, or application. For example, your company decides to launch a new marketing campaign selling its most popular widgets at 50 percent off. This sale causes a dramatic increase in traffic to the company's Web site. Logging performance data will allow you to compare and contrast the effects of the increased user transaction before, during, and after the sale. This information can then be analyzed to determine whether the Web site is suffering from any bottlenecks or whether you have adequate hardware to support future marketing campaigns.

You can capture System Monitor data for a specific period of time and then analyze and compare the performance log files later on. This will allow you to view the system behavior over time, which can reveal trends in system usage that you might not see when viewing real-time data. For example, in your log files you might find that disk utilization is typically high from 8 P.M to 10 P.M and lower for the remainder of time. You might be able to equate this trend to heavy data entry or a database backup during these times.

> **Note**   When you use System Monitor, it is most efficient to start the log locally on the server you want to collect data from. You can access the log file later from a remote system if you need to. If you must log over the network, reduce the number of objects and counters to the most critical ones.

To start logging information on a Windows 2000 server using System Monitor, follow these steps:

1. Click Start, Programs, then point to Administrative Tools, and click Performance.

2. Expand Performance Logs And Alerts in the left pane of the performance window.

3. Select Counter Logs in the console tree.

4. In the right pane, right-click and choose New Log Settings from the shortcut menu as shown in Figure 4-4.

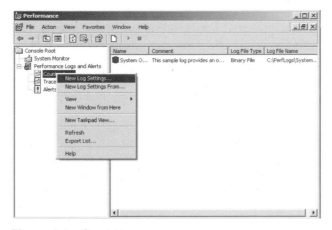

Figure 4-4   Create log

5. Enter a name to identify the log settings in the New Log Settings dialog box as shown in Figure 4-5, and then click OK. We chose IBuyspy for the name of this log setting.

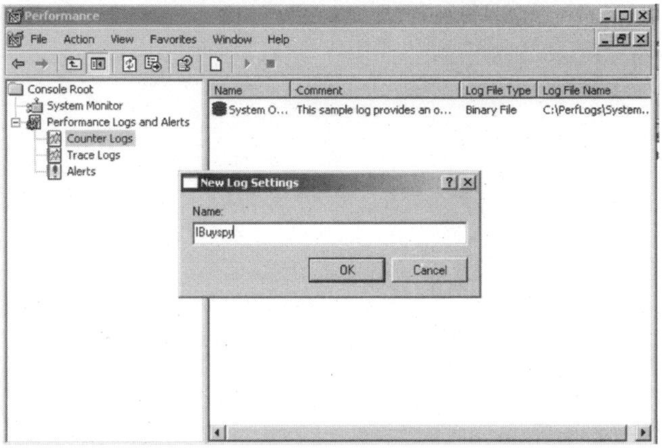

Figure 4-5   New Log Settings

6. The name you choose for the log setting will appear as the title for the Performance Log dialog box. Click the Add button to open the Select Counters dialog box.

7. Add the counters that you want saved to the log file by highlighting them and then clicking the Add button. When finished adding counters, click Close in the Select Counters dialog box. On the General tab of the Performance Log dialog box, you can also set the interval for sampling data.

8. Click the Log Files tab to set log file–specific information, such as location, file name, file type, and maximum file size limit. Use CSV files for the default file type, especially if you are collecting data for a long period of time, in order to maintain manageability. As shown in Figure 4-6, in this example we save the file locally.

> **Note**   It is always a good idea to select a high interval for the sampling data value when collecting performance data over a long period of time. This is most important to note when saving data as a binary file—binary files are always larger than CSV files.

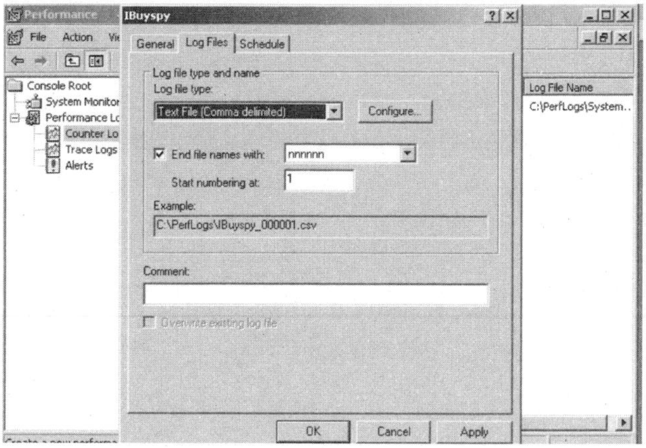

Figure 4-6   Log file information

9. Click the Schedule tab to set the schedule for logging. If you do not enter a time for the logging to stop, it will continue until you stop it manually.

10. Click OK. The log file name should appear in the right pane. The green icon next to the log name shows logging has started, as shown in Figure 4-7.

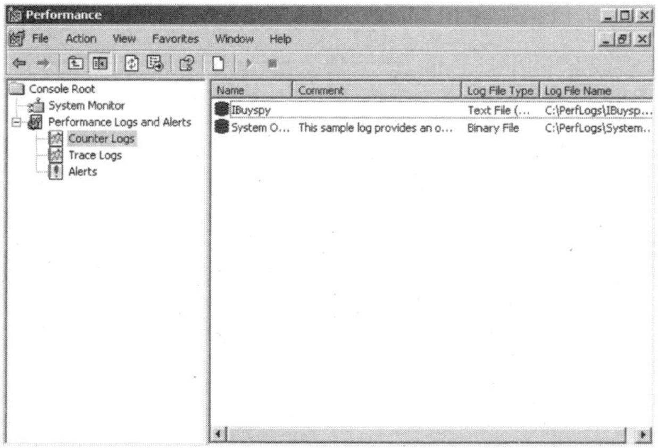

Figure 4-7   Log file started

The icon will be red if the logging is stopped. You can start and stop logging manually in this window by right-clicking the name of the log setting and choosing Start or Stop from the shortcut menu.

After you have collected information and stopped the logging process, use the following steps to load logged data into the system and view it.

1. Click System Monitor in the left pane to view System Monitor in the right pane.

2. Click the View Log File Data button at the top of the right pane to open the Select Log File dialog box, as shown in Figure 4-8. Navigate to the folder and select the log file you want to view and then click open.

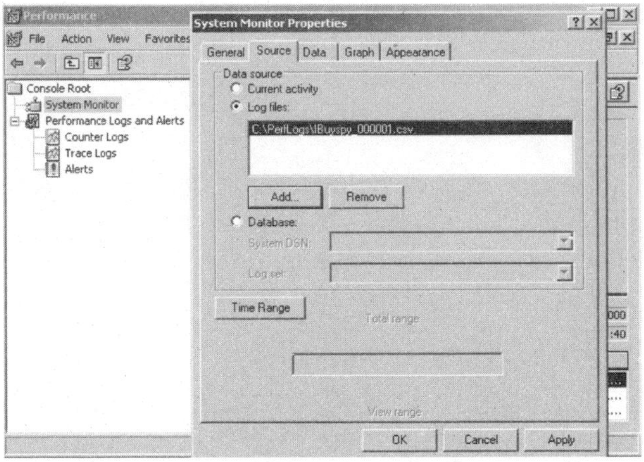

Figure 4-8 Log File dialog box

3. Click the Add button to add the counters you want to view from the selected log file. When you close the Add Counters dialog box you will see the selected counters in System Monitor, as shown in Figure 4-9. Only the counters selected for initial logging will be available for viewing.

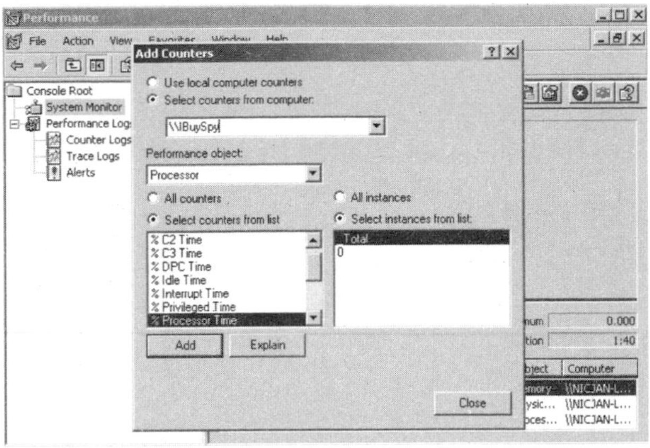

Figure 4-9   Add Counters

You can narrow your view of the log file by following these additional steps:

1.   After you have loaded your log file into System Monitor, click the Properties button at the top of the right pane.

2.   In the System Monitor Properties dialog box, click the Source tab.

3.   Near the bottom of the Source tab, slide both ends of the slide window to include the times that you want to see in the View range as shown in Figure 4-10.

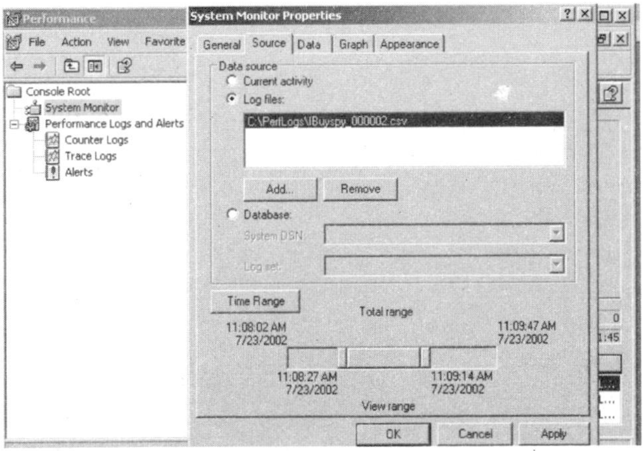

Figure 4-10   Log file information

4. (Optional) Use the other tabs in System Monitor Properties dialog box to change the different characteristics of the output.

5. Click OK to return to System Monitor and view the selected range of the data.

Monitoring Remote Computers

With System Monitor you can remotely collect and monitor data from multiple machines. There could be several reasons why you would want to monitor remote machines—for example, the server in question could be located in a lab or production environment across the country.

Before you start monitoring remote computer performance you must have Access This Computer from the Network rights. These rights are granted by following these steps:

1. From the Administrative Tools folder, launch the Local Security Policy program.

2. Double-click the Local Policies folder to expand it.

3. Double-click the User Rights Assignment folder. The currently defined list of policy rights will be displayed.

4. Find the policy Access This Computer from the Network and double-click to open it. A list of users and groups assigned to the policy will be displayed.

5. To assign additional users or groups to the policy click the Add User or Group button.

To monitor a remote computer follow these steps:

1. Start System Monitor and then press Ctrl+I to open the Add Counters dialog box.

2. In the Select Counters From Computer list, select or type the name of computer you want to monitor.

You should keep your connection speed in mind when monitoring computers remotely. If you have a slow connection speed (128 Kbps or slower) you may want to switch from the default chart view to report view. This way you'll be passing far fewer graphics over the wire, and avoiding delays in results being displayed on your screen.

Monitoring Objects, Counters, and Instances for Performance Bottlenecks

In this section we elaborate on some of the most commonly used performance counters. These counters are key when you're attempting to determine processor, memory, and disk bottlenecks. We provide some real world examples that show how to determine each bottleneck. We do not cover all of the system counters, as they would require a book of their own.

> **Note**   If you don't see a counter mentioned that you need information on, you can use online help to get a description of each counter. To access this information, open System Monitor, follow the steps to add a counter, which are described earlier in this chapter. When the Add Counters dialog box opens, click on the counter you want information on and then click the Explain button.

Processor Bottlenecks

When analyzing the performance of a Web application, one of the most commonly observed components is CPU utilization. The server's CPU is performing complex operations and therefore is a logical place to start when observing the performance of the Web server. The general processor information is contained in the *processor* object. The primary objective of monitoring processor-specific counters is to identify any potential processor bottlenecks on the server. As a best practice you should limit CPU utilization to an average of 75 percent or below for each processor, although short bursts of 100 percent utilization could be tolerable depending on the nature and user base of the application. High CPU utilization can lead to high context switching (discussed later in the chapter) which causes undesirable overhead. So, though you may be running at 90 percent CPU utilization, you might not be getting optimal throughput compared to when you're running at 70 percent or 75 percent utilization.

For a system with multiple processors, System Monitor lists an instance of each processor in the Add Counters dialog box. You can also view the average value of all processors by monitoring the *Total instance*. In a single processor system, System Monitor lists the total and one processor instance; both refer to the single processor.

Below is a list of counters that should be monitored when investigating a processor level bottleneck. Additionally, we describe best practices when using the *Processor* object counters.

- **% Processor Time**   The percentage of elapsed time that the processor spends to execute a non-idle thread. It is calculated by measuring the duration of the idle thread that is active in the sample interval, and subtracting that time from interval duration. (Each processor has an idle thread that consumes cycles when no other threads are ready to run). This counter is the primary indicator of processor activity, and displays the average percentage of busy time observed during the sample interval. It is calculated by monitoring the time that the service is inactive and subtracting that value from 100 percent.

- **% Privileged Time**   The percentage of elapsed time that the process threads spent executing code in privileged mode. When a Windows system service is called, the service will often run in privileged mode to gain access to system-private data. Such data is protected from access by threads executing in user mode. Calls to the system can be explicit or implicit, such as page faults or interrupts. Unlike some early operating systems, Windows uses process boundaries for subsystem protection in addition to the traditional protection of user and privileged modes. Some work done by Windows on behalf of the application might appear in other subsystem processes in addition to the privileged time in the process.

- **% User Time**   The percentage of time the thread is running in the code of a user mode process or code other than the operating system's code. *% User Time* should always be viewed for sanity against *% Privileged Time* on *System* and *Processor* objects, as they are measures of non-idle time and sum the total of non-idle time.

- **% Interrupt Time**   The time the processor spends receiving and servicing hardware interrupts during sample intervals. This value is an indirect indicator of the activity of devices that generate interrupts, such as the system clock, the mouse, disk drivers, data communication lines, network interface cards and other peripheral devices. These devices normally interrupt the processor when they have completed a task or require attention. Normal thread execution is suspended during interrupts. Most system clocks interrupt the processor every 10 milliseconds, creating a background of interrupt activity. This counter displays the average busy time as a percentage of the sample time.

- **Interrupts/sec**   The average rate, in incidents per second, at which the processor received and serviced hardware interrupts. It does not include deferred procedure calls (DPCs), which are counted separately. This value is an indirect indicator of the activity of devices that generate interrupts, such as the system clock, the mouse, disk drivers, data communication lines, network interface cards, and other peripheral devices. These devices normally interrupt the processor when they have completed a task or require attention. Normal thread execution is suspended. The system clock typically interrupts the processor every 10 milliseconds, creating a background of interrupt activity.

To observe the efficiency of a multiprocessor computer, use the counters listed in Table 4-1.

Table 4-1   Counters for Multiprocessor Computers

Counter	Description
Process\ % Processor Time	The sum of processor time on each processor for all threads of the process.
Processor(_Total)\ % Processor Time	Lists activity for all processors in the computer. It's the average non-idle time of all processors during the time interval divided by the number of processors. It should be noted that the counter will have a value of 50% if all processors are busy for half of the sample interval and if half of the processors are busy for the entire interval.
Process\ % Processor Time	The sum of processor time on each processor for all threads of the process.

Typical Processor-related Problems and Solutions

A processor bottleneck occurs when the demand is overshooting supply of processor threads of the system or applications being deployed. This is caused by processor demands being queued and thus maintaining high CPU utilization until the queue is being emptied, which causes the system response to degrade.

When you find that the processor utilization on a server is consistently high (90 percent or higher) it usually leads to processes queuing up, waiting for processor time, and causing a bottleneck. Such a sustained high level of processor usage is unacceptable for a server.

Let's discuss an example of high processor utilization. If you are monitoring an IIS server hosting a single Web site that relies upon a legacy COM+ application written in Visual Basic 6 to parse through extensive XML documents, you may find that the COM+ application is utilizing more than 90 percent of the processor's time. This high processor utilization by the COM+ application affects the Web application's ability to handle new connections to the site. If you understand the type of bottleneck (in this case, a processor bottleneck) and the root cause of the bottleneck (processor hungry COM+ application), you can decide how to handle the resource problem. One solution may be to physically separate the COM+ application from the Web server, or to convert your code to more efficient and faster performing managed code.

> **Note** When examining processor usage, keep in mind the role of the computer and the type of work being done. High processor values on a SQL server are less desirable than on a Web server.

There are two methods for correcting most processor bottlenecks. The first is to add faster or additional processors to your system. The downside to this option is that its not cost effective and is a temporary solution. The next surge in traffic to your Web site will cause you to scramble to add additional hardware or replace the old servers with newer faster servers. The other and more appropriate route is to analyze the software to see which specific process or portion of the application is causing this bottleneck. As a rule, you should always try to performance tune your software before reverting to the more costly route of adding additional hardware. In addition to monitoring counters found under the *Processor* object, there are other counters found under the *System* object that you should monitor when verifying the existence of a processor bottleneck.

System Object

The *System* object and its associated counters measure aggregate data for threads running on the processor. They provide valuable insights into your overall system performance. The following system counters are the most important to monitor.

- ***Processor Queue Length***   The number of threads in the processor queue. Unlike the disk counters (discussed later in the chapter), this counter shows ready threads only, not threads that are running. There is a single queue for processor time even on computers with multiple processors. Therefore, if a computer has multiple processors, you need to divide this value by the number of processors servicing the workload.

    One way to determine if a processor bottleneck exists with your application is to monitor the *System\ Processor Queue Length* counter. A sustained queue length along with an over-utilized processor (90 percent and above) is a strong indicator of a processor bottleneck.

    When monitoring the *Processor Queue Length* counter we generally do not want to see a sustained processor queue length of 2 or more along with high processor utilization. If you find that the queue length is 2 or higher, but your processor utilization is consistently low, you may be dealing with some form of processor blocking rather than a bottleneck.

    You can also monitor *Processor\ % Interrupt Time* for an indirect indicator of the activity of disk drivers, network adapters, and other devices that generate interrupts.

- ***Context Switches/sec***   The combined rate at which all processors on the computer are switched from one thread to another. Context switches occur when a running thread voluntarily relinquishes the processor, is pre-empted by a higher priority ready thread, or switches between user-mode and privileged (kernel) mode to use an Executive or subsystem service. It is the sum of *Thread\\Context Switches/sec* for all threads running on all processors in the computer and is measured in numbers of switches. There are context switch counters on the *System* and *Thread* objects. This counter displays the difference between the values observed in the last two samples, divided by the duration of the sample interval.

    A system that experiences excessive context switching due to inefficient application code or poor system architecture can be extremely costly in the terms of resource usage. Your goal should always be to decrease the amount of context switching occurring at your application or database servers. Context switches essentially prevent the server from getting any real work done as valuable processor resources are taken up dealing with a thread that is no longer able to run because it is blocked waiting for a logical or physical resource, or the thread puts itself to sleep. Symptoms of high context switching can include lower throughput coupled with high CPU utilization, which begins to occur at switching levels of 15,000 or higher. You can determine whether context switching is excessive by comparing it with the value of *Processor\ % Privileged Time*. If this counter is at 40 percent or more and the context-switching rate is high, then you should investigate the cause for the high rates of context switches.

Finally, when monitoring your system you should make sure that the *System\Context Switches/sec* counter that reports system wide context switches is close to, if not identical to, the value provided by the *_Total instance* of the *Thread\Context Switches/sec* counter. Monitoring this over time can help you determine the range by which the two counters' value might vary.

Disk Bottlenecks

Disk space is a recurring problem. No matter how much drive space you configure your servers or network storage devices with, your software seems to consume it. However, disk bottlenecks problems are related to time, not disk space. When the disk becomes the limiting factor in your server, it is because the components involved in reading from and writing to the disk cannot keep pace with the rest of the system.

The parts of the disk that create a time bottleneck are less familiar than the megabytes or gigabytes of space. They include the I/O bus, the device bus, the disk controller, and the head stack assembly. Each of these components contributes to and, in turn, limits the performance of the disk configuration.

System Monitor measures different aspects of physical and logical disk performance. To truly understand the state of disk resource consumption you will need to monitor several disk counters, and in some instances you will need to monitor them for several days. On top of this, you will probably find yourself churning through some mathematical formulas to determine whether or not a disk bottleneck exists at your server. These formulas are detailed in the real world example below. However, before we delve into these formulas let's review some of the counters you will monitor when hunting down a disk bottleneck. These counters will allow you to troubleshoot, capacity plan and measure the activity of your disk subsystem. In the case of some of the counters the information they provide is required for the aforementioned disk bottleneck formulas.

- *Average Disk Queue Length*   The average number of both read and writes requests that were queued for the selected disk during the sample interval.

- *Average Disk Read Queue Length*   The average number of read requests that were queued for the selected disk during the sample interval.

- *Average Disk Write Queue Length*   The average number of write requests that were queued for the selected disk during the sample interval.

- *Average Disk sec/Read*   The average time, in seconds, of a read of data from the disk.

- *Average Disk sec/Transfer*   The time, in seconds, of the average disk transfer.

- *Disk Reads/sec*   The rate of read operations on the disk.

- *Disk Writes/sec*   The rate of write operations on the disk.

How the ACE Team Discovered a Disk Bottleneck

An internal product team at Microsoft was interested in evaluating server hardware from two different vendors. These servers would be used to host the SQL database for a Web application they were designing. This Web application would be accessed by several thousand customers simultaneously; therefore, selecting the right hardware was critical for the success of their project. The product team was interested in conducting several stress tests and monitoring the effect these tests had on the SQL server's resources. A stress test harness was developed that simulated production environment activity. The stress harness was written using Visual Basic and run on client machines as a Win32 application. One hundred client machines were configured to execute the stress test harness. The stress harness was designed to spawn instances that simulated five users per instance, each connecting to a different database (that is, db1 through db5) on the server. The workflow used results in each client executing a SQL batch file via ADO or an OSQL instance for each operation. These batch files were generated using SQL Profiler to trace manual user navigation of the site then saving the trace as a SQL batch file. The operations performed in this manner for these tests were:

- Load the login page

- Select a user name and hit enter

- Load the tasks page
- Submit actual work times to the manager
- Load the resource views page
- Set and save notification reminders
- Delegate one task to another resource

The client machines were configured so that all of the 500 databases at the SQL server would be accessed during the tests. This helped prevent any one of the databases from receiving a majority of the SQL transactions. After configuring the client machines, the stress test harness was started and run for 20 minutes (15 minutes were set aside as a warm up period). During these 20 minutes, performance data at the SQL server was collected for benchmark purposes.

A wait time of 10 and 60 seconds was used when executing the load against the targeted databases. Each simulated user started the test at a random offset from the global start time of the test and performed one operation. The user would then wait either 10 or 60 seconds before beginning the next operation.

On executing both scenarios a significant disk read times and write times was noticed which prompted an investigation as to the disk capacity of the hardware being utilized. The calculations indicated the I/O per disk exceeded the manufacturer's specified I/O that the disk can successfully handle.

The performance data collected during the 10 second and 60 second wait-time benchmark indicated the existence of a disk bottleneck at Server 1. In order to verify this, our team applied the performance data gathered from the physical disk activity to the following formula:

I/Os per Disk = [Reads + (4×Writes)] / Number of Disks

If the calculated I/Os per disk exceeded the capacity for the server, this would verify the existence of a disk bottleneck. The disk I/O capacity and calculated disk I/O per disk is outlined below. It should be noted that for each of the calculations, 85 random I/Os per disk is used as the capacity for a disk in a RAID 5 configuration.

10-Second Wait Time Test Scenario on Server 1

Disk I/O capacity = 85 random I/Os per disk
Calculated I/Os per disk = [269.7 + (4×74.6)] / 5

Calculated I/Os per disk = 113.62 random I/Os per disk

At 113.62 random I/Os per disk Server1 is suffering from a disk bottleneck as the capacity for each disk in the server was only 85 random I/Os per disk.

10-Second Wait Time Test Scenario on Server 2

Disk I/O capacity = 85 random I/Os per disk

Calculated I/Os per disk = [138.3 + (4×43.0)] / 4

Calculated I/Os per disk = 77.7 random I/Os per disk

At 77.7 random I/Os per disk Server 2 is below the capacity of 85 random I/Os per disk, therefore no disk bottleneck exists.

60-Second Wait Time Test Scenario on Server 1

Disk I/O capacity = 85 random I/Os per disk

Calculated I/Os per disk = [294.8 + (4×71.8)] / 5

Calculated I/Os per disk = 116.4 random I/Os per disk

At 116.4 random I/Os per disk Server 1 is suffering from a disk bottleneck as the capacity for each disk in the server is only 85 random I/Os per disk.

60-Second Wait Time Test Scenario on Server 2

Disk I/O capacity = 85 random I/Os per disk

Calculated I/Os per disk = [68.9 + (4×24.0)] / 4

Calculated I/Os per disk = 41.2 random I/Os per disk

At 41.2 random I/Os per disk Server 2 is significantly below the capacity of 85 random I/Os per disk, therefore no disk bottleneck exists. At 113.62 and 116.4 random I/Os per disk respectively Server1 is suffering from a disk bottleneck as the capacity for each disk in the server is only 85 random I/Os per disk thus exceeding the manufacturer's specified number of disk I/Os the hardware can sustain.

Disk Architecture Matters to Performance

Today, many Web applications are built to interact with database server. Many if not all of the applications we test use SQL Server 2000, and in most cases we find some significant performance gains by tuning the SQL server. These wins come through optimization of the SQL code, database schema, or disk utilization. When designing the architecture of your database, you will be required to select how data and log files are read and written from disk. For example, do you want to write your log files to a RAID device versus a non-RAID device? If you do not make the right choices, this can lead to a disk bottleneck. In one such case we were able to apply formulas that proved or disproved the existence of a disk bottleneck. You will find details of the project and formulas utilized in the real world example above.

Memory

When analyzing the performance of your Web applications, you should determine if a system is starving for memory due to a memory leak or other application fault, or if the system is simply over-used and requires more hardware. In this section we discuss the counters you should monitor to determine the existence and then cause of the memory bottleneck. (Note that there are tools available to you other than System Monitor to analyze memory utilization of a server. It may be worth your while to investigate some of these tools, as they can save time when monitoring the system.)

- ■ *Page faults/sec* The average number of pages faulted per second. It is measured in number of pages faulted per second because only one page is faulted in each fault operation; hence this is also equal to the number of page fault operations. This counter includes both hard faults (those that require disk access) and soft faults (where the faulted page is found elsewhere in physical memory.) Most processors can handle large numbers of soft faults without significant consequences. However, hard faults, which require disk access, can cause significant delays.

- ■ *Available Bytes* Indicates how many bytes of memory are currently available for use by processes. Pages/sec provides the number of pages that were either retrieved from disk due to hard page faults or written to disk to free space in the working set due to page faults.

- ■ *Page Reads /sec* The rate at which the disk was read to resolve hard page faults. It shows the number of read operations, without regard to the number of pages retrieved in each operation. A hard page fault occurs when a process references a page in virtual memory that is not in the working set or elsewhere in physical memory, and must be retrieved from disk. This counter is a primary indicator of the kinds of faults that cause system-wide delays. It includes read operations to satisfy faults in the file system cache (usually requested by applications) and in non-cached mapped memory files. Compare the value of *Memory\\Pages Reads/sec* to the value of *Memory\\Pages Input/sec* to determine the average number of pages read during each operation.

- ■ *Page writes /sec* The rate at which pages are written to disk to free up space in physical memory. Pages are written to disk only if they are changed while in physical memory, so they are likely to hold data, not code. This counter shows write operations, without regard to the number of pages written in each operation. This counter displays the difference between the values observed in the last two samples, divided by the duration of the sample interval.

■ ***Pages/sec*** The rate at which pages are read from or written to disk to resolve hard page faults. This counter is a primary indicator of the kinds of faults that cause system-wide delays. It is the sum of *Memory\\Pages Input/sec* and *Memory\\Pages Output/sec*. It is counted in numbers of pages, so it can be compared to other counts of pages, such as *Memory\\Page Faults/sec*, without conversion. It includes pages retrieved to satisfy faults in the file system cache (usually requested by applications) non-cached mapped memory files.

How the ACE Team Discovered a Memory Leak

In this example we discuss how we were able to determine the existence of a memory leak in an application that was submitted to our team for performance testing. Performance analysts on our team met with the development team to understand some of the common user scenarios for the Web application. The analyst discussed existing performance issues the development team was aware of. The developers were concerned about memory usage by COM+ applications running on the Web server. Keeping this in mind, the analyst thought the best approach in ruling out memory issues would be to execute a series of stress tests. These tests would help to uncover memory utilization issues at the server if they truly existed. The analyst built test scripts of the user scenarios provided by the development team and executed a short stress test. Performance logs recorded resource utilization at the server hosting the COM+ application. During this one-hour test the analyst observed a memory consumption of approximately 20 MB. He noted that this memory was still not released three hours after the test was stopped. These findings prompted a further investigation into the application's memory consumption (see Table 4-2). A 12-hour continuous stress test was conducted to analyze the applications memory behavior. At the end of the 12-hour continuous test it was discovered that in addition to heavy CPU activity, growth in private bytes was significant for the test period and the server was extremely low on virtual memory (see Table 4-3). Of the 671 MB acquired by the dllhost private bytes, 640 MB was still allocated three hours after the test ended. Virtual memory growth appeared to be centered almost entirely on private bytes for the dllhost process. For the 1-hour test, the memory only grew from between 38 to 58 megabytes. For the 12-hour test, this growth was much higher, from 368 to 671 megabytes. The memory was not released until the server was rebooted. The dllhost process was then analyzed to identify the processes that were involved in the execution of the dllhost to narrow down the potential memory leak to a specific process. After identifying the exact process causing the memory leak, the code for that process was profiled and the developer was able to pinpoint exactly where in his code memory was not being managed correctly. Of course with managed code, you won't find yourself running into the slew of memory management issues you did in the days of unmanaged code.

Table 4-2 Summary of 1-hour Test Results

Windows 2000 IIS 5.0	~ Average-IIS	~Maximum / Total-IIS
System-% Total Processor Time	55%	100%
Inetinfo-% Total Processor Time	.5%	1%
Dllhost-% Total Processor Time	41%	100%
Memory: Available in Megabytes	164 MB	185 MB
Memory: Pages/sec	0	.2
Inetinfo: Private in Megabytes	14 MB	14 MB
Dllhost: Private in Megabytes	38 MB	56 MB

Table 4-3 Summary of 12-hour Test Results

Windows 2000 IIS 5.0	~ Average-IIS	~Maximum / Total-IIS
System-% Total Processor Time	69%	100%
Inetinfo-%Total Processor Time	.6 %	1.5%
Dllhost-% Total Processor Time	71%	100%
Memory: Available in Megabytes	56 MB	196 MB
Memory: Pages/sec	51	295
Inetinfo: Private in Megabytes	14 MB	14.4 MB
Dllhost: Private in Megabytes	368 MB	671 MB

Memory leaks should be investigated by monitoring *Memory\ Available bytes, Process\ Private Bytes* and *Process\ Working Set*. A memory leak would typically indicate *Process\ Private Bytes* and *Process\ Working Set* increasing while *Memory\Available bytes* would be decreasing. This should be verified in Task Manager by identifying PID and then trace this back to your application. Memory leaks should always be verified by running a performance test for an extended period of time to verify the applications reaction when all available memory is depleted.

Create and Configure Alerts

You can configure the Performance Logs and Alerts service to fire off alerts when a specified performance event has occurred at the server. For example, if the available memory at the Web server drops below 20 MB, an event could be trigged that satisfies one or all of the following conditions:

- Logs an entry to the application event log
- Sends a network message to a specified user
- Starts a performance data log
- Runs a specified program

There are several instances when configuring an alert to trigger an event helps increase your testing efficiency. One is when you are running an extended stress test. Let's say the stress test must be run over a 24-hour period and you are particularly interested in what happens with the Web server's memory. You could configure an alert that records an event to the application event log each time a spike occurs with the *Pages/Sec* counter. This way, you don't have to try to count the number of spikes in an enormous log file. You can simply sort the application event log for each instance you are most concerned with.

To create an alert follow these steps:

1. Open Performance and click Start, point to Programs, point to Administrative Tools, and then click Performance.

2. Double-click Performance Logs and Alerts, and then click Alerts. Any existing alerts will be listed in the details pane. A green icon indicates that an alert is running; a red icon indicates an alert has been stopped or is not currently active.

3. Right-click a blank area of the details pane and click New Alert Settings.

4. In Name, type the name of the alert, and then click OK.

5. To define a comment for your alert, along with counters, alert thresholds, and the sample interval, use the General tab. To define actions that should occur when counter data triggers an alert, use the Action tab, and to define when the service should begin scanning for alerts, use the Schedule tab.

Note You must have Full Control access to a subkey in the registry in order to create or modify a log configuration. The subkey is:

HKEY_LOCAL_MACHINE\SYSTEM\CurrentControlSet\Services\SysmonLog\Log Queries

In general, administrators have this access by default. Administrators can grant access to users using the Security menu in Regedt32.exe. In addition, to run the Performance Logs and Alerts service (which is installed by Setup and runs in the background when you configure a log to run), you must have the right to start or otherwise configure services on the system. Administrators have this right by default and can grant it to users by using Group Policy.

Caution Incorrectly editing the registry may severely damage your system. Before making changes to the registry, you should back up any valued data on the computer.

To define counters and thresholds for an Alert, follow these steps:

1. Open Performance.

2. Double-click Performance Logs and Alerts, and then click Alerts.

3. In the details pane, double-click the alert.

4. In Comment, type a comment to describe the alert as needed.

5. Click Add.

For each counter or group of counters that you want to add to the log, perform the following steps:

1. To monitor counters from the computer on which the Performance Logs and Alerts service will run, click Use Local Computer Counters.

    Or, to monitor counters from a specific computer regardless of where the service is run, click Select Counters From Computer and specify the name of the computer you want to monitor.

2. In *Performance* object, click an object to monitor.

3.   In *Performance* counters, click one or more counters to monitor.

4.   To monitor all instances of the selected counters, click All Instances. (Binary logs can include instances that are not available at log startup but subsequently become available.)

 Or, to monitor particular instances of the selected counters, click Select Instances From List, and then click an instance or instances to monitor.

5.   Click Add.

6.   In Alert When The Value Is, specify Under or Over, and in Limit, specify the value that triggers the alert.

7.   In Sample Data Every, specify the amount and the unit of measure for the update interval.

8.   Complete the alert configuration using the Action and Schedule tabs.

Note   When creating a monitoring console for export, be sure to select Use Local Computer Counters. Otherwise, counter logs will obtain data from the computer named in the text box, regardless of where the console file is installed.

To define actions for an alert, follow these steps:

1.   Open Performance.

2.   Double-click Performance Logs and Alerts, and then click Alerts.

3.   In the details pane, double-click the alert.

4.   Click the Action tab.

5.   To have the Performance Logs and Alerts service create an entry visible in Event Viewer, select Log An Entry in the Application Event Log.

6.   To have the service trigger the messenger service to send a message, select Send a Network Message to and type the name of the computer on which the alert message should be displayed.

7.   To run a counter log when an alert occurs, select Start Performance Data Log and specify the counter log you want to run.

8. To have a program run when an alert occurs, select Run This Program and type the file path and name or click Browse to locate the file. When an alert occurs, the service creates a process and runs the specified command file. The service also copies any command-line arguments you define to the command line that is used to run the file. Click Command Line Arguments and select the appropriate check boxes for arguments to include when the program is run.

To start or stop a counter log, trace log, or alert manually, follow these steps:

1. Open Performance.

2. Double-click Performance Logs and Alerts, and click Counter Logs, Trace Logs, or Alerts.

3. In the details pane, right-click the name of the log or alert you want to start or stop, and click Start to begin the logging or alert activity you defined, or click Stop to terminate the activity.

> **Note**   There may be a slight delay before the log or alert starts or stops, indicated when the icon changes color (from green for started to red for stopped, and vice versa).

To remove counters from a log or alert, follow these steps:

1. Open Performance.

2. Double-click Performance Logs and Alerts, and then click Counter Logs or Alerts.

3. In the details pane, double-click the name of the log or alert.

4. Under Counters, click the counter you want to remove, and then click Remove.

To view or change properties of a log or alert, follow these steps:

1. Open Performance.

2. Double-click Performance Logs and Alerts.

3. Click Counter Logs, Trace Logs, or Alerts.

4. In the details pane, double-click the name of the log or alert.

5. View or change the log properties as needed.

To define start or stop parameters for a log or alert, follow these steps.

1. Open Performance.

2. Double-click Performance Logs and Alerts, and then click Counter Logs, Trace Logs, or Alerts.

3. In the details pane, double-click the name of the log or alert.

4. Click the Schedule tab.

5. Under Start log, click one of the following options:

   ❑ To start the log or alert manually, click Manually. When this option is selected, to start the log or alert, right-click the log name in the details pane, and click Start.

   ❑ To start the log or alert at a specific time and date, click At, and then specify the time and date.

6. Under Stop Log, select one of the following options:

   ❑ To stop the log or alert manually, click Manually. When this option is selected, to stop the log or alert, right-click the log or alert name in the details pane, and click Stop.

   ❑ To stop the log or alert after a specified duration, click After, and then specify the number of intervals and the type of interval (days, hours, and so on).

   ❑ To stop the log or alert at a specific time and date, click At, and then specify the time and date. (The year box accepts four characters; the others accept two characters.)

   ❑ To stop a log when the log file becomes full, select options as follows:

      ❑ For counter logs, click When the Log File is Full. The file will continue to accumulate data according to the file-size limit you set on the Log Files tab (in kilobytes up to two gigabytes).

      ❑ For trace logs, click When the n-MB Log File is Full. The file will continue to accumulate data according to the file-size limit you set on the Log Files tab (in megabytes).

7. Complete the properties as appropriate for logs or alerts:

    When setting this option, take into consideration your available disk space and any disk quotas that are in place. An error might occur if your disk runs out of disk space due to logging.

    ❑   For logs, under When a Log File Closes, select the appropriate option:

        ❑   If you want to configure a circular (continuous, automated) counter or trace logging, select Start a New Log File.

        ❑   If you want to run a program after the log file stops (for example, a copy command for transferring completed logs to an archive site), select Run This Command. Also type the path and file name of the program to run, or click Browse to locate the program.

    ❑   For alerts, under When An Alert Scan Finishes, select Start a New Alert Scan if you want to configure continuous alert scanning.

    To delete a log or alert, follow these steps:

1. Open Performance.

2. Double-click Performance Logs and Alerts.

3. Click Counter Logs, Trace Logs, or Alerts.

4. In the details pane, right-click the name of the log or alert, and click Delete.

When you schedule a log to close at a specific time and date or close the log manually, the Start a New Log File option is unavailable.

Conclusion

This chapter discussed how to utilize System Monitor to assist you in performance testing applications and identifying system level bottlenecks. We reviewed several sets of objects and counters one must monitor to find these system level bottlenecks. Understanding System Monitor is critical to successful performance testing and analysis.

5

Application Network Analysis

The approach to performing an application network analysis of Web-based applications remains unchanged between operating systems (Microsoft Windows NT, Windows 2000, and Windows XP), development technologies (static HTML, ASP, Windows DNA, and now .NET), and data access technologies (RDO, ADO and ADO.NET). This process has remained consistent because the primary protocol used to communicate over the Internet (TCP/IP) has not changed. With the advent of .NET and software as a service, this approach can be used to identify network-related bottlenecks and improve the network performance of both legacy applications and those built with the .NET Framework.

Conducting an Application Network Analysis

Many Internet users still use modems that connect at painfully slow speeds, and they probably will for the foreseeable future. The goal of an *application network analysis* is to identify slowly executing pages or code and fix them to provide a better end user experience. We assume that you are familiar with networking basics, such as the Open Systems Interconnection (OSI) model, but do not expect you to be as familiar with conducting a network analysis. Therefore, before we delve into the process of conducting a network analysis, it's imperative that you become familiar with the concepts and terminology behind the application network analysis process. If there are terms discussed in this chapter that are unfamiliar to you, please refer to the *Microsoft Encyclopedia of Networking, Second Edition* written by Mitch Tullock (Microsoft Press, 2002). You should also become familiar with the type of questions you'll be facing from the customer's perspective. For example, questions you'll hear from application owners may include: How does *network latency* impact my global users? What is a *network round trip* and how does it affect my end user experience? How do I determine the amount of *data transferred* for each *page view* and other *content* loaded when my customers access my Web application? My users are complaining of long *response times*. What can I do? How do I identify and avoid *processing delays* on my IIS server or SQL server?

As we progress through the chapter, we will answer questions such as these. We will define these terms and provide examples that will help illustrate these concepts and their effect on application performance. Also, we will provide an introduction to tools used to perform an application network analysis: Microsoft Network Monitor, and Compuware's Application Expert.

> **Note** We use the term *page view* to refer to the actual page plus elements or file types associated with it. For example, the Default.aspx will include this file and any image files, style sheets, java scripts, etc. that accompany it.

Network Latency

The simplest definition of *network latency* is the time it takes for a data packet to move across a network connection. The lower the latency between your Web application tiers, the faster the response times. Latency and bandwidth are two factors that determine the speed of a network connection. An easy way to determine the network latency between your client and a Web application is to use the pathping utility, or other utilities such as the Visual Trace Route feature provided in Application Expert. A PowerPoint presentation of Compuware's Application Expert can be found on this book's companion CD.

> **Note**   The pathping utility is a command-line tool that combines features of the *ping* and *tracert* commands. To use, open a command prompt and type **pathping *servername***. The output from the *pathping* command will show you the hops or network routers between the client you are using and the server you are pinging, along with the latency or round trip time for the particular hop.

Every local area network (LAN) and wide area network (WAN) connection is constrained by network latency. Factors that cause latency to increase are poor quality network devices, longer distances causing communication travel through more hops or network devices, and network congestion. For example, a typical 56-kbps local modem connection may have 200 milliseconds of latency, while a similar connection traveling a farther distance may pass through more network devices, which increases the latency to 500 milliseconds. In Table 5-1, we captured a trace with Network Monitor to measure the impact of network latency when requesting the 46-kilobyte home page of IBuySpy with our Microsoft Internet Explorer Web browser. The capture was imported into Application Expert's Response Time Predictor, and we are able to extrapolate the response times for both a 200-millisecond and 500-millisecond latency 56-kbps connection. We'll discuss this Application Expert feature and others in the "Using Compuware Application Expert" section later in this chapter.

Table 5-1 Latency and Response Time

Connection Speed	Latency	Response Time
10 mbps	10 milliseconds	0.5 seconds
56 kbps	200 milliseconds	6 seconds
56 kbps	500 milliseconds	8.5 seconds

The impact of the additional 300 milliseconds of latency for this particular page view and all associated elements is 2.5 seconds, not 300 milliseconds. The reason for this is latency affects every application round trip.

> **Note**   One way to deal with the impact of latency is to locate your Web application closer geographically to your user base. This does not guarantee a better connection between your user base and Web application but will typically reduce the amount of latency.

Network Round Trips

A network round trip is a client-server request-response pair generated by an application. A request-response pair sent from a Web browser to a Web server and back is considered a single round trip. For example, when you type in a URL in your Web browser, such as *http://www.microsoft.com*, each image, style sheet, or other page element defined in the response to your request (from the Web server) is counted as a separate network round trip. Additional round trips are involved in the setup of each connection to the Web server in this example. Later in this chapter we will discuss how Application Expert can be used to quickly obtain the number of round trips your ASP pages are consuming. Combined with latency, round trips have a profound effect on application response time. Imagine that your IIS servers are located on both the US East and West Coasts. You are located in Mountain View California and viewing your IBuySpy Login ASPX page on the West Coast IIS server takes 4 seconds while viewing it from the East Coast IIS server takes 6.5 seconds. Further investigation shows the latency for your connection to the East Coast server is 500 milliseconds while that to the West Coast server is 200 milliseconds. Because every round trip is affected by network latency, the East Coast response time is longer by approximately 2 seconds.

For most application developers, network latency on the Internet is out of their control. This is why it is important to develop applications that use as few round trips as possible to keep response times quick even under high network latency conditions.

Reducing Network Round Trips

The most effective method for reducing round trips is to reduce the number of objects per page. Table 5-2 shows two home pages for major Internet search sites that many of you have probably used before. The first home page has fewer than six objects and loads very quickly. The second home page has approximately 15 objects and loads much more slowly. Notice the difference in the number of round trips that are generated when each of these home pages are loaded.

Table 5-2   How Objects per Page Affect Round Trips

Sites	Number of Objects	Number of Round Trips
Search Site 1 (Optimized)	6	8
Search Site 2 (Slow)	15	19

Search Site 1 used in Table 5-2 was able to limit the number of objects to six and has a less than 10-second response time on most 56-kbps connections. They limit the number of objects to six by creating one large graphic at the top of their home page, which consists of eight images. Considering each object requested will create a network round trip, they have saved seven round trips by merging their eight small graphics into a single request.

Data Transferred

Data transferred is the amount of data moved between a client Web browser and Web server and is often measured in kilobytes. The best approach for measuring data transferred is to break down the scenarios within your application by page views including their associated elements. For example, the IBuySpy home page transfers 46 kilobytes of data non-cached the first time you access it and 24 kilobytes of data cached (subsequent requests with many objects loaded from your Web browser cache located in the temporary Internet folder). Based on our experience, the amount of data transferred for a page view and associated elements of 50 kilobytes or less will give an acceptable response time. This allows low speed Internet connections like 56-kbps modems the best chance of having fast response times. This chapter uses several terms to quantify data, such as *kilobits per second* and *kilobytes of data transferred*. Therefore to better illustrate how these metrics relate, Table 5-3 shows the conversion from bits to bytes, kilobits to kilobytes, and kilobytes to megabytes.

Table 5-3   Conversion Metrics

Measured Value	Converted Value
8 bits	1 byte
1 kilobyte	1024 bytes
1024 kilobytes	1 megabyte

Reducing the Quantity of Data Transferred

There are several techniques for reducing the amount of data being transferred between Internet Explorer and the IIS tier. These methods include IIS compression, removing unnecessary characters and white space, reducing the number of objects on pages, and optimizing images.

HTTP Compression is a built-in feature of IIS and Internet Explorer. This tool works well for static content like HTM files, HTML files, CSS files, JS files, and uncompressed images. However, with dynamic content you may run into some problems, such as pages rendering incorrectly or becoming nonfunctional. There is also additional overhead associated with resources on your IIS server if you choose to use IIS compression. By default, HTTP Compression is disabled and can be enabled using the WWW Service Master Properties Services tab, shown in Figure 5-1.

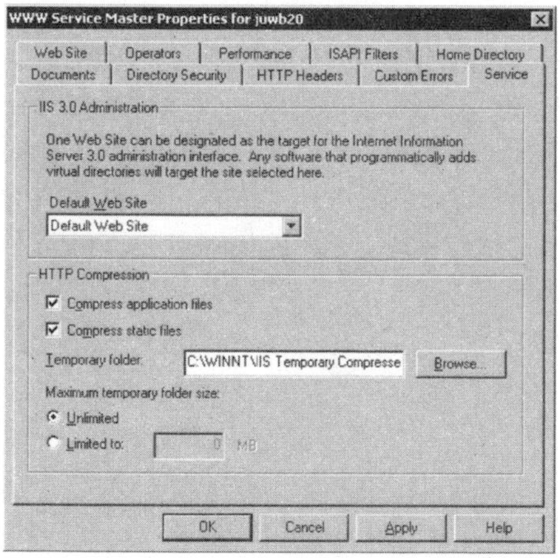

Figure 5-1   Enabling IIS compression

Once HTTP Compression is enabled, you must specify the file types to be compressed by editing the *metabase*. The following steps show how to edit the metabase settings to compress static TXT, JS, CSS, DOC, and XLS files:

1. Enable HTTP Compression as shown in Figure 5-1.

2. Open a command prompt and navigate to the adminscripts folder.

3. Execute the following command: cscript.exe adsutil.vbs set W3Svc/ Filters/Compression/GZIP/HcFileExtensions "txt" "js" "css" "doc" "xls"

4. Execute the following command: cscript.exe adsutil.vbs set W3Svc/ Filters/Compression/DEFLATE/HcFileExtensions "txt" "js" "css" "doc" "xls"

5. Execute the following command: iisreset.exe /restart

Another method to trim down the amount of data transferred between the browser and IIS tier is to package the data more tightly by removing all unnecessary characters and white space from your code. This is particularly useful around loops when a lot of data is returned to the client. Also, many developers put comments into their code, which adds additional characters and lines to the page, resulting in more data transferred.

> **Note**   If you are very conscious about reducing your page size as much as possible, use short variable and filenames as well as a flat directory structure. This will slightly reduce the amount of data transferred because you are passing less text to the client.

Reducing the number of objects on your page will decrease the amount of data transferred. Many sites use images for bullets and text instead of using formatted text. By limiting the number of elements and using colored text and background colors to make sections of the page stand out, you can reduce the amount of data transferred and network round trips.

Images make a Web site or application more visually appealing but there is a significant performance cost associated with using them. Use Graphics Interchange Format (GIF) images whenever possible. Using optimized or compressed images will reduce the amount of data transferred and typically does not impact the clarity of your pictures much. Most high quality imaging software suites will include a tool to optimize and compress your image files. Reuse images for your company logo, navigational bars or other images that are used throughout your application. Make sure you use the exact same name and path or Internet Explorer will treat it as a new image. After the initial fulfillment of the request Internet Explorer will cache the images locally. Another option is to preload images using JavaScript. This will load the images in the background while the rest of the page loads. Subsequent requests for the cached image will appear more quickly to the end user because the images will be cached locally in Internet Explorer.

> **Note** Make sure you set the height and width attributes of each image. It will load faster because the Internet Explorer client does not have to determine the dimensions.

Processing Delay

When client requests spend unnecessary time on the middle or back-end tier of an application, it is considered a *processing delay*. This can be due to poorly written code that can take several seconds to process, or poor SQL tuning and improper indexing causing stored procedures and other SQL commands to consume valuable time. Processing delays directly impact response times. To get the most gain out of our tuning efforts, we typically focus on delays longer than 1 second. However, your application may have stricter or higher standards depending on a number of variables including type of application and size of your user base. For example, if your application is designed to render large reports to a small group of decision support analysts, response time may be expected to be slower. This is because larger reports may take longer to process on your database server, and given that your user base is small, budget constraints may limit the amount of time you can spend optimizing this application. However, if your user base is very large and consists of customers ordering your products, you will spend more time optimizing the application's response time to ensure that no sales are lost because customers are frustrated about slow response times.

Reducing Processing Delays

The most common way to speed the response time of your application is to reduce application-processing delays. This is accomplished by speeding up slowly executing ASPX, Managed Code, and poor SQL code. More details are available in the IIS, Managed Code, and SQL sections of this book. As discussed earlier in the "Identifying Application Processing Delays" section, by using Network Monitor display data view or Application Expert bounce diagrams, you can identify whether or not your page view and associated elements have processing delays and which tier is causing it. Next, determine where in your application's code the processing delay is happening. There are several methods for profiling and identifying the code causing processing delays:

■ With .NET applications you can enable tracing on your ASPX pages. After you request an ASPX page with your browser, the statistics and timing will be located at the bottom of your page view. To enable tracing at the page level, add the ASPX page directive `Trace="True"`, as shown in Figure 5-2.

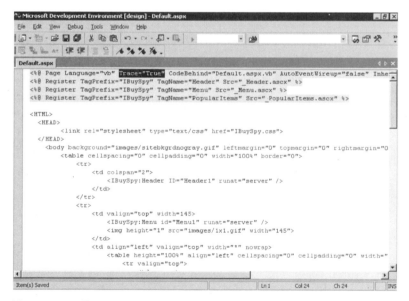

Figure 5-2 Enabling tracing on ASPX pages

■ With standard ASP applications, you can use timers in your code to identify problems. Simply add timing variables throughout your script and write the values to a text file. This method of ASP profiling will allow you to narrow processing delays to a particular function or line of code. This book's companion CD includes examples of the ASP timing code for VBScript and JScript, which are called ACETimerVB.doc and ACETimerJS.doc. Many times these delays are related to a specific call to a custom component that is inefficient or a SQL command that is taking several hundred milliseconds or even several seconds to execute.

> **Note**   A simple profiling approach is to insert `response.end` in your ASP page where you suspect the processing is occurring. When this ASP page is loaded, the script will exit when this command is executed, exposing your processing delay. If no delay occurred, move the *response.end* command farther down in your ASP page and load again. Eventually you will narrow down the portion of your script causing the processing delay.

■   The easiest way to identify SQL bottlenecks and processing delays is to use SQL Profiler. Simply create a SQL Profiler trace file while you request your page view. Any delays caused by SQL commands or stored procedures will show up in the Duration field of the trace file in milliseconds. Once you have identified these poorly performing SQL commands or stored procedures, you can work on optimizing them. For more information on optimizing your SQL commands and stored procedures, see Chapter 8.

Response Times

In reference to performing an application network analysis, *response time* refers to how long it takes data to travel from the client's initial request to the completion of the request. Improving performance of your application is synonymous with reducing the overall response time for each of your application's page views including associated elements. Some factors that constrain response times are a high number of round trips, low bandwidth, end users with high latency connections, a large amount of data transferred, and processing delays on the IIS code, managed code, or SQL code. We describe the process of using Application Expert to quickly calculate response times later in this chapter.

Response time acceptability depends on a variety of factors including the type of application, the function of each requested page within the application, the bandwidth and latency of your Internet connection. For instance, a requested page that has no interaction with a back-end database (that is, a static page view) or has a small amount of content should load faster than requested pages that are heavy in content or constantly retrieve or update data from a database (that is, a dynamic page view) will be slower. Table 5-4 shows the response times we consider acceptable when performing an application network analysis. Low response times represent applications with small static page views or very light interaction with a database. High response times represent applications with large page views or heavy interaction with a database.

Table 5-4   Acceptable Response Times

Connection Speed	Low Response Time	High Response Time
Low speed (modems)	10 seconds	15 seconds
High speed (DSL, cable, or higher)	5 seconds	10 seconds

User Scenarios

User scenarios are a collection of page views, including their associated elements, that implement business or functional processes. For example, searching the IBuySpy site (discussed in Chapter 3) is a good example of a real-world user scenario. The search scenario consists of several steps, such as loading the home page, entering a search string, clicking the GO button, selecting a product from the search results and viewing the product detail page. This scenario consists of two page views. Instead of capturing the entire user scenario, we recommend you conduct this analysis by separating the scenario into distinct user actions, like clicking a button or link to submit a form that makes a request to the Web server. The reason we isolate the user scenarios into separate page views or user actions is to help identify the exact causes of slow response times.

Identify User Scenarios

The IBuySpy .NET sample application utilizes typical e-commerce functionality. In the following example we have broken the search user scenario into three separate page views, including their associated elements:

- **Step 1** The user views the home page, loading the Home.aspx or Default.aspx page.

- **Step 2** The user enters a search string in the search field and clicks GO, loading the "SearchResults.aspx" page.

- **Step 3** The user selects or clicks a product returned by the search, loading the ProductDetails.aspx page.

If your application is already deployed, you can identify scenarios by either focusing on pages that users have complained about, or by walking through the application and identifying pages that load or execute more slowly. The second method requires that every application page is hit. In some applications this may be unreasonable. However, if you have never performed an application network analysis on the application, this is a good way to establish a response time baseline. Also, if you are working on a new application, this method is more useful because you can identify and fix poorly performing pages before going live.

Now that we have defined the terminology, the next section of this chapter describes the tools available with which to conduct an application network analysis.

Using Microsoft Network Monitor

Network Monitor is a software-based network sniffer that can be used to analyze and troubleshoot data transferred between nodes and devices on a network. This tool is designed for several types of Information Technology (IT) disciplines. Network administrators often use Network Monitor to capture and monitor overall network utilization. Network Engineers may use Network Monitor to assist in troubleshooting potential bottlenecks in network designs and architecture. Developers may use Network Monitor to troubleshoot their code. In an application network analysis, Network Monitor is primarily used to identify the amount of data transferred and count the number of round trips used in response time calculations per page view, including associated elements or user actions performed that generate activity to the Web server.

Network Monitor for Windows 2000 is available in two versions:

■   Network Monitor 2 Lite is available with Windows 2000 Advanced Server and Data Center editions. This version can only sniff network traffic from the local Network Interface Card (NIC) to other nodes communicating with it.

■   Network Monitor 2 Full is available with Microsoft System Management Server (SMS) 2. This version allows traffic to be captured for all traffic on a network from a single location that has the Network Monitor driver installed.

Network Monitor captures frames of network data to help you detect and analyze network problems. It aids in tracking down problems with network applications by capturing data transferred between application tiers, network round trips, network time, and processing delays.

MAC Address and IP Address Setup

In preparing for your network captures, you should document all node MAC addresses and IP addresses. To do this, open a command prompt and type **ipconfig/all** from each back-end server and client. The output from this command will show the IP address information, DNS servers, DNS suffix, physical or MAC address, and other valuable information. This will make it easier to set up your capture filter and isolate network traffic created by the application. Often you can use a host file entry to force nodes to communicate with the correct NIC and IP addresses you are capturing on. The hosts file is typically located in the C:\windows\system32\drivers\etc folder and does not have a file extension. To add or change entries you can open the hosts file with Microsoft Notepad and follow the examples provided within the file.

Note   If you are using a client or server that has more than one NIC, make sure you either disable the extra NIC or ensure all traffic communicates on the same NIC.

Configuring Network Monitor Settings

Network Monitor needs to be properly configured before capturing data from your user scenarios. There are three key settings—the capture filter, capture buffer, and network—that can be adjusted to make sure you are creating a correct and complete capture.

Capture filters allow you to narrow down your network captures to the tiers or nodes that are used by your application. This makes it easier to isolate data transferred and round trips without analyzing unnecessary network traffic in the trace file. Figure 5-3 shows a typical capture filter.

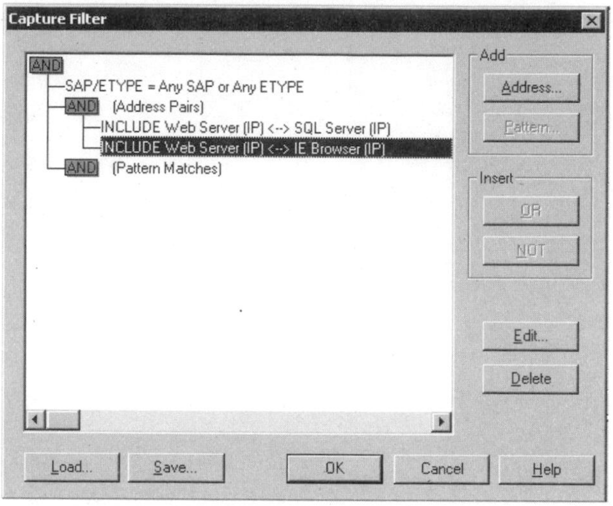

Figure 5-3 Network Monitor capture filter

The *capture buffer* is an important setting to adjust. By default the buffer is set to 1 megabyte. If a page is transferring a large amount of data you may exceed this 1 megabyte limit. Typically we adjust the capture buffer to 10 megabytes to accommodate any large captures. Figure 5-4 shows the Network Monitor Capture Buffer Settings dialog box.

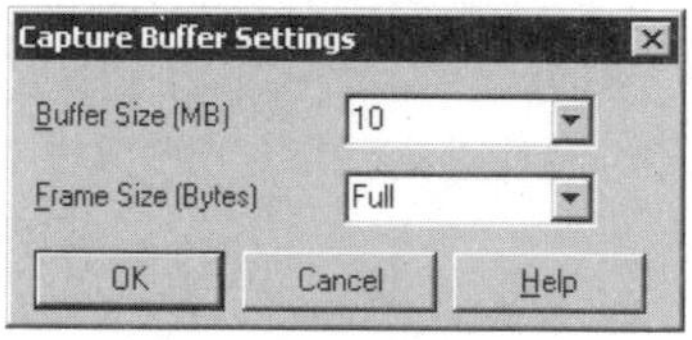

Figure 5-4 Network Monitor Capture Buffer Settings dialog box

It's important to make sure you capture on the correct *network*. With clients and servers that have more than one NIC, you need to set which network you want to capture on. To verify you are capturing on the correct network, start a Network Monitor trace and ping the IP address or URL of the Web application you are testing. Next, stop your Network Monitor trace and verify you collected the ping traffic. If not, switch Network Monitor to capture a different network and repeat until you capture on the correct network. Figure 5-5 shows where you set Network Monitor to capture on the proper network.

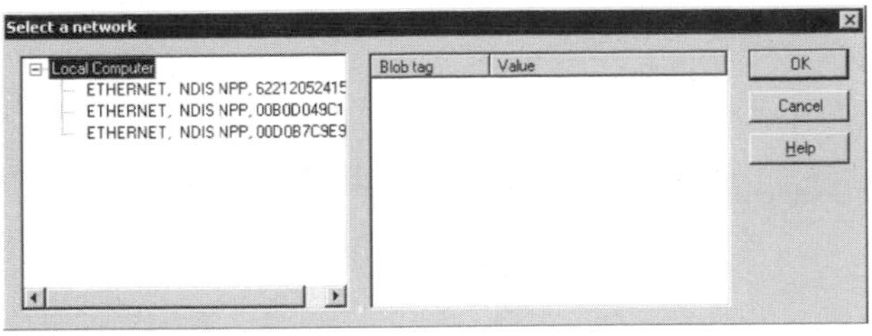

Figure 5-5   The Network Monitor Select A Network dialog box

Environment Setup

The hardware used in an application network analysis includes the test client, and all of the back-end servers that make up the application (IIS Server, SQL Server, Application Server) and any other network devices used (switch, hub, router, bridge, load balancer, etc.). Applications that require high availability and scalability typically use more than one identical Web server to load balance traffic volume. If your application is load balanced, you should ensure that only a single node (front-end Web server) is enabled during an application network analysis. The purpose of this is to make sure you are capturing traffic on the correct Web server. There are numerous ways to use Network Monitor to capture traffic created by your application. Here are a few:

■   Most applications are made up of servers connected by a network switch, because every port has dedicated bandwidth and performance is better. Network switches isolate traffic from each port, which makes it impossible for Network Monitor to see traffic from each application tier. However, through port spanning or port mirroring you can configure most network vendor switches to copy or mirror all traffic from each port you assign. Consult your network hardware vendor for instructions on configuring port spanning. By using the SMS version of Network Monitor and plugging the network monitor capture client into this port, you can see all the traffic from each of your application tiers. Figure 5-6 illustrates this model.

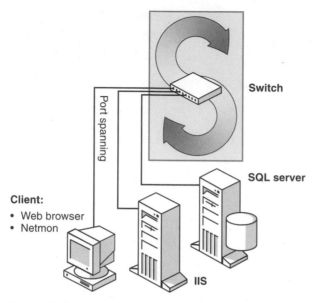

Figure 5-6   Using port spanning on your switch

■   If you do not have access to your switch configuration or if port spanning is not an option available with your network switch, another simple approach is to plug all back-end servers that make up your application into a hub. Hubs share bandwidth amongst all ports; therefore, the machine you use as your network monitor client will be able to capture traffic from all tiers. Figure 5-7 illustrates this model.

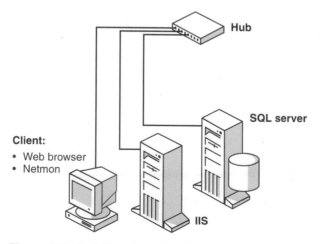

Figure 5-7   Isolating your network with a hub

■ The full version of Network Monitor allows you to install a Remote
Network Monitor Driver on each tier of your application to capture
traffic remotely. If you choose this method, install the Remote Network Monitor driver on each of your application tiers. From the Start
menu, choose Control Panel, and then choose Add/Remove Programs.
In the Add/Remove Programs dialog box, click Add New Program.
Navigate to Windows Components, then choose Management and
Monitor Tools, select Network Monitor Tools, and click OK. This
method allows you to gather the captures from all remote agents to
one client. The benefit of this approach is that it's quicker than performing separate captures to get the data from all of your Web applications tiers. However, the disadvantage is it takes longer to setup
since you have to install an additional component on each server.
Figure 5-8 illustrates this model.

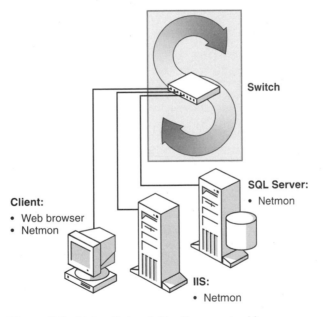

Figure 5-8   Using Network Monitor remote drivers

■ The easiest method for capturing traffic is to use the Network Monitor 2 Lite version on the IIS tier as your capture client. The IIS tier is
typically located between the Internet Explorer client and SQL tier.
Therefore, when the network monitor client is located on your IIS
server you will be able to see all the traffic coming to and from it.
Figure 5-9 illustrates this model.

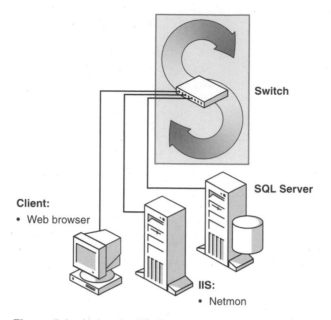

Switch

SQL Server

Client:
• Web browser

IIS:
• Netmon

Figure 5-9   Using the IIS tier as your Network Monitor client

Capturing Network Traffic

Now that Network Monitor is installed and configured correctly and your environment is set up, you are ready to begin capturing network traffic. We have discovered a few tricks that will assist you in gathering captures:

■ Because we typically break user scenarios down into individual user actions, we recommend creating a separate capture for each page view. Using this method easily identifies how much data is being transferred for each page view including associated elements. If you are looking for scenarios that are expensive in terms of data transferred or round trips you can sum the individual page views.

■ Perform your Network Monitor captures several times to verify their integrity. In approximately 90 percent of the network analyses we have performed, the network capture is accurate, however, unless you do your captures a few times to verify, you can't be sure. We re-run each capture at least three or four times until we get consistent and repeatable results. Each sample should be similar if not identical in terms of round trips and data transferred.

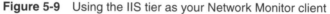

■   Network Monitor allows you to save the captures files (CAP), which can be used for further analysis or importing into third-party tools such as Application Expert.

■   Save your Network Monitor filters and address database (discussed above) in case you need to recapture. Saving your filters will save time reconfiguring Network Monitor. Figures 5-10 and 5-11 show the Save Capture Filter and Save Address As dialog boxes.

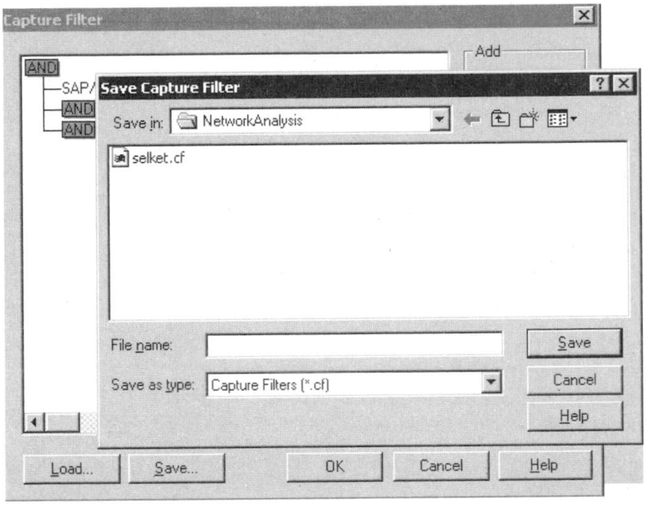

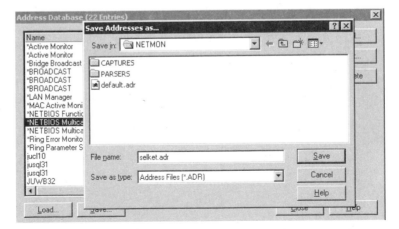

Figure 5-10   The Network Monitor Save Capture Filter dialog box

Figure 5-11   The Network Monitor Save Addresses As dialog box

■ The goal of the capture is to record only pertinent application data transferred between nodes. To achieve this, start the Network Monitor capture, request a page by typing a URL in the address window of a browser, then stop the Network Monitor capture as soon as the page finishes loading. The page is considered finished when your Internet Explorer client displays Done in the lower left-hand corner of the status bar. This will allow you to avoid excess traffic transferred after the page view is loaded.

Network Monitor Capture Structure

A Network Monitor capture file consists of two views, the capture window and the display data view. As illustrated in Figure 5-12, the capture window calculates the amount of data transferred between nodes.

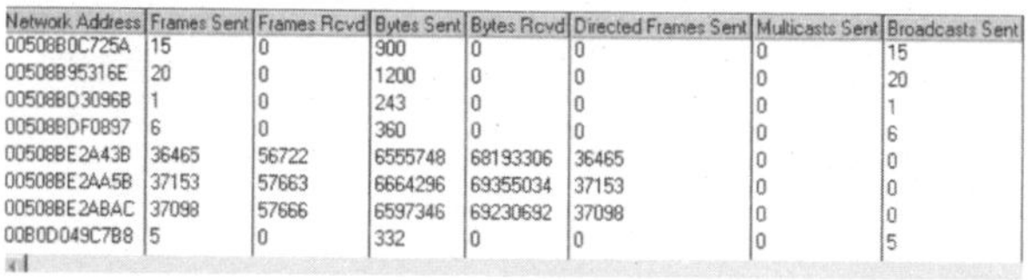

Network Address	Frames Sent	Frames Rcvd	Bytes Sent	Bytes Rcvd	Directed Frames Sent	Multicasts Sent	Broadcasts Sent
00509B0C725A	15	0	900	0	0	0	15
00508B95316E	20	0	1200	0	0	0	20
00508BD3096B	1	0	243	0	0	0	1
00508BDF0897	6	0	360	0	0	0	6
00508BE2A43B	36465	56722	6555748	68193306	36465	0	0
00508BE2AA5B	37153	57663	6664296	69355034	37153	0	0
00508BE2ABAC	37098	57666	6597346	69230692	37098	0	0
00B0D049C7B8	5	0	332	0	0	0	5

Figure 5-12   The Network Monitor capture window

The display data view contains nine columns and can contain many rows, depending on the amount of data collected. By default the trace file will show the MAC address of the NIC. To make the trace easier to read, edit the address to show the machine name or machine type. Figure 5-13 illustrates a raw capture from a client browser to an IIS server to a SQL server and back.

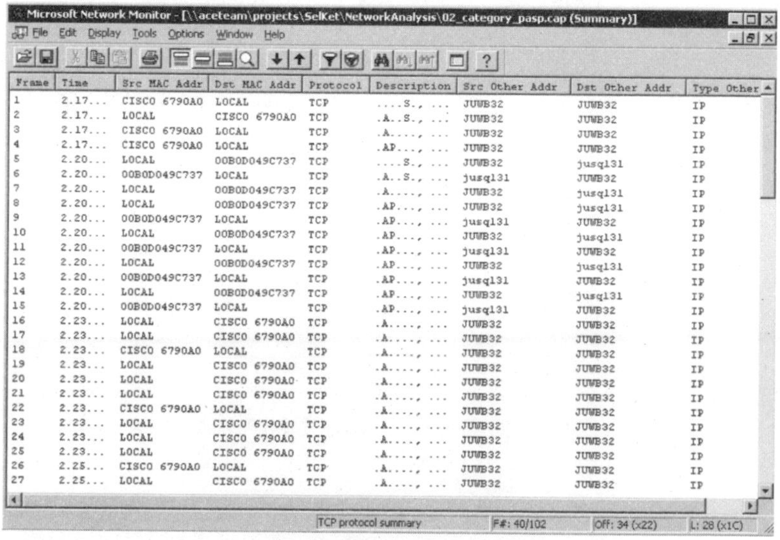

Figure 5-13   The Network Monitor display data view

All data in these views is important, however, the critical data to focus on identifies the amount of data transferred, number of round trips, and total time.

Using Compuware's Application Expert

Application Expert provides advanced response time prediction capabilities and granular application-level details for tuning distributed applications to ensure optimal network performance. Application Expert is used as a packet sniffer or for importing binary capture files obtained through Network Monitor. Application Expert also can be used as a fully functional packet sniffer. We find the following features of Application Expert to be particularly useful when performing a network analysis:

Conversation Map

Once a network capture has been imported into Application Expert, you can model the conversation between applications tiers. Figure 5-14 shows the conversation map of IBuySpy home page (no cache). This figure shows how quickly the conversation map is used to determine the amount of data transferred and number of round trips for a page view including its associated elements.

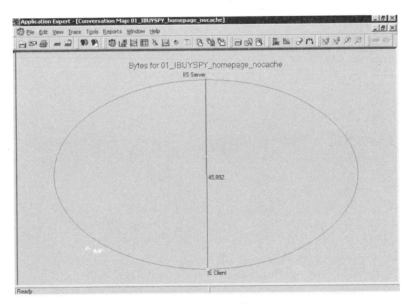

Figure 5-14   Application Expert conversation map

The conversation map provides a top-level view of the nodes (Client, IIS, and SQL) and conversations associated with hitting the home page. The conversation is defined as the data transferred or communication between the various nodes in your application. You can view the conversations by bytes or select your choice of display metric, such as payload bytes, frames, or application turns or round trips by right-clicking to open the Conversation Map context menu. Referring back to Figure 5-6, we see a total of 46 kilobytes of data being transferred between the IE client and IIS server and a total of 18 round trips.

Bounce Diagram

The bounce diagram is an excellent feature that gives you the packet level view of your application tiers and allows you to identify processing delays. Figure 5-15 shows the IBuySpy Default.aspx bounce diagram.

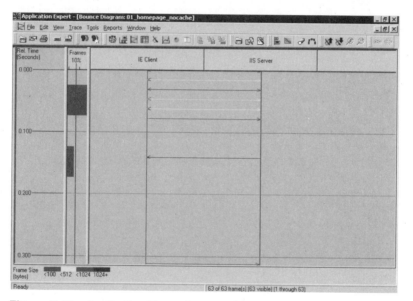

Figure 5-15   Application Expert bounce diagram

The bounce diagram is a packet flow timing diagram for client/server conversations on the network. This view shows individual frames between nodes in the sequence in which they occurred during the capture. In Figure 5-15, the IBuySpy login page shows a very small processing delay of approximately 170 milliseconds between the Internet client and Web server.

In the bounce diagram, each vertical line represents a node and the horizontal lines on the grid represent relative time increments in seconds. The time is relative to the start of the trace, which is designated 0.00. Within the diagram, the colored horizontal lines represent captured frames. The size of each frame is indicated by a color described in the legend at the bottom of the window: red for fewer than 100 bytes, yellow for up to 512 bytes, green for up to 1024 bytes, and blue for more than 1024 bytes.

Thread Analysis

It is helpful to look at the threads and thread timing using the thread analysis view in conjunction with the bounce diagram to identify which requests are causing processing delays. This combination view lets you focus thread-by-thread. The panes are dynamically linked, so an action in the upper pane affects the display and data in the lower pane to give you multiple views. For example, when you click a thread in the upper pane, the display in the lower pane changes to show the frames associated with the selected thread. If necessary, Application Expert automatically zooms into the bounce diagram for you. When you click a frame displayed in the bounce diagram, you get the detailed information on that thread. Figure 5-16 shows a thread analysis of the IBuySpy Default.aspx page. Using the thread analysis feature in Application Expert, you can quickly identify all 16 objects associated with this page view. Identifying this information from the raw Network Monitor capture or Application Expert packet trace view takes much longer.

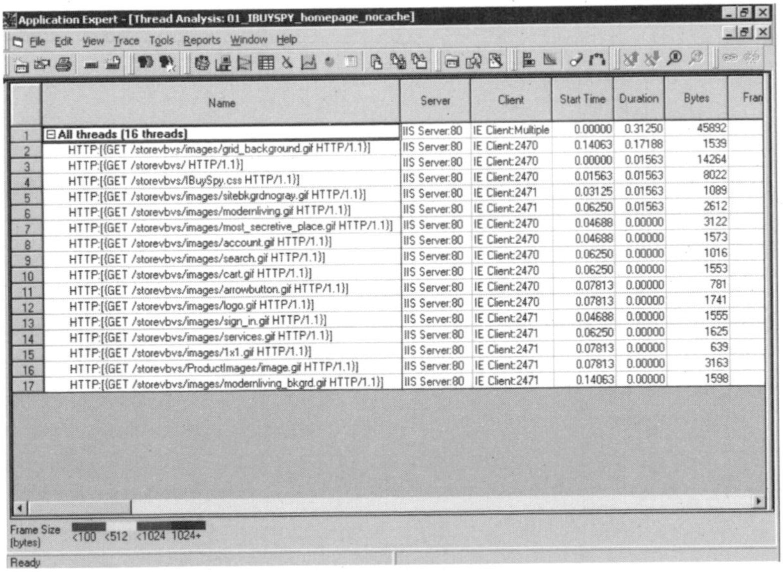

	Name	Server	Client	Start Time	Duration	Bytes	Fran
1	⊟ All threads [16 threads]	IIS Server:80	IE Client:Multiple	0.00000	0.31250	45892	
2	HTTP:[{GET /storevbvs/images/grid_background.gif HTTP/1.1}]	IIS Server:80	IE Client:2470	0.14063	0.17188	1539	
3	HTTP:[{GET /storevbvs/ HTTP/1.1}]	IIS Server:80	IE Client:2470	0.00000	0.01563	14264	
4	HTTP:[{GET /storevbvs/IBuySpy.css HTTP/1.1}]	IIS Server:80	IE Client:2470	0.01563	0.01563	8022	
5	HTTP:[{GET /storevbvs/images/sitebkgrdnogray.gif HTTP/1.1}]	IIS Server:80	IE Client:2471	0.03125	0.01563	1089	
6	HTTP:[{GET /storevbvs/images/modernliving.gif HTTP/1.1}]	IIS Server:80	IE Client:2471	0.06250	0.01563	2612	
7	HTTP:[{GET /storevbvs/images/most_secretive_place.gif HTTP/1.1}]	IIS Server:80	IE Client:2470	0.04688	0.00000	3122	
8	HTTP:[{GET /storevbvs/images/account.gif HTTP/1.1}]	IIS Server:80	IE Client:2470	0.04688	0.00000	1573	
9	HTTP:[{GET /storevbvs/images/search.gif HTTP/1.1}]	IIS Server:80	IE Client:2470	0.06250	0.00000	1016	
10	HTTP:[{GET /storevbvs/images/cart.gif HTTP/1.1}]	IIS Server:80	IE Client:2470	0.06250	0.00000	1553	
11	HTTP:[{GET /storevbvs/images/arrowbutton.gif HTTP/1.1}]	IIS Server:80	IE Client:2470	0.07813	0.00000	781	
12	HTTP:[{GET /storevbvs/images/logo.gif HTTP/1.1}]	IIS Server:80	IE Client:2470	0.07813	0.00000	1741	
13	HTTP:[{GET /storevbvs/images/sign_in.gif HTTP/1.1}]	IIS Server:80	IE Client:2471	0.04688	0.00000	1555	
14	HTTP:[{GET /storevbvs/images/services.gif HTTP/1.1}]	IIS Server:80	IE Client:2471	0.06250	0.00000	1625	
15	HTTP:[{GET /storevbvs/images/1x1.gif HTTP/1.1}]	IIS Server:80	IE Client:2471	0.07813	0.00000	639	
16	HTTP:[{GET /storevbvs/ProductImages/image.gif HTTP/1.1}]	IIS Server:80	IE Client:2471	0.07813	0.00000	3163	
17	HTTP:[{GET /storevbvs/images/modernliving_bkgrd.gif HTTP/1.1}]	IIS Server:80	IE Client:2471	0.14063	0.00000	1598	

Figure 5-16 Application Expert thread analysis

To analyze your capture in more detail, drill into the packet trace for a specific frame by selecting the Drill Into Packet Trace option in the context menu or, in a bounce diagram view, double-clicking a frame. This view is similar to the way Network Monitor displays the raw capture. The packet trace view lists all of the packets and provides important information about each one including the frame number, acknowledgement number, window size, and total bytes (data transferred) versus payload bytes (total bytes minus overhead of headers and acknowledgement frames). The bounce diagram view, thread analysis view, and conversation map are visual representations of the raw data provided in the packet trace view. Figure 5-17 displays a packet trace of the IBuySpy Default.aspx page.

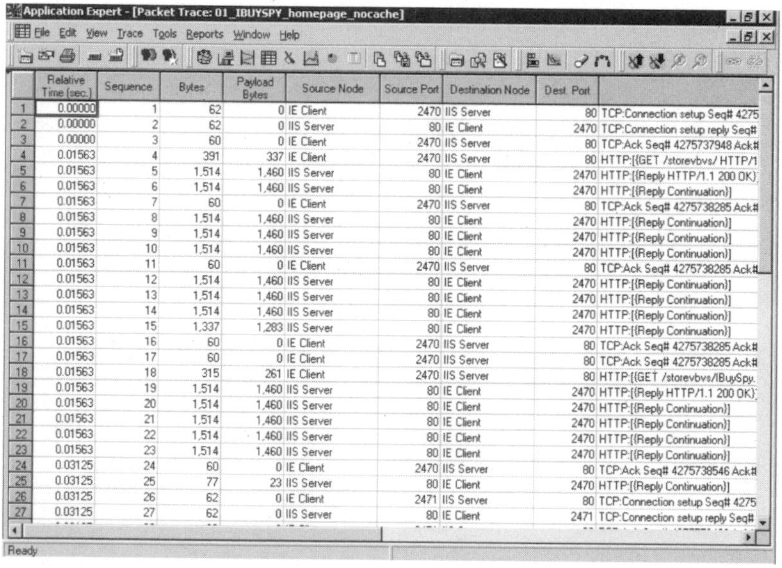

Figure 5-17   Application Expert packet trace view

Response Time Predictor Tool

The Response Time Predictor allows you to predict the impact of bandwidth and latency for overall response time. This is very useful in determining response times of your Web pages in a pre-production test environment. Having this data you can identify and fix performance problems before your customers begin using your application. For instance, if you have several page views that do not meet your criteria for response time acceptability, you have a chance to optimize them before your customers begin using your Web application. The predicted response time depends on a number of factors, including the number of network round trips, amount of data transferred, and processing delays which are modeled using algorithms developed by Compuware. In the Response Time Predictor, you specify the bandwidth and the latency parameters to characterize the production network. The bandwidth and latency should be defined for the slowest link between the communicating end nodes. Figure 5-18 shows a Response Time Predictor model for IBuySpy Home page.

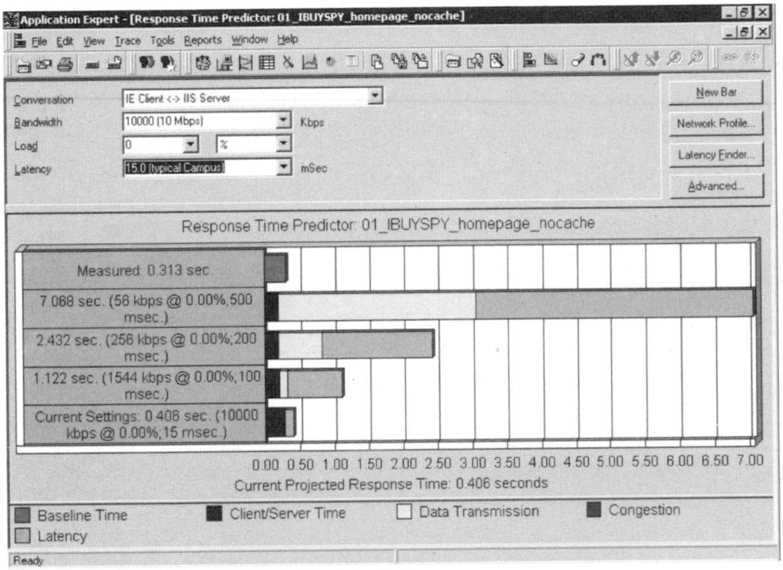

Figure 5-18   Application Expert Response Time Predictor

Interpreting Network Captures with Application Expert

In previous sections of this chapter we identified and defined key components that are used throughout the application network analysis. We introduced Network Monitor, the application used to capture the network traffic between application tiers. Next, we will provide our method for analyzing applications for network efficiency and identifying response time bottlenecks.

The capture file is in a format that can be viewed in Network Monitor or imported into Application Expert. The capture file is not easily interpretable and can be intimidating for novice users. By using Application Expert to interpret the capture, valuable time can be saved. To import your Network Monitor capture files into Application Expert, follow these steps:

1. Open Application Expert.

2. Create a new application.

3.   Open Windows Explorer and browse to the location of your capture files.

4.   Drag and drop your capture files onto your newly created application.

Calculating Data Transferred

After performing the network captures, we isolate traffic between application tiers. Calculating data transferred with Application Expert is accomplished using the conversation map. Figure 5-19 shows there are approximately 15 kilobytes of data transferred between the Internet Explorer client—IIS server tier and 4 kilobytes of data transferred between the IIS server—SQL server tier for the IBuySpy Checkout.aspx page view including their associated elements.

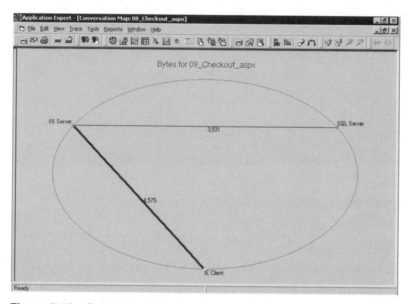

Figure 5-19   Calculating data transferred with Application Expert

Counting Network Round Trips

Counting the number of network round trips is accomplished using the Application Expert conversation map. Figure 5-20 shows there are five round trips between the Internet Explorer Client—IIS server and 10 round trips between the IIS server—SQL server for the IBuySpy Checkout.aspx page.

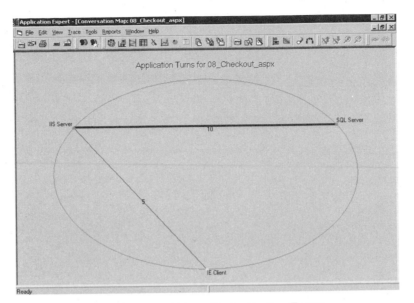

Figure 5-20   Counting round trips with Application Expert

Identifying Application Processing Delays

Processing delays on the IIS or SQL server tiers will critically impact end user response time performance. These delays are caused by several factors such as slowly executing scripts or components in your ASPX pages, SQL stored procedures requiring optimization, or improper SQL indexes that add seconds to your page load time. There are a number of tools and methods you can use to determine if your application has a processing delay. One such tool is SQL Profiler to monitor the SQL server tier, looking at the IIS logs "time taken" field to estimate IIS processing duration, or using the Application Expert bounce diagram feature to identify excessive time between network frames.

> **Note**   For debugging and testing purposes we recommend enabling logging within IIS and using the W3C Extended Log file format. This includes enabling all of the extended properties, such as time taken, bytes sent, and bytes received. For more information relating to the W3C Log file format, see Chapter 6.

If you find delays of more than a second between frames, this should be flagged and investigated for optimization. If you reduce this delay by making code changes, the overall response time for that particular page view will be reduced by the same amount. Figure 5-21 shows a 1.3-second processing delay on the IIS server tier for the IBuySpy update cart page.

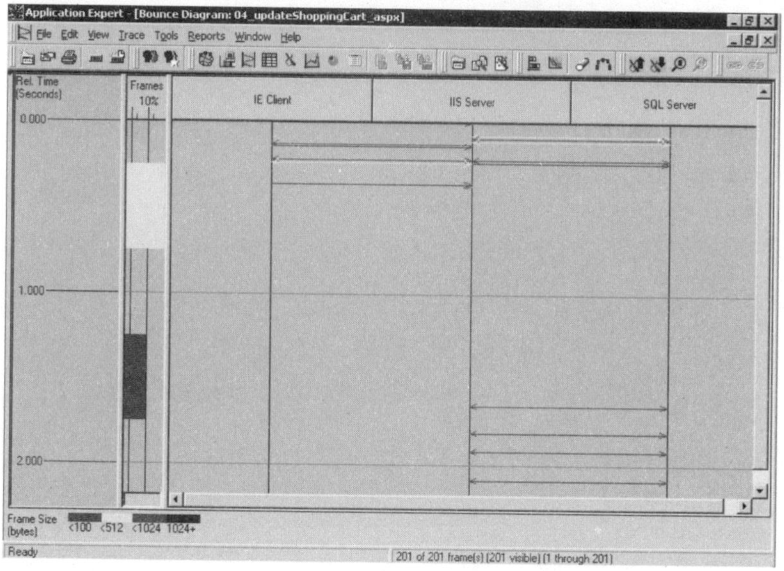

Figure 5-21 Processing delay shown in Application Expert

Predicting Response Times

The Application Expert Response Time Predictor allows us to model response times using the quantity of data transferred, round trips, and processing delays in our network capture. These models show the response time predictions for different line speeds and network latencies, allowing you to discover if your application will perform as you expect before you roll it out to your customers.

> **Note** An alternate method for predicting response times at various connections speeds and latency is to use a hardware-based WAN simulator. Hardware WAN simulators are located between your Web application tiers and suppress the network signal to the programmed specification. For example, you can place the simulator between your test client and Web server tier and program it to reduce your connection to 56 kbps and 500 milliseconds of latency.

We typically use a mix of slow modem connections, high-speed broadband connections (DSL or cable modems), and typical office connections like T1, and LAN connections. For each of these connections you can do a best case and worst case latency. Keep in mind, the bandwidth and latency metrics used in these models are not set in stone. From our experience we use the following connection speeds and latency to simulate users:

- 56-kbps modem connections have a 200-millisecond latency best case and a 500-millisecond latency in poor conditions.

- 256-kbps DSL and cable modems have a 50-millisecond latency best case and 200-milliseconds in poor conditions.

- T1 (1.54-mbps) connections have a 50-millisecond latency best case and 100-milliseconds in poor conditions.

- LAN connections represent a 10- or 100-mbps connection, depending on your network infrastructure. Commonly you will have a 10-millisecond latency or less and 50-milliseconds in poor conditions.

As shown in Figure 5-18, the Application Expert Response Time Predictor allows you to change the line speed and latency for each of your applications tiers. The response time formula utilizes connection speeds, data transferred, round trips, latency, and processing delays. Table 5-5 demonstrates a typical response time model for the IBuySpy home page (no cache page) using our model with varying connection speeds and latency metrics.

Table 5-5 Modeling Response Times

Line Speed	56 kbps Modem	256 kbps DSL	1.54 mbps T1	10 mbps LAN
Latency	200–500 ms	50–200 ms	50–100ms	10–50ms
Response Time	6–9 seconds	2–3 seconds	1–1.5 seconds	.5–1second

Conclusion

An application network analysis is useful for identifying performance bottle-necks and improving end-user response time. Incorporating this into your development process helps detect performance issues in terms of response times, processing delays, and quantity of data transferred. Now that you have used the techniques in this chapter to identify where your application needs to be optimized for improved response time performance, the next three chapters will help you identify specific areas in each tier that can be tuned for performance.

6

Analyzing and Performance Tuning the Web Tier

We use the term *Web tier* to refer to the front-end Web server used to satisfy HTTP requests from remote browser clients, such as Internet Explorer. Many different Web servers are available for various platforms. Microsoft's implementation of a Web server is called Internet Information Server (IIS), and it is essentially a file and application server for Internet and private Intranet Web sites or applications. IIS is a very powerful Web server capable of hosting both static and dynamic content. Static content typically consists of images or simple text files created using HTML that rarely change. To the end user, dynamic content may appear to be static because the request that generated server-side scripting activity is executed on the server, and only the response is returned to the client. Dynamic content usually provides a far richer user experience than static content. Dynamic content can be highly customizable for each request. It is usually generated by some additional component or scripting language, which is processed by the Web server originating from a remote request. The types of dynamic applications discussed in this chapter are ASP.NET or traditional ASP Web applications. This chapter refers to the sample storefront IBuySpy ASP.NET Web application coded in the VB.NET language.

Getting Started

This chapter describes a process of identifying application bottlenecks that can occur on the Web tier. Rather than list every possible bottleneck, an impossible task, we will show you how to analyze your Web application. By sharing our experiences and method of profiling ASP.NET Web applications, we hope to help you quickly identify some common Web tier bottlenecks that may cause scalability issues with your Web application. After you have identified a bottleneck in your Web application, it is much easier to research the problem or seek help.

Although we began this chapter with a brief introduction to what a Web server is, we assume you have some knowledge and experience with IIS and Web-based applications. It is beyond the scope of this chapter to go into detail about Web server administration and configuration, but here is a list of resources for in-depth information on each topic.

- **IIS**   Microsoft Internet Information Services 5.0 documentation

- **ASP.NET**   *Microsoft ASP.NET Step by Step* by G. Andrew Duthie (Microsoft Press, 2002); *Web Database Development Step by Step .NET Edition* by Jim Buyens (Microsoft Press, 2002); *Professional ASP.NET* (Wrox Press, 2001).

- **ADO.NET**   *Programming Microsoft Visual Basic .NET* by Francesco Balena (Microsoft Press, 2002); *Web Database Development Step by Step .NET Edition* by Jim Buyens (Microsoft Press, 2002); *Professional ADO.NET* (Wrox Press, 2001).

Understanding Configuration and Performance

Before you begin performance testing it is very important you become familiar with several performance-related configuration aspects of your Web application. Configuration aspects such as the method of authentication and other global application settings help to give you a quick understanding of how your Web application works.

ASP.NET and ASP Web applications, while very different, can coexist on the same Web server because their file extensions are mapped to different DLLs within IIS. One major difference between ASP.NET and ASP applications is how they are configured. ASP.NET Web applications are configured by XML-based text files, where traditional ASP Web applications have many configurable parameters located in the metabase and the Registry. Storing configuration information in XML-based files makes it much easier to maintain the data in a readable format and update it on the fly without restarting the Web server.

ASP.NET File Extensions

When you first look at an ASP.NET Web application like the IBuySpy sample site you will notice many different file extensions. Some of the new file extensions that you should be familiar with are as follows:

- **ASPX**   This extension is used for Web form pages and is very similar to the traditional ASP pages.

- **ASCX**   These files hold the Web forms user controls. This provides one of the ways that ASP.NET reuses code.

- **ASMX**   Files with this extension are for files that implement XML Web services.

- **VB**   These files are for Visual Basic .NET code behind modules. When you create a Web application using Visual Basic .NET you will have a Visual Basic file associated with each Web form. These files allow for a separation of user interface elements and application logic.

- **CS**   This extension is similar to the VB extension except that the code is written in the new C# language. Code behind modules written in C# will have the same name as the Web form with a CS extension.

- **Global.asax**   This file is used to define application- and session-level variables and procedures when the Web application starts up or receives a request from a new user.

Authentication in ASP.NET

The three different types of authentication to use with ASP.NET Web applications are Windows, Passport, and Form-based. ASP.NET does not do all the authenticating; there are two distinct layers of authentication: IIS and ASP.NET application level. ASP.NET uses the *<authentication>* tag in the Web.config file to set the mode (more information on this in the next section).

Windows-based Authentication

The first authentication mode is for Microsoft Windows-based machines, where ASP.NET relies on IIS to authenticate the incoming requests. This form of authentication is primarily used for Intranet applications. The three different methods available for this configuration are Basic, Digest, and Integrated Authentication.

- **Basic Authentication**   This method works with most browsers, but it sends all passwords in clear text. For Internet sites, this method is tolerated as long as you have enabled SSL encryption, but it is not recommended.

- **Digest Authentication**   This method requires Windows 2000 Domain Controller and HTTP 1.1 (so it may not be supported by all browsers). The password is not sent in clear text—it is a hashed value, making it a little more secure. However, the domain controller has to store a clear-text password so it can validate the password. Thus the domain controller must be safe from outside attacks.

- **Integrated Windows (NTLM) Authentication**   This method is only available with Internet Explorer and is the most secure because it never sends the username and password over the network. It requires all users to have a Windows NT account on the Web server or the domain controller.

Passport Authentication

The second authentication mode is Passport. Passport is a centralized service provided by Microsoft which allows you to log in to any Passport-enabled site or Web application by simply using a single username and password (that is, single sign-in, or SSI).

Form-based Authentication

The last form of authentication is called form-based. This allows developers to create their own authentication within their Web applications. However, passwords are sent in clear text so make sure you add a SSL layer to protect your password. You simply create a login page and link it to ASP.NET in the Web.config file where you can set security restrictions. You can verify that username and password against a database or Windows 2000 Active Directory.

Configuration Files

ASP.NET uses a series of XML-based files to configure the Web application. The highest level configuration file is the machine.config file, which by default is located in [Your system folder]\Microsoft.NET\Framework\versionx.x.x\CONFIG\. This file contains the default settings for all ASP.NET applications on your server.

> **Note**   You must exercise great caution when editing this file because it affects all ASP.NET Web applications on the server.

There is another configuration file named Web.config that is specific to each application you create. Every Web application you create using Visual Studio .NET automatically creates this file for you. Do not worry if you are not using Visual Studio .NET to create your application. If there is no Web.config file, the application will inherit default values from the machine.config file. We will take a quick run through some of the values represented in these files to provide better understanding of the power of these files.

Now let's dive down into the other tags that you will find within the configuration files. If you wish to find more information about the attributes for each of these elements please refer to your .NET Framework documentation.

Table 6-1   Configuration File Tags

Tag	Description
\<trace>	This element can help when you are trying to get more information about how your Web application is performing. It enables you to gather information about requests received by the Web server. (*http://\<servername>/\<appname>/trace.axd*.) Be sure to set this attribute to false when you deploy your Web application.
\<globalization>	Specifies how Web requests and local searches are handled; for example, what language the requests are handled in.
\<httpRuntime>	Controls parts of the ASP.NET and HTTP runtime engine, including attributes for number or requests before returning a 503, maximum size of incoming files and minimum number of threads that will be kept free for processing new requests.
\<compilation>	One of the most extensive elements, which includes settings that determine how your code is compiled, such as debug. This will include debug information within the compiled assemblies. The debug attribute should be set to false when you deploy your Web application.
\<pages>	Allows ways to configure the SessionState, ViewState and other settings that will enable you to get more out of your Web application.
\<customErrors>	This element allows you to customize how your Web applications respond to errors in terms of what the user sees.
\<authentication>	Allows you to choose the authentication mode you want to use.
\<identity>	Allows your Web application to use impersonation.
\<authorization>	Specifies accounts that are authorized to access resources.
\<machinekey>	Specify keys for encryption and decryption of cookie data. However it can not be used at the subdirectory level.
\<securityPolicy>	Allows the choice of several named security policies.
\<trust>	Implements the security policy stated in the securityPolicy element.
\<sessionState>	Used to configure the HttpModule element, mainly the state management to be used.
\<httpHandlers>	Allows you to assign certain requests to different types of resources to handler classes. This can be used to limit the HTTP access to certain file types.

(continued)

Table 6-1 Configuration File Tags   *(continued)*

Tag	Description
<processModel>	This setting deals with how the Web application is run and provides many features such as automatic restart and allowed memory size to help improve performance.
<webControls>	Allows the use of client-side implementations of ASP.NET server controls by specifying script files.
<clientTarget>	Allows you to use a single alias for your application.
<browserCaps>	Allows the application to gather information about the user's browser.

Understanding Your Web Application

Some of the configuration settings listed above have adverse effects on your Web application or even generate problems when you're creating test scripts for your Web application. For example, many people might find the <custom-Errors> element in the Web.config file useful because you can set up a custom error page to redirect to when an error occurs. When you build a test script in ACT, by default you do not get a visual indication of what is displayed on the page. If an error occurs in your test script while recording, you could be redirected to the custom error page, which receives a 200 status code (success) according to the IIS log file. The page that had the error would only show a 302 (redirect) instead of the true error. So you must be careful and understand your application, otherwise you could waste a lot of time trying to solve the problem.

> **Note** If you see a large percentage of page views occurring on one page, verify in the Webconfig file to make sure it is not the Custom Error Handling file for your ASP.NET Web application.

Profiling a .NET Web Application

There are several tools readily available to help you monitor and identify performance problems which occur on the Web tier. The profiling tasks discussed in this section include analyzing IIS log files, using the new tracing feature in ASP.NET, viewing performance data with the infamous System Monitor (which you should be very familiar with by now).

IIS Log Files

IIS log files serve many purposes, including analyzing user behavior or traffic patterns, monitoring activity for security exploits, and aiding in troubleshooting or identifying problems with your Web applications. The purpose of the following IIS log file discussion is to first give you a quick overview and then to demonstrate how to quickly identify performance problems at a high level (the page level) on the Web tier. After you have identified the poorly performing pages within your Web application, you can drill deeper to identify the specific code that is causing the problem and fix it. Let us begin by becoming more familiar with the log files generated by IIS in response to client activity.

Log File Formats

There are various logging modules and formats available with IIS. With the exception of the ODBC logging module, which is written to a database, all of the other log files are ASCII text files. The NCSA Common Log File Format and the Microsoft IIS Log Format are both fixed ASCII formats that are not customizable. We always use the W3C Extended Log File Format for our testing efforts because you can customize it by selecting the fields you want to monitor. From an administrative point of view this is very useful because you log less data, you can conserve more available disk space and keep your log files more readable without sacrificing functionality. All of the ASCII text-based modules discussed above can be set to create new logs when the file size reaches a certain threshold or timeframe (hourly, daily, weekly, monthly). We are not going into great detail about every available log file format in IIS, but we do discuss more information relating to the W3C Extended Log File Format because we use it for identifying problems in Web applications that we encounter.

By default the W3C Extended Log File Format uses Greenwich Mean Time (GMT) for times listed by each request, where all of the other formats use the local time. Keep in mind that the times listed in the log files are generated by the server after processing a request but do not reflect network travel time to the client or client processing time.

Tip   If you are building a test script or debugging your Web application, we recommend selecting every field. Otherwise, select only the relevant fields required to profile your Web application. This will conserve disk space and make parsing or navigating around the log file much quicker and easier.

Below is a sample from one of our log files in the W3C Extended Log File Format. It is worth mentioning that we did not select every available field to be logged, but only the relevant fields for this Web application.

```
#Software: Microsoft Internet Information Services 5.0
#Version: 1.0
#Date: 2002-05-24 17:25:01
#Fields: date time c-ip cs-method cs-uri-stem cs-uri-query sc-
status sc-bytes cs-bytes time-taken
2002-05-24 17:25:01 181.39.207.242 GET /storevbvs/default.aspx -
 200 12893 373 2516
```

The first four lines of a properly formatted W3C Extended log, which begin with a pound sign (#), contain directives or header information such as the version of the log file format, the date and time the file was created, and field identifiers for various information which is logged for each entry. The field identifiers are prefixed in Table 6-2.

Table 6-2   W3C Extended Log File Field Identifiers

Prefix	Meaning
s-	Server actions
c-	Client actions
cs-	Client-to-server actions
sc-	Server-to-client actions

Table 6-3 contains a complete list of available properties, definitions, and reference information for each field in the W3C Extended Log File Format.

Table 6-3   W3C Extended Log File Format Reference Table

Field	Appears As	Description
Date	Date	The date on which the activity occurred.
Time	Time	The time the activity occurred.
Client IP Address	c-ip	The IP address of the client that accessed your server.
User Name	c-username	The name of the authenticated user who accessed your server. This does not include anonymous users, who are represented by a hyphen.

Table 6-3   W3C Extended Log File Format Reference Table   *(continued)*

Field	Appears As	Description
Service Name and Instance Number	s-sitename	The Internet service and instance number that was running on the client computer.
Server Name	s-computername	The name of the server on which the log entry was generated.
Server IP	s-ip	The IP address of the server on which the log entry was generated.
Method	cs-method	The action the client was trying to perform (for example, a *GET* method).
URI Stem	cs-uri-stem	The resource accessed; for example, Default.htm.
URI Query	cs-uri-query	The query, if any, the client was trying to perform.
Http Status	sc-status	The status of the action, in HTTP terms.
Win32 Status	sc-win32-status	The status of the action, in terms used by Windows.
Bytes Sent	sc-bytes	The number of bytes sent by the server.
Bytes Received	cs-bytes	The number of bytes received by the server.
Server Port	s-port	The port number the client is connected to.
Time Taken	time-taken	The length of time the action took.
Protocol Version	cs-protocol	The protocol (HTTP, FTP) version used by the client. For HTTP this will be either HTTP 1.0 or HTTP 1.1.
User Agent	cs(User-Agent)	The browser used on the client.
Cookie	cs(Cookie)	The content of the cookie sent or received, if any.
Referrer	cs(Referer)	The previous site visited by the user. This site provided a link to the current site.

Logging is enabled within IIS by default and can be disabled at the site, directory, or file level by right-clicking the element and clearing the Log Visits checkbox in the IIS MMC snap-in Properties dialog box, as shown in Figure 6-1.

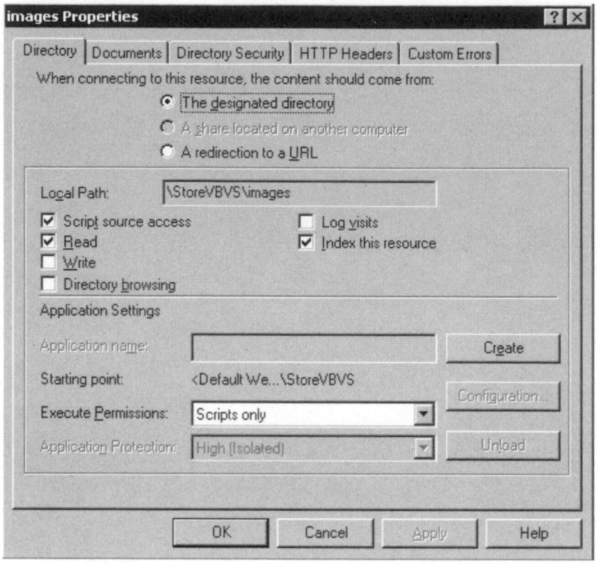

Figure 6-1 Clearing the Log Visits checkbox

Disabling logging on certain directories that contain static or rarely changing files is another useful method of reducing your Web server log file size and saving valuable disk space. For example just by browsing the IBuySpy Web application home page *http://localhost/storevbs/Default.aspx,* you write 16 different entries in the IIS log file for that one request. Fourteen images, one style sheet, and the actual Default.aspx page are referenced in the code. Keep in mind that as far as the user is concerned, it is only one URL request, even though it's several HTTP requests to the Web server (one request for Default.aspx, one for the style sheet, and 14 for the images). You can imagine how large the log file can grow and how much disk space can be consumed from a stress test script that requests multiple pages using several browser connections for an extended period of time.

There are several ways to verify how many items are referenced by a page and the size of each file. One such method useful in checking a single page is to first clear your browser cache and then request the page from your browser. You should see all of the different file elements referenced from the page from that one request. Add up the total number of file elements and their file size by viewing the file properties. This is a tedious method when you have many files to investigate. An alternative method that makes more sense to use when you have several files is to use a log parser and view the results in a report format. There are several commercial log parsers available today.

Identifying Problem Pages from a Log File

Now that we have presented some background information on what to look for in the log file let's look at a somewhat real-world example of how to use the IIS log file to quickly identify errors occurring on the Web tier. The next four steps are necessary for us to demonstrate this example.

1. The code in the IBuySpy sample site is very efficient, so we must first introduce a problem into the code of the ProductList.aspx page to simulate a page delay. We mentioned above that this is a somewhat real-world example because the code causes similar results on many different machines. If we tried to create a demo using code that performs poorly implemented string concatenation or some looping logic that returns many rows from a database, the performance and ASPX execution time from the ProductList.aspx page would vary depending on different hardware configurations. On the ProductList.aspx page, comment out line four as shown below.

    ```
    <%'@ OutputCache Duration="6000" VaryByParam="CategoryID" %>
    ```

    Then insert the code below between the <% to %> on line five of the ProductList.aspx page.

    ```
    <%
    '////////////////////////////////////////////////////////////
    ' TODO: -Comment out line 4 on ProductList.aspx.  This will
    '       -disable the OutputCache so we can introduce a delay.
       System.Threading.Thread.Sleep(7000)       '7 second delay
    '////////////////////////////////////////////////////////////
    %>
    ```

2. Next, we disabled logging on the IBuySpy.css file, the Images subdirectory, and the ProductImages subdirectory in order to focus on tuning the code, which occurs on the ASPX file type.

    > **Note**   It is still important to optimize or reduce the size of your images and stylesheets to ensure that this does not become the bottleneck on your Web application.

3. Verify that you have installed the IBuySpy sample site correctly. Then, within IIS, verify that you have selected W3C Extended Log File Format and selected the following fields: date, time, c-ip, cs-method, cs-uri-stem, cs-uri-query, sc-status, sc-bytes, cs-bytes, time-taken.

4. Finally, we ran the Browse test script using Microsoft ACT for one iteration. The Browse test script is included on this book's companion CD and is discussed in more detail in Chapter 3. This is not really considered a stress test but more of an automated walkthrough of our user scenario because we only ran through one iteration with one browser connection.

The results of the script playback from the IIS log file are as follows:

```
#Software: Microsoft Internet Information Services 5.0
#Version: 1.0
#Date: 2002-05-30 18:36:11
#Fields: date time c-ip cs-method cs-uri-stem cs-uri-query sc-status sc-
bytes cs-bytes time-taken
2002-05-30 18:36:11 181.39.207.242 GET /storevbvs/Default.aspx - 200 0 346 15
2002-05-30 18:36:18 181.39.207.242 GET /StoreVBVS/
productslist.aspx CategoryID=20&selection=2 200 0 377 7016
2002-05-30 18:36:18 181.39.207.242 GET /storevbvs/
Default.aspx test=count 200 0 357 16
```

Note that there are three requests in the above log. The first thing you should look for is to verify that the requests were successful and there were no errors generated. This is accomplished by looking at the field labeled sc-status, also known as the status code. Table 6-4 below is a useful table to reference HTTP status codes.

Table 6-4   HTTP Status Codes

Status	Description
2xx	**Success.**
200	OK: The request has succeeded.
201	Created: The request has been fulfilled and resulted in a new resource being created.
202	Accepted: The request has been accepted for processing, but the processing has not been completed.
203	Non-authoritative Information.
204	No Content: No response-request received but no information to send back.
3xx	**Redirection.**
301	Moved: The data requested has a new location and the change is permanent.
302	Found: The data requested has a different URL temporarily.

Table 6-4   HTTP Status Codes   *(continued)*

Status	Description
303	Method: Under discussion, a suggestion for the client to try another location.
304	Not Modified: The document has not been modified as expected.
4xx	**Error seems to be in the client**
400	Bad Request: Syntax problem in the request or it could not be satisfied.
401	Unauthorized The client is not authorized to access data.
402	Payment Required: Indicates a charging scheme is in effect.
403	Forbidden: Access not required even with authorization.
404	Not Found: Server could not find the given resource.
5xx	**Error seems to be in the server.**
500	Internal Error: The server could not fulfill the request because of an unexpected condition.
501	Not Implemented: The server does not support the facility requested.
502	Server Overloaded: High load (or servicing) in progress.
503	Gateway Timeout: Server waited for another service that did not complete in time.

All three of the log entries are GET requests (indicated by the method) and they appear to be successful with 200 status code. Also, there appears to be very little data transferred (indicated by the Bytes Sent and Received fields). The ASPX execution time or the Time Taken field for the Default.aspx page was quick, but the ProductList.aspx took over seven seconds (7016 milliseconds, to be exact). Voilà, we have identified a problem. The IIS logs are very useful in helping you to identify pages that are executing slowly, transferring a lot of data and identifying errors in your Web application. Now that we have successfully identified a problem at the page level, we will discuss a new feature available in ASP.NET that will help us to trace the problem down to the line of code causing the delay.

Tracing Problems to the Code Level

Tracing is a useful new feature in ASP.NET for debugging or profiling problems which occur at the application, page, and code level of a Web application. You can print statements during code execution to help identify exactly what is happening at a certain point within your code. With traditional ASP pages, debugging or troubleshooting code is accomplished by inserting text or logic with multiple `Response.Write` statements at different points within the code as placeholders. To help you fully appreciate the new tracing feature in ASP.NET, we offer a brief discussion of our method to isolating slowly executing code within traditional ASP pages.

Tracing in Traditional ASP Pages

After the files with high execution times are identified from the IIS logs, we typically add several timers throughout the page to pinpoint the slowly executing code. When the page is requested the timers are written to a text file using the local file system of the Web server. Finally, you simply open the text file to view the timer information that was written between each block of code separated with a timer. Below is an example written in VBScript to illustrate this point.

```
<% Dim t1, t2
  'Timer 1 - start timer for section 1
 t1=Timer
%>
INSERT CODE BLOCK HERE
<% 'Timer 2 - start timer for section 1
 t2=Timer
'The following code can be placed at the end of the ASP file.
Dim fso, filename, fileref
filename =  "C:\temp\" + cstr(Timer) + ".txt"
'A new file is created each time the page is executed.
SET fso = createobject("Scripting.FileSystemObject")
SET fileref = fso.createtextfile(filename  )

'Write timer values to the file - time is in milliseconds.
fileref.writeline("1," + cstr(t1) + "," + cstr(t2) + "," +  cstr(t2-t1))
'Close the file.
fileref.close
%>
```

Another method for finding slowly executing code within traditional ASP pages is to first make a note of how long it takes the page to execute without modifying the code. Then place the *Response.End* method at different places within your code and request the page again noting the execution time. The *Response.End* method stops the execution of the code so you can compare the time against the time taken from the original request. This method often takes several tries to identify the culprit and might end up generating errors, because you are not executing the code in its entirety.

Tracing in ASP.NET

Tracing in ASP.NET can be performed at either the page or application level. Page-level tracing is implemented by adding `Trace="True"` to the `@ Page` directive at the top of an ASPX file. The complete syntax is as follows:

```
<%@ Page  Trace="True"%>
```

This will append an HTML table to the browser once the original content has rendered. The HTML table will contain detailed information on the request itself: timing information, server control tree (with rendering viewstate size), header, cookies, querystring along with form parameters, server variables, and of course, the ability to add custom messages. The syntax to add custom tracking information is `Trace.Write()` or `Trace.Warn()`. Both methods create the same output but `Trace.Warn()` writes the output in red text.

Tip   We want to caution you about only enabling tracing when you need to debug your Web application. When trace was enabled on the ProductList.aspx page, the server-to-client bytes transferred for this page changed from 13628 bytes to 32695 bytes according to the IIS logs. This is nearly three times the amount of data in the original request and this can easily skew a stress test.

Enabling tracing at the application level is accomplished by adding or modifying the following statements to the Web.config file.

```
<configuration>
    <system.Web>
        <trace enabled="true"
            requestlimit="15"
            pageOutput="true"
            traceMode="SortByTime"
            localOnly="true"/>
    </system.Web>
</configuration>
```

After *trace* is enabled in the Web.config file, you can view the results of various requests by browsing to a special HttpHandler (Trace.axd) to view the output. The *requestLimit* parameter will control the number of requests to log for which trace information will be collected. You should also be aware that page-level tracing will override application-level tracing.

Identifying Problem Code in ASPX Pages

Let's take the above example, in which we used the IIS log file to identify a slow executing page, a step further and use the new *Trace* method discussed above to isolate the code that is causing a delay in our ProductList.aspx page.

1. Make sure you enabled tracing at the application level by adding or modify the following syntax to the Web.config file located in the IBuySpy Web application root directory.

    ```
    <configuration>
        <system.Web>
            <trace enabled="true"
                requestlimit="15"
                pageOutput="true"
                traceMode="SortByTime"
                localOnly="true"/>
        </system.Web>
    </configuration>
    ```

2. Modify the following code block, which introduces the page delay by adding both statements beginning with `Trace.Warn`. These statements will write our custom messages around the suspected problematic code.

    ```
    <%
    '////////////////////////////////////////////////////////////////
    ' TODO: -Comment out line # 4 on ProductList.aspx.  This will
    '          -disable the OutputCache so we can introduce a delay.
      Trace.Warn("Find Delay", "Timer 1: Begin")
        System.Threading.Thread.Sleep(7000)          '7 second delay
      Trace.Warn("Find Delay", "Timer 1: End")
    '////////////////////////////////////////////////////////////////
    %>
    ```

3. Run the same Browse test script discussed above using Microsoft ACT for one iteration. This will simulate someone walking through our user scenario.

4. Finally, on the Web server that contains the IBuySpy sample site, type in the following URL from within your browser: *http://localhost/ StoreVBVS/trace.axd*. The three requests that our script made should be displayed as in Figure 6-2 below.

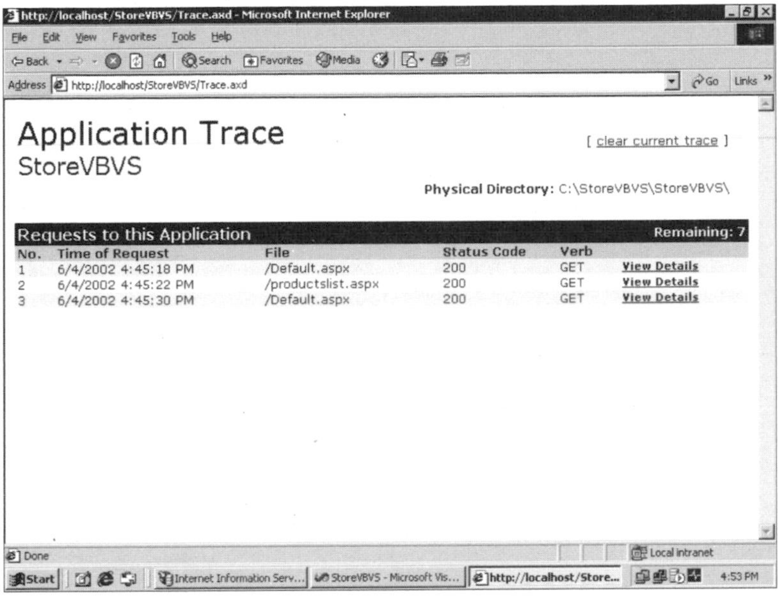

Figure 6-2   Browse test script results

You should notice similar information displayed in the HTTP Handler (Trace.axd) compared to what we saw previously in the IIS log file. We already identified the ProductList.aspx page as the problematic page because it is taking more than seven seconds to load. Now click the View Details hyperlink for the ProductList.aspx page.

Because we used `Trace.Warn` the code we added should immediately stand out when you look at it online because the syntax is in red text. In Figure 6-3 below you can identify the code we added under the Trace Information heading and the Find Delay Category. From the Timer 1: Begin message to the Timer 1: End, it took around seven seconds to execute the code between the two statements we added. Voilà! Once again we successfully pinpointed the problem causing the delay. Now, you can verify that this is the problem by simply commenting out the suspected line of code and browsing directly to the ProductList.aspx page. The execution time should be reduced by seven seconds, indicating that indeed this was the problem causing the delay.

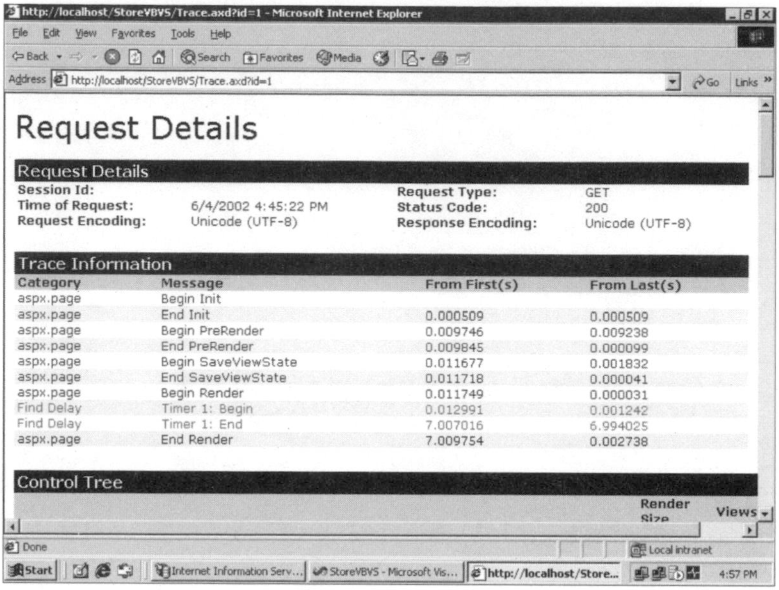

Figure 6-3   The problem code is in red text.

System Monitor Counters

System Monitor is an essential tool that can be used for monitoring and analyzing ASP.NET Web application performance. During performance testing, performance data can be analyzed in real time or collected for processing at a later time using System Monitor. Performance data is used in locating possible performance issues such as an inefficient processor, memory usage and any other factors that prohibits the application from performing and utilizing its targeted performance goals on the Web tier.

Performance Counters for IIS

In the following sections, we discuss the IIS counters and ASP.NET performance counters that our team uses in performance testing.

■ **Internet Information Services Global: File Cache Flushes and File Cache Hits**   These counters can be compared to see the ratio of hits to cache clean up. A flush occurs when a file is removed from the cache. These global counters provide some indication of the rate at which objects are being flushed from the cache. Memory is wasted when flushes are occurring too slowly.

- **Internet Information Services Global: File Cache Hits %**   Displays the ratio of cache hits to total cache requests. This should stay around 80 percent on Web sites that have mostly static content.

- **Web Service: Bytes Total/sec**   Shows the total number of bytes sent and received by the Web server. A low number indicates IIS is transferring data at a low rate.

- **Web Service: Connection Refused**   Lower is better. High numbers indicate network adapter card or processor bottlenecks.

- **Web Service: Not Found Errors**   Shows the number of requests that could not be satisfied by service because the requested document could not be found (HTTP status code 404).

Performance Counters for ASP.NET

There are two sets of performance counters in ASP.NET that can be used in diagnosing and monitoring Web application performance. They reside under ASP.NET, and ASP.NET application performance objects. If you have multiple versions of ASP.NET installed, there may be multiple instances of these counters, each with a version stamp on them. The names without versions will always give you performance data for the highest version installed on the machine.

ASP.NET System Performance Counters   We will not discuss all performance objects and counters in the .NET Framework. All performance counters for ASP.NET information are found on the Microsoft MSDN Web site, and .NET Framework help file. In this chapter, we discuss in some detail the system performance counters, and application performance counters that our team uses in monitoring and analyzing performance of a .NET Web application.

- **Application Restarts**   Indicates the number of times and how often a Web application has been restarted. An application restart can occur because of changes in configuration, bin assemblies and too many page changes. This value is reset every time to 0 when the IIS host or w3svc restart.

- **Requests Queued**   The number of requests waiting for service from the queue. When the number of requests queued starts to increment linearly with respect to client load, this is an indication of reaching the limit of concurrent requests processed on the Web server.

- **Requests Rejected**   Shows the total number of requests not executed due to insufficient server resources to process the requests. This counter represents the number of requests that return a 503 HTTP status code "Server is too busy". The value of requests rejected counter should ideally be 0.

- **Request Wait Time**   The number of milliseconds that the most recent request waited for processing in the queue. The average request should ideally spend very little time waiting to be processed.

ASP.NET Application Performance Counters   ASP.NET supports the application performance counters that can be used to monitor the performance of a single instance of an ASP.NET application. A unique instance appears for these counters, named _Total_, which aggregates counters for all applications on a Web server. The _Total_ instance is always available. The counters will display zero when no applications are present on the server.

- **Cache Total Turnover Rate**   The number of additions and removals to the total cache per second. Large turnover indicates the cache is not being used efficiently.

- **Errors Total**   The total number of parser, compilation, or runtime errors that occur during the execution of HTTP requests. A well-functioning Web server should not be generating errors.

- **Request Execution Time -**   The number of milliseconds taken to execute the last request. The value of this counter should be stable.

- **Requests Failed**   The total number of requests that have timed out, requests that are unauthorized (HTTP status code 401), requests that are not found (HTTP status code 404 or 414), or that resulted in a server error (HTTP status code 500).

- **Requests Not Found**   The number of requests that have failed due to resources not being found (HTTP status code 404, 414).

- **Requests Not Authorized**   The number of requests that have failed due to unauthorized access (HTTP status code 401).

- **Requests Timed Out**   The number of requests that have timed out.

- **Requests/Sec**   The number of requests executed per second. Under constant load, the number of requests/sec should remain within a certain range.

The above section covered the IIS counters, and ASP.NET performance counters that our team regularly uses in monitoring and analyzing ASP.NET Web applications.

Performance Tuning Tips

Performance tuning involves fixing bottlenecks and tweaking code to achieve your desired throughput rate or response time criteria while maintaining scalability. Using new features in ASP.NET, such as caching and new data access methods, can help you realize greater performance gains and scalability. Disabling certain default features, like Session State and ViewState whenever they are not used can have a positive affect on the performance of your Web application too.

Application and Session State

Maintaining state without creating performance and scalability problems in a Web application distributed among multiple Web servers proved to be challenging in the past. There are more options available for ASP.NET Web applications compared to traditional ASP Web applications, but you still must be aware of the performance versus scalability tradeoffs for each option.

Application State

Traditionally application variables were used to store information like connection strings or as a caching mechanism for storing variables and recordsets among multiple users requests. They still exist in ASP.NET but many of the functions previously served in traditional ASP have been replaced with newer more effective methods. Use the Web.config file to store and retrieve database connection strings or use a trusted connection with a SQL server. Utilize the new caching engine discussed below to store frequently accessed data. Application state still has the limitation and cannot be shared across multiple Web servers.

Session State

Session information is data stored in memory of the Web server for each user making a request. In the past, many problems have been associated with enabling and using session state within a Web application. The underlying protocol used in making each request (HTTP) is stateless, so to overcome this in traditional ASP Web applications an HTTP cookie was assigned to the client and would be passed back to the server for subsequent requests within a certain time frame. For a Web application located on multiple machines or a Web farm, the user may be redirected to a different machine between requests and the session cookie would be lost because it could not be passed among multiple machines.

ASP.NET addresses some of the scalability issues previously associated with using session data in Web farms by offering the option to store it out-of-process in a Windows service or to store it in a SQL server. Keep in mind that scalability is gained but there is a performance hit associated with running the session out-of-process. Session state is enabled by default in the Machine.config file and is set to run in-process. Running *Session InProc* has the same limitations for ASP.NET Web applications as discussed above for traditional Web applications, however it is the fastest most efficient method to use if session state is required. Our recommendation is if you do not absolutely have to use session state, then disable it in the Web.config file or at the page level. You can disable it at the page level by using `<%@ Page EnableSessionState = "False" %>`.

Caching in ASP.NET

Caching has been greatly improved with ASP.NET and when used properly can boost application performance significantly. With traditional ASP, caching was implemented by either storing all of your data in session variables, application variables, or by using a custom caching solution. These methods are still available in ASP.NET, but ASP.NET has even more options available to the developer. With the new caching mechanisms the output of entire pages can be cached via a simple directive. Additionally, there is an advanced caching engine and a caching API that can be used to store any arbitrary piece of information that will be reused often.

> **Note**   We recommend output caching frequently accessed pages in your ASP.NET Web application whenever possible, but you should always follow up your tuning efforts with testing. Be careful not to go overboard because caching too much data can use valuable memory resources. To ensure that your caching implementation is effective, you can monitor the performance counter *ASP.NET Applications\Output Cache Turnover Rate\Total.* This counter should remain low or commensurate with the expiration or invalidation rate of the cached pages.

Output Caching

The ASP.NET output cache can use memory on the server to store the output of processed and rendered pages. If output caching is enabled, the output of a page is saved after the first request. Subsequent requests for the same page are then retrieved from the cache, if the output is still available, and returned to the user bypassing all the overhead of parsing, compiling and processing. This greatly improves the response time and reduces utilization of the server's resources.

This feature can easily be enabled for pages by including the *OutputCache* directive within the page. For example, to save the output of a processed page for a maximum of 60 seconds, using the most basic syntax, you can include the following directive in the page:

```
<%@ OutputCache Duration="60" VaryByParam="None"%>
```

The *Duration* and *VaryByParam* attributes are required.

> **Note**   It is recommended that pages which are output cached have a *Duration* of at least 60 seconds, or the turnover rate of the page may hinder rather than benefit performance.

For pages that are short lived but have potentially expensive-to-obtain data, it may be better to utilize the *Cache* object to cache and update the data as needed (see the section on "Cache API" below). The *VaryByParam* attribute allows you to save multiple versions of a page. For example, pages can be designed to produce varying output based on the values of the parameter sent. Specifying a value of *None* for the *VaryByParam* attribute saves the output for the page if it is accessed without any parameters. To save versions of the page for all combinations of parameters, you can pass a value of ***. You must, however, be aware that caching multiple versions of a page will consume additional memory. To cache output based on a specific querystring parameter or form field within the page, you can specify the name of the parameter. Multiple parameters can be included by separating them with a semicolon. For example, if a page has a form with ProductCategory and Product fields, you can cache the output based on values supplied for these parameter with the following syntax:

```
<%@ OutputCache Duration="10" VaryByParam="ProductCategory;Product"%>
```

Besides the two required attributes that are supported by the *OutputCache* directive, there are three additional attributes all of which are optional; these are *Location*, *VaryByCustom*, and *VaryByHeader*. The *Location* attribute controls where the data will be cached (for example, the server or client). *VaryBy-Header* can cache based on specific headers sent with the request, and *Varyby-Custom* can be used to cache based on browser type when specified with a value of *Browser* or can be used to implement custom logic when supplied with any other value.

Fragment Caching

Fragment caching is similar to output caching in the sense that the directive is the same. This level of caching is used to cache portions of a page that are implemented as user controls and is also referred to as partial page caching or user controls caching. Fragment caching should be considered whenever there is a lot of information to cache and caching at the page level is prohibitive in terms of server memory and cache utilization. Again, as with output caching, fragment caching is best used to cache output that does not vary tremendously or for output that is resource intensive.

The *Output* directive to implement fragment caching has to be included as part of the file implementing the control. The *Duration* and *VaryByParam* attributes are required and are exactly the same as in output caching. Addition-ally, there is the *VaryByControl* attribute, which is specific to fragment caching and can be included only in the user control file.

```
<%@ OutputCache Duration="60" VaryByParam="None"%>
```

Caching API

The caching API lets you save any piece of information in server memory that you want to reuse. For example, let us say that you need to display the product categories on a page in addition to other information. Rather than retrieving this information from the database with every request to the page, you can save the categories via the caching API. The most basic syntax to cache something is:

```
Cache("mydata"}() = "some data"
```

You can store entire data sets besides just strings and numeric data. Retrieving the cached data is just as simple:

```
X = Cache("mydata")
```

Other useful methods to be aware of are the *Remove* method, used to remove an item from the cache and the *Insert* method to add items to the cache. The syntax for the *Remove* method is:

```
(Cache.Remove("mydata"))
```

The *Insert* method is an overloaded method of the *Cache* object and has several versions. For example, the following version of the *Insert* method can be used to add an item to the cache with no external dependency and with an absolute expiration time of 120 minutes from the first time the page is cached:

```
Cache.Insert("mydata", mydata, nothing, _
        DateTime.Now.AddMinutes(120), TimeSpan.Zero)
```

The last parameter in the previous example is known as the sliding window and can be used to set an expiration for a cached item relative to the time the item was first placed in or last retrieved from the cache The sliding value parameter can be thought of as the maximum length of time between successive calls that need to elapse before a cached item is removed from the cache. For example, to place an item in the cache for a maximum of 10 minutes between successive retrievals, you can use the following syntax of the *Cache* object's *Insert* method:

```
Cache.Insert("mydata", mydata, nothing, DateTime.MaxValue, _
        TimeSpan.FromMinutes(10))
```

Disabling ViewState

ViewState saves the properties from one page (usually from a form) to the next by saving and encoding the data for each server control to a hidden form field rendered to the browser. The size and contents of the ViewState data can be determined by using the *Trace* directive at the page or application level as discussed in the previous section, "Profiling a .NET Web Application." If many server controls are used, the size of the ViewState data can become quite large and hinder performance of your Web application. As a best practice it is advisable to disable ViewState unless you absolutely need to use it. You can disable ViewState by setting the property `EnableViewState="false"` at the page or control level.

ADO.NET Tips

Most Web applications are built with a back-end database management system. Connecting to this data tier and manipulating the data is critical to application performance, among other factors such as the amount of data being transferred and the database design. This is where an understanding of the object model of ADO.NET becomes important. Using the correct object and right method can make a difference to application performance, especially under load. This section will highlight some of the recommended practices for retrieving and affecting data at the data source but is by no means exhaustive. The references listed at the beginning of the chapter are suggested for more detailed information on ADO.NET.

The .NET Framework ships with two .NET data providers: The OLE DB .NET Data Provider and the SQL Server .NET Data Provider. The OLE DB .NET Data Provider can be used to connect to any data source for which there exists an OLE DB Provider, for example Microsoft SQL Server or an Oracle database, but is primarily intended for non-SQL Server databases. For applications that use Microsoft SQL Server versions 7.0 or higher, the SQL Server .NET Data Provider is the better choice. This provider has been optimized specifically for SQL Server and implements some SQL Server–specific functionality.

> **Note** Use the SQL Server .NET Data Provider with SQL Server versions 7.0 and higher.

SqlConnection Object

The first step in communicating with the data tier is to establish a connection with the database server. The SQL Server .NET Data Provider gives us the *SqlConnection* object for this purpose. Creating a connection is fairly straight forward; the following VB.NET sample code demonstrates opening a connection to the SQL server on the local machine and connecting to the Pubs database:

```
Dim strCnStr As String = "Data Source =.;" _
          & "Integrated Security=SSPI;" _
          & "Initial Catalog = Pubs"
Dim objCn as New SqlConnection(strCnStr) _
    objCn.Open()
```

By default, this data provider takes advantage of connection pooling. This helps reduce the overhead of establishing a connection each time it is requested because all of the work is done up-front when the first connection is established. It is important, to understand when this feature is taken advantage of. For a pooled connection to be utilized, the connection strings of all new connections has to match that of the existing pooled connections exactly. Even an extra space in the string will cause the .NET runtime environment to create a separate pool. In fact, the .NET runtime creates a separate connection pool for every distinct connection string. This implies that connections utilizing different usernames and password will fail to take advantage of pooled connections.

> **Note** It is recommended that applications either use integrated security whenever possible or implement a common application username/password that is shared by all users in order to improve the efficiency of the connection pooling usage.

The other factor that determines whether a pooled connection is utilized is the transaction context. A second connection will use a pooled connection as long as the transaction context is the same as the initial connection or does not have one at all.

Controlling the size of the connection pool is affected by specifying the *min* and *max* properties. This is important if you need to control the amount of memory utilized at the Web tier. If all pooled connections are active, any extra connection request will be blocked until one is relinquished or the connection time out has expired (the default is 15 seconds). The following code demonstrates setting these properties as part of the connection string:

```
Dim strCnStr As String = "Data Source =.;" _
                & "Integrated Security=SSPI;" _
                & "Initial Catalog = Pubs;" _
                & "Min Pool Size=10;" _
                & "Max Pool Size =100"
```

Another property that can have an effect on performance is the packet size. For applications that transfer large blob or image fields, increasing the packet size can be beneficial. In cases where the amount of data transferred is small, a smaller value for the packet size may be more efficient. The following code demonstrates setting this property as part of the connection string:

```
Dim strCnStr As String = "Data Source =.;" _
                & "Integrated Security=SSPI;" _
                & "Initial Catalog = Pubs;" _
                & "Packet Size=32768"
```

SqlCommand Object

A common scenario for Web applications is the retrieval/modification of data from the data source. The SQL Server .NET provider implements the *SqlCommand/DataReader* and the *DataAdapter /DataSet* classes that allow the user to retrieve/modify the data. We only briefly discuss the *SqlCommand/DataReader* in this book; information on the *SqlDataAdapter/DataSet* classes can be obtained from other sources that deal specifically with ADO.NET.

The *SqlCommand/DataReader* is connection oriented and provides certain methods that can be leveraged to improve application performance. These methods include the *ExecuteNonQuery*, *ExecuteScalar* and *ExecuteReader*. Additionally the *SqlCommand* class implements the *ExecuteXmlReader* method for data returned in XML format. A description of these four methods along with an example (VB.NET Console application) for each follows. The examples make a connection to the NorthWind database, which by default is installed with Microsoft SQL Server.

***ExecuteNonQuery* Method**   This method is typically used with Insert, Update, and Delete operations. The only piece of information that is most useful in these cases, and that is returned to the client, is the number of rows that are affected. This method will also work with stored procedures that contain output/return parameters, which can be returned to the client. The following Visual Basic .NET code demonstrates this method by calling a stored procedure that returns a count of the number of customers in the Customer table in the NorthWind database as a return value:

```
Imports System
Imports System.Data
Imports System.Data.SqlClient

Module ExecuteNonQuery

    Sub Main()
        Dim strConnString As String = "Data Source=.;" _
                & "Initial Catalog=Northwind;" _
                & "Integrated Security=SSPI"
        Dim strSQL As String = "GetNumberOfCustomers"
        Dim sqlConn As New SqlConnection(strConnString)

        Dim sqlComd As New SqlCommand(strSQL, sqlConn)
        sqlComd.CommandType = CommandType.StoredProcedure
        sqlComd.Parameters.Add(New _
            SqlParameter("@i", SqlDbType.Int))
        sqlComd.Parameters(0).Direction = _
            ParameterDirection.ReturnValue

        sqlConn.Open()
        sqlComd.ExecuteNonQuery()
        sqlConn.Close()

        Console.WriteLine("Number of customers = {0}", _
            CType(sqlComd.Parameters(0).Value, Integer))
    End Sub
End Module
```

***ExecuteScalar* Method**   This method should be used whenever you need to retrieve a single value from the data tier, for example, if you need a count of customers or the customer ID of a single customer. To demonstrate this method, the following Visual Basic .NET code retrieves the count of customers from the Customers table in the NorthWind database:

```
Imports System
Imports System.Data
Imports System.Data.SqlClient

Module ExecuteScalar

    Sub Main()
        Dim strConnString As String = "Data Source=.;" _
                & "Initial Catalog=Northwind;" _
                & "Integrated Security=SSPI"
        Dim strSQL As String = "select count(*) from customers"
        Dim sqlConn As New SqlConnection(strConnString)
        Dim sqlComd As New SqlCommand(strSQL, sqlConn)

        sqlConn.Open()
        Dim o As Object= sqlComd.ExecuteScalar()
        sqlConn.Close()

        Console.WriteLine("Number of customers = {0}", _
            CType(o, Integer))
    End Sub
End Module
```

***ExecuteReader* Method**   Any time you need to return a single data row or multiple data rows containing a lot of columns, you should use this method. This method is useful for a one-time pass of the returned data only. To demonstrate this method, the following Visual Basic .NET code retrieves the customer ID, contact names, and phone number of customers in the Customers table in the NorthWind database.

```
Imports System
Imports System.Data
Imports System.Data.SqlClient
Imports Microsoft.VisualBasic

Module ExecuteReader

    Sub Main()
        Dim strConnString As String = "Data Source=.;" _
                & "Initial Catalog=Northwind;" _
```

(continued)

```
                          & "Integrated Security=SSPI"
        Dim strSQL As String = _
            "select customerid,contactname,phone from customers"
        Dim sqlConn As New SqlConnection(strConnString)
        Dim sqlComd As New SqlCommand(strSQL, sqlConn)

        sqlConn.Open()

        Dim sqlDR As SqlDataReader = _
            sqlComd.ExecuteReader(CommandBehavior.CloseConnection)

        Do While sqlDR.Read()
            Console.WriteLine(sqlDR("customerid").ToString() _
                & ControlChars.Tab _
                & sqlDR.GetSqlString(1).ToString() _
                & ControlChars.Tab _
                & sqlDR.GetSqlString(2).ToString())
        Loop

        sqlDR.Close()
    End Sub

End Module
```

In cases where you are sure only one row is returned to the client, you can call this method by supplying the *SingleRow* value of the *CommandBehavior* enumeration as a parameter. The syntax with this optional parameter is:

```
Dim sqlDR As SqlDataReader = _
    sqlComd.ExecuteReader(CommandBehavior.SingleRow);
```

Data values in each row can be referenced either by name or ordinal position as illustrated in the example shown above. In general using the ordinal position of a data item achieves slightly better performance. Additionally, if you know the data types being returned, a further gain can be achieved by using the SQL Server .NET Providers type-specific methods to return data values. There are several such methods, such as *GetSqlString* and *GetInt32*.

> **Tip** Try to use the type-specific methods of the SQL Server .NET Provider whenever possible.

ExecuteXMLReader Method This method is useful when data is returned from SQL Server in XML format. For example, to return the data in XML format, the

SQL statement can be modified to instruct SQL Server to return the data in XML format. The example that follows demonstrates using this method:

```
Imports System
Imports System.Data
Imports System.Data.SqlClient
Imports System.Xml

Module ExecuteXmlReader

    Sub Main()
        Dim strConnString As String = "Data Source=.;" _
                & "Initial Catalog=Northwind;" _
                & "Integrated Security=SSPI"
        Dim strSQL As String = "SELECT customerid," _
                & "contactname," _
                & "phone " _
                & "From customers " _
                & "FOR XML AUTO"
        Dim sqlConn As New SqlConnection(strConnString)
        Dim sqlComd As New SqlCommand(strSQL, sqlConn)

        sqlConn.Open()

        Dim xmlR As XmlReader = sqlComd.ExecuteXmlReader()

        Do While xmlR.Read()
            Console.WriteLine(xmlR.ReadOuterXml())
        Loop

        xmlR.Close()
        sqlConn.Close()
    End Sub

End Module
```

Common Web Tier Bottlenecks

Web tier bottlenecks can occur due to many reasons such as configuration problems, lack of hardware resources, inefficient design, or use of code. It is always useful to eliminate configuration issues by keeping your build documentation and build scripts up-to-date and verifying your configuration, especially when major code changes occur.

Effective stress testing can assist you in determining if your Web application will scale up or out by adding additional hardware. Assuming your Web application can scale, one method is to throw more hardware at your application. The downside to this is that it often requires more support hours, because there is more hardware to manage. There is a more detailed discussion on scalability at the end of this chapter. The best method of meeting or exceeding your performance goals is to identify the bottlenecks and fix or tune the code. This method is a cyclical process and requires performance testing and tuning throughout the software development life cycle. In this section we discuss some general best practices and also share our experiences with some of the newer, more effective coding techniques currently available.

Real World Configuration Problem

To illustrate a possible configuration problem, let's say you recently deployed a Web application from your development environment to your production environment. Of course you completed performance testing of your Web application in the development environment and have benchmark results or numbers that you can compare against a test in your production environment. In analyzing the performance data (counters and IIS logs), you notice much more data being passed from the test conducted in your production environment. Also, the throughput numbers for the test in your development environment are much higher. You expected much more throughput in your production environment because the hardware is more powerful and you used the same test scripts and the same amount of stress clients for both tests. You then log on to your production Web server to troubleshoot configuration differences between each environment. Finally you discover that *Trace* and *Debug* were both enabled in the Web.config file on your development environment just before it was copied up to the production servers.

Limiting Page Size

One of the most common bottlenecks we often encounter from the Web tier is a result of the dreadful never-ending page. Passing too much data per page can cause performance issues on both the IIS server and network tier. This may seem very obvious, but many Web applications we analyze suffer from slow response times as a result of having pages that are simply too large. Do not be afraid to divide up the content when necessary. This may cost your users an additional click to get to the data they are looking for but your content will load much quicker. Here are some other tips which can help to provide your end users with a better experience and quicker response times:

- If your Web application returns huge record sets, look into paging the results.

- Remove white space and comments from your code or HTML. This sends less data over the wire.

- Remove unused styles from your stylesheets.

Limiting Images

Optimize all images and use them sparingly or when they provide some kind of value to your Web application. Reusing the same image causes less network round trips because most browsers can cache the image on the client, and not have to go to the Web server to get the image each time. It is more efficient to use one larger image than multiple smaller images. Quite often images are used for advertisements and are loaded from another site outside of your control. You should be aware that this creates a dependency on another site that you cannot control and in extreme cases can cause your page to timeout if the resource becomes unavailable or becomes extremely slow when loading. If your site is very dynamic and graphically intensive, consider splitting your dynamic content and your images to separate Web servers and tune each accordingly.

Using Naming Conventions

Come up with a naming convention that makes sense and is readable but keep the directory structure as flat as possible. Keep file, directory, and variable names short and sweet, and abbreviate whenever possible. By doing this you will pass less data in each request, which can really make a difference because it is common to reference many file types (like images, StyleSheets, client side scripts, and so on) within HTML. You should avoid a directory structure like the following URL, which contains 68 characters:

http://yoursite/goodoldunitedstatesofamerica/northcarolina/pictures/

Just by abbreviating the directory structure you can eliminate 41 characters for just one request.

http://yoursite/us/nc/pics/

Disabling SSL

Use SSL only when necessary or required within your Web application. Test your pages with and without SSL enabled to determine the impact of encrypting your data. Generally speaking we notice a 20 to 30 percent decrease in performance by using SSL. If you organize your content effectively you can create distinct folders which house content so you can enable or disable SSL per directory. In most cases there is no need to enable SSL for images, stylesheets or other file types such as client-side scripts.

Trying New Features

As new programming methods and features become available, do not be afraid to test them out. Many new coding features are designed not only to provide additional functionality but to gain performance over previous methods used to solve various problems. For example, *Response.Execute* has been available for some time now, but we still frequently see people using *Response.Redirect* within their ASP/ASPX code. When you use *Response.Redirect* your users will incur an additional network round trip for the same operation. We have also seen many .NET Web applications which suffer major performance problems stemming from inefficient string manipulation or concatenation within loops. Using the new *.NET StringBuilder* class often resolves this problem and can add huge performance gains when concatenating many strings together in a loop.

Scaling the Web Tier

Scalability is defined as having the ability to add resources to a system that increase its performance (decrease response times or increase throughput). From the performance testing perspective, this means adding more hardware or redesigning your Web application to allow more users to access your Web application more efficiently. To cover scalability we will focus on the Web tier and a methodology to know when and how to scale it.

Scale Out, Scale Up, or Performance Tune?

The term scalability typically is covered by two distinct yet similar methods, scaling up and scaling out. These methods should only be used after your Web application has been performance tested and performance tuned. Performance testing helps you identify bottlenecks and limitations of your current Web application. Through performance tuning you will increase throughput, decrease your response times, or both. The following list definitions and the pros and cons for scaling out, scaling up, and performance tuning.

Scaling Out

Scaling out your Web tier is adding extra Web servers to your application to overcome a bottleneck or limitation caused by this tier. The benefit of scaling out your Web tier is an increase in throughput, provided there are no network, SQL, or other bottlenecks external to your Web server. The downside of scaling out is that it can be expensive in terms of hardware cost, software cost, and production support cost (power, rack space, cooling, and so on). Additionally, this puts more of a burden on support staff and deployment.

Scaling Up

Scaling up your Web tier means adding extra hardware like memory and CPU capacity to your servers to overcome a bottleneck or limitation caused by this tier. This method is less expensive then scaling out because memory and CPU costs are relatively inexpensive compared to buying the whole machine. However, this approach may not give you linear gains in performance. To justify scaling up, performance testing is required both before and after scaling up to determine the overall impact.

Performance Tuning

Performance tuning is simply fixing bottlenecks on your application to achieve your desired throughput rate or response time criteria. In other words, fix the code instead of scaling your hardware. This method can be the most expensive if not performed during the software development life cycle, because it involves high labor cost for software developers, test engineers, and support engineers.

When to Scale your Web Tier?

A common mistake when building and deploying a Web application is using an unnecessary amount of hardware to solve issues and overcome bottlenecks. Performance tuning your application will save time and money because it can give you a better idea of when additional hardware via scaling up or scaling out is required. By using steps detailed in Chapter 2, you can identify the business requirements for the approximate number of customers who will access your Web application. Then you can run performance tests and tune your Web application to meet and exceed these estimates. You can also perform a transaction cost analysis, which is outlined in Chapter 9, to determine the maximum number of users your Web application can handle and to help with capacity planning

You should scale your Web tier only after all other performance constraints are identified and resolved. For example, if your SQL tier has several performance issues that limit the number of users to a quantity that a single IIS Server can handle you should fix your SQL issues first. There is no point in scaling out your Web tier by adding more IIS servers or upgrading your existing servers with more and faster CPUs and memory if your SQL tier is at peak capacity.

How Big is Big Enough?

Say you are in the travel and cruise ship industry and you are trying to determine what is the largest ship possible to obtain the maximum number of customers. If you scale your ship out and up too much to accommodate as many passengers as possible, you may not be able to travel to certain places that have size limitations, like the Panama Canal. If you are not sold out for every trip the unnecessary space and weight may cause your business to incur extra expenses. The best approach would be to build the ship to meet your peak passenger and profit requirements with five percent extra capacity perhaps. This same principle applies when you are trying to determine how much hardware is needed to deploy a Web application.

How to Scale Out your Web Tier?

To have fault tolerance and redundancy every Web application should have a minimum of two Web servers. You may build redundancy into a single machine but just having one Web server limits your application to a single point of failure. The simplest way to scale out your Web tier is by adding additional Web servers and to use a hardware or software based load balancing solution.

Software-based Load Balancing

Microsoft's implementation of a software-based load balancing solution is called Network Load Balancing (NLB). Using NLB is typically the least expensive method of load balancing and uses services bundled in Windows 2000 Advanced Server, Windows 2000 Data Center Edition, and Windows .NET Server. This method is good for most Web applications and allows you to scale out several nodes in your Web tier. For detailed instructions and implementation practices visit *http://www.microsoft.com*.

Hardware-based Load Balancing

A hardware-based load balancing solution is optimal because it is a layer separate from your Web application's code, so it does not use resources from your Web server. Many companies, such as Cisco, F5 Labs, and Extreme Networks, provide hardware-based load balancing products and solutions. For detailed information on configuring and installing a load balancing solution, visit the Web sites of the vendors listed above.

Conclusion

After you understand your Web application's configuration, you can begin to identify bottlenecks at the Web tier. You profile your .NET Web application by monitoring the IIS log files and System Monitor data, and pinpoint delays or other bottlenecks within the code by using the new trace feature in ASP.NET. You can make large performance gains by tuning your code and using new methods or features in ASP.NET, like output caching, whenever possible and appropriate.

Performance Analysis of Managed Code

In this chapter, we will explore the performance considerations relevant to the .NET common language runtime environment (CLR). First we will review the CLR features that have the most influence on the performance of .NET Web applications, and go into detail about specific performance counters used to analyze typical .NET Web application behavior. Next, we will discuss two applications that Microsoft uses when profiling managed code: Compuware's Dev-Partner Studio, and Xtremesoft's Appmetrics.

CLR and Performance

The common language runtime is the part of the .NET Framework that provides the management we refer to when we speak of *.NET managed code*. For .NET applications, CLR stands in for the Windows kernel, providing vital services such as loading, memory management and protection, exception handling, and the means to easily interoperate with other components and applications. In addition to reprising the features of a classic runtime environment, CLR also takes on the job of compiling .NET applications on the system where they will actually be running.

Microsoft's reasons for creating a new runtime environment go beyond the scope of this book, but many of the particular features and trade-offs of CLR's design are of immediate interest.

Microsoft Intermediate Language

The biggest difference between traditional applications and .NET applications is that .NET applications are not directly compiled into native instructions for the processor on which they will eventually run. Instead, .NET applications are compiled from any number of .NET languages (such as Visual Basic .NET, C++ .NET, or C#) into Microsoft Intermediate Language (MSIL), which is then packaged and distributed in the form of *assemblies*. An assembly is a file or set of files containing objects compiled into MSIL and a *manifest* that describes them.

> **Note**   You can browse the contents of an assembly using the tool ildasm.exe, which Microsoft provides with the .NET Framework.

With this design, code represented as MSIL can be analyzed and managed by CLR. Its benefits include garbage collection, whereby CLR determines which objects in memory are no longer in use and automatically de-allocates them, and memory type safety, meaning that CLR knows how a given object in memory is meant to be accessed and can verify in advance that no executable code will misuse it. In addition, managed code simplifies interoperability between applications and components written in different languages.

The Just-in-Time Compiler

Code written in MSIL is never executed. Instead, CLR uses a built-in compiler called the Just-in-Time Compiler (JIT) to generate native machine instructions for execution.

Code is typically compiled only as needed. When a process calls a method for the first time, the JIT steps in and compiles the method on the spot. (If another application or instance of the same application later calls the same method, it will have to compile its own instance of the method as well.) One part of this process is *verification*, in which CLR verifies that the code is safe, meaning it only accesses objects in memory as they are intended to be accessed. After the code is compiled, execution proceeds from the address where the generated native instructions are located. Finally, when the process terminates, the native instructions that were generated are discarded.

This process provides a huge performance advantage when measured against classic Web applications written using ASP. Until now, ASP has been an interpreted language, meaning that it has carried the overhead cost of having to interpret code as it goes along, never reducing that code to a more efficient compiled form the way ASP.NET does.

However, the case is not as clear cut when measured against classic compiled applications. Compiling code at run time, instead of ahead of time, obviously incurs a performance impact. Microsoft has taken measures to minimize the impact, and in a few cases, JIT compiled code can even outperform its unmanaged counterpart.

One performance benefit of compiling code at run time is that so much more is known about the operating environment at run time than the developer could possibly have known at design time. Certain optimizations may be available to the JIT based on the number of system processors and their individual features, as well as what other system resources are available and how they are being used at the time.

On the other hand, only a limited amount of optimization can be done before the time required to optimize the code has the potential to outweigh the benefit of optimization. Recognizing this, the JIT implements certain algorithms to avoid optimizations that are unlikely to save as much time as it costs to attempt them.

> **Note**   If you're interested in quantifying exactly how the JIT affects performance, you'll find a number of helpful performance counters in the *.NET CLR Jit* performance object.

The Pre-JIT Alternative

Included with the .NET Framework is the tool ngen.exe, used to compile assemblies from MSIL into native instructions at the time they are installed, in a process referred to as Pre-JIT. At first glance, Pre-JITting looks like the best of all worlds—why compile at run time when the compiler can still benefit from knowing the details of the system at install time?

The truth is that the impact of JITting at run time is most noticeable when the application is first loaded. Since Web applications rarely reload, if ever, there's little reason to Pre-JIT them. Another reason not to Pre-JIT is that you miss out on the optimizations made available by knowing the state of the system at run time.

> **Note**   On the other hand, the JIT could afford to spend more time computing code optimizations at install time than it can at run time. The current version of .NET does not take advantage of this, but future versions may do so, possibly making Pre-JIT more suitable for Web-based applications.

The Life and Times of a .NET Web Application

Now that we've introduced JIT, we will explore some of the other ways CLR influences the performance of an application over the course of its execution. Bear in mind that as far as CLR is concerned, it does not matter which high-level programming languages the application components were written in. By the time CLR encounters them, they are either managed assemblies written in MSIL, or they are unmanaged code to be run outside of CLR.

Load Time—AppDomains

When CLR loads a new application, applications are placed in special memory areas set aside for them called AppDomains. Because CLR provides memory type safety, it is possible for multiple applications to safely cohabit within the same AppDomain. Applications in the same AppDomain function as a group in the sense that they can share data quickly and efficiently, and if the AppDomain is unloaded, all applications and assemblies loaded into that domain are unloaded together.

Run Time—Interoperability

As a .NET application runs, it may make calls into unmanaged code, such as COM components or standard Windows DLLs. Whenever execution of a thread passes between managed code and unmanaged code, a transition is said to occur. These transitions carry certain costs.

One cost of making a transition is that the arguments and return values being passed between the caller and callee must be marshaled. Marshaling is the process of arranging the objects in memory according to the expectations of the code that will process them. Naturally, data types such as strings and complex structures are more expensive to marshal than simple types like integers.

> **Note**   In the case of strings, it is often necessary to convert them to different formats such as ANSI and Unicode. This is an example of an expensive marshalling operation.

Another cost of transitioning concerns CLR's memory manager, known as the garbage collector. (The garbage collector will be discussed in more detail later in the chapter.) Whenever a transition into unmanaged code occurs, CLR must identify all the objects referenced by the call to unmanaged code, to ensure the garbage collector does not move them and thereby disrupt the unmanaged thread. Objects that have been identified as possibly in use by unmanaged code are said to be *pinned*.

> **Note**   Obviously, the most desirable behavior for an application is to minimize the number of transitions needed to do a given amount of work. When testing, use the *# of marshalling* counter in the *.NET CLR Interop* performance object to locate areas where application threads are repeatedly transitioning between modes and doing only a small amount of work before transitioning back.

Run Time—Garbage Collection

One of CLR's most prominent features is automatic memory management, better known as garbage collection. Rather than requiring developers to implement their own memory management, CLR automatically allocates memory for objects when they are created, and periodically checks to see which objects the application is done using. Those objects that are no longer in use are marked as garbage and collected, meaning that the memory they occupy is made available for use by new objects.

Generations and Promotion

Naturally, garbage collection needs to be fast, since time spent managing memory comes at the expense of time spent letting the application do its job.

One assumption about memory management that has withstood considerable scrutiny can be summarized by simply saying that the vast majority of objects are usually needed for only a short amount of time. Microsoft's garbage collector (GC) makes the most of this by sorting objects into three categories, or generations, numbered 0, 1, and 2. Each generation has a heap size, which refers to the total number of bytes that can be occupied by all objects in that generation. These heap sizes change over the course of an application's execution, but their initial sizes are usually around 256 KB for generation 0, 2 MB for generation 1, and 10 MB for generation 2.

Objects in generation 0 are youngest. Any time an application creates a new object, the object is placed in generation 0. If there is not enough room on the generation 0 heap to accomodate the new object, then a generation 0 garbage collection occurs. During a collection, every object in the generation is examined to see if it is still in use. Those still in use are said to survive the collection, and are promoted to generation 1. Those no longer in use are de-allocated. You will notice that the generation 0 heap is always empty immediately after it is collected, so there is always room to allocate a new object—that is, unless the system is out of memory, as we discuss below.

> **Note**   You may wonder what happens if a new object is so large that its size exceeds the space available on the generation 0 heap all by itself. Objects larger than 20 KB are allocated on a special heap all their own, known as the large object heap. You'll find performance counters to track the large object heap size in the *.NET CLR Memory* performance object.

In the course of promoting objects from generation 0 to generation 1, the GC must check to see if there is room to store the promoted objects in generation 1. If there is enough room on the generation 1 heap to accomodate objects promoted from generaton 0 the true GC terminates, having only collected generation 0. If, on the other hand, the capacity of the generation 1 heap will be exceeded by promoting objects into it from generation 0, then generation 1 is collected as well. Just as before, objects that are no longer in use are de-allocated, while all surviving objects are promoted, this time to generation 2. You'll notice that after generation 1 is collected, its heap is occupied only by those objects newly promoted from generation 0.

Just as generation 1 must sometimes be collected to make room for new objects, so must generation 2. Just as before, unused objects in generation 2 are de-allocated, but the survivors remain in generation 2. Immediately after a collection of generation 2, its heap is occupied by surviving as well as newly promoted objects.

Immediately following a collection, a heap's contents are re-arranged so as to be adjacent to each other in memory, and the heap is said to be compacted.

Notice that any time generation 1 is collected, so is generation 0, and whenever generation 2 is collected, the GC is said to be making a full pass because all three generations are collected.

As long as only a few objects need to be promoted during a collection, then the garbage collector is operating efficiently, making the most memory available with the least amount of work. To optimize the likelihood that the garbage collector will operate efficiently, it is also self-tuning, adjusting its heap sizes over time according to the rate at which objects are promoted. If too many objects are being promoted from one heap to another, the GC increases the size of the younger heap to reduce the frequency at which it will need to collect that heap. If, on the other hand, objects are almost never promoted out of a heap, this is a sign that the GC can reduce the size of the heap and improve performance by reducing the application's working set. The exception here is generation 2: since objects are never promoted out of generation 2, the GC's only choice is to increase the size of the generation 2 heap when it starts getting full. If your application's generation 2 heap grows too steadily for too long, this is probably a sign that the application should be reviewed for opportunities to reduce the lifetime of objects. When generation 2 can no longer accommodate promoted objects, this means the garbage collector cannot allocate space for new objects, and attempts to create new objects will cause a *System.OutOfMemoryException*.

The GC also attempts to keep the size of the generation 0 heap within the size of the system's L2 cache. This keeps memory I/O costs to a minimum during the most frequent collections. When monitoring your application, it may be helpful to see if it allows the GC to take advantage of this optimization.

Pinned Objects

As mentioned earlier, pinned objects are those that have been marked as possibly in use by threads executing unmanaged code. When the GC runs, it must ignore pinned objects. This is because changing an object's address in memory (when compacting or promoting it) would cause severe problems for the unmanaged thread. Objects therefore survive any collection that occurs while they are pinned.

When monitoring application performance, pinned objects indicate memory that cannot be managed or reclaimed by the garbage collector. Pinned objects are usually found in places where the application is using significant amounts of unmanaged code.

Finalization

Some objects might store references to unmanaged resources such as network sockets or mutexes. Since de-allocating such an object would result in loss of the reference to the unmanaged resource, developers might specify that the GC must cause the object to clean up after itself before it can be de-allocated, in a process called finalization.

Finalization carries several performance costs. For example, objects awaiting finalization cannot be de-allocated by the garbage collector until they are finalized. Moreover, if an object pending finalization references other objects, then those objects are considered to be in use, even if they are otherwise unused. In contrast to the garbage collector, the programmer has no way to directly control the finalization process. Since there are no guarantees as to when finalization will occur, it is possible for large amounts of memory to become tied up at the mercy of the finalization queue.

When a garbage collection occurs, objects pending finalization are promoted instead of collected, and tracked by the *Finalization Survivors* counter in the *.NET CLR Memory* performance object. Objects referenced by finalization survivors are also promoted, and tracked by the *Promoted Finalization* counters in the *.NET CLR Memory* performance object.

When monitoring an application that uses objects that require finalization, it is important to watch out for excessive use of memory by objects that are pending finalization directly or otherwise.

Differences Between Workstation and Server GC

Whenever a collection occurs, the GC must suspend execution of those threads that access objects whose locations in memory will change as they are promoted or compacted. Choosing the best behavior for the GC depends on the type of application.

Desktop applications that interact directly with individual users tend to allocate fewer memory objects than Web-based applications that serve hundreds or even thousands of users, and so minimizing the latency involved in a garbage collection is a higher priority than optimizing the rate at which memory is reclaimed.

Therefore, Microsoft implements the GC in two different modes. Note that the best GC is *not* chosen automatically - CLR will use the Workstation GC (mscorwks.dll) unless the developer specifies that the application requires the Server GC (mscorsvr.dll) instead.

Note   In our experience, with most Web application scenarios, we have found that the Server GC out performs the Workstation GC.

Run Time—Exceptions

Whenever a method encounters a situation it can't deal with in the normal course of execution, it creates an exception object that describes the unexpected condition (such as out of memory or access denied). The exception is then *thrown*, meaning the thread signals CLR that it is in a state of distress, and cannot continue executing until the exception has been handled.

When an exception is thrown, the manner of its disposal will depend on whether or not the application has code to handle the exception. Either CLR will halt the application because it cannot handle the exception gracefully, or CLR will execute the appropriate exception handler within the application, after which the application may continue execution. (An application could be designed to terminate gracefully after handling certain exceptions; in that case we would say that the application continues, if only to terminate as intended.)

Suppose method *main()* calls method *foo()*, which in turn calls method *bar()*, and *bar()* throws a *System.FileNotFoundException*. The CLR suspends execution of the thread while it looks for an exception filter that matches the thrown exception. Method *bar()* might have an exception handler whose filter specifies *System.DivideByZeroException*. The *FileNotFoundException* would not match this filter, and so CLR would continue in search of a matching exception filter. If none of the exception filters specified by function *bar()* matched the exception, the system would recurse up the call stack from *bar()* to the function that called it, in this case, *foo()*. Now, suppose *foo()* has an exception handler that specifies *System.FileNotFoundException*. The exception handler in *foo()* will execute, thereby catching the exception.

When we speak of *throw-to-catch depth*, we refer to the number of layers up the call stack CLR had to traverse to find an appropriate exception handler. As it was in our hypothetical example, the throw-to-catch depth was 1. If *bar()* had caught its own exception, the depth would have been 0. And if CLR had needed to recurse all the way up to *main()*, the depth would have been 2.

Once an exception has been caught, execution of the application resumes inside a block of code called a *finally block*. The purpose of a finally block is to clean up after whatever operations might have been interrupted by the exception. Finally blocks are optional, but every finally block that exists between the method that threw the exception and the method that caught it will be executed before the application resumes regular execution.

Therefore, in our example above, if functions *foo()* and *bar()* each implement a finally block, both will execute before program flow returns to normal. If the developer chose not to write a finally block for *bar()*, but did write one for *foo()*, the finally block in *foo()* would still execute.

Exceptions in Unmanaged Code

When managed code calls unmanaged code, and that unmanaged code throws an exception which it does not catch, the exception is converted into a .NET exception, and the CLR becomes involved in attempting to handling it. As with any other. NET exception, CLR will halt the application if it is not handled.

Unmanaged exceptions, which do not concern CLR, won't be tabulated by any of the .NET CLR performance counters. On the other hand, .NET exceptions which originated in unmanaged will be tabulated by the *# of Exceps Thrown* counters once they are converted. When tabulating .NET exceptions converted from unmanaged code, the *Throw to Catch Depth* performance counter will only count stack frames within the .NET environment, causing the throw-to-catch depth to appear shorter than it actually is.

Exceptions and Performance

Exception handling is expensive. Execution of the involved thread is suspended while CLR recurses through the call stack in search of the right exception handler, and when it is found, the exception handler and some number of finally blocks must all have their chance to execute before regular processing can resume.

Exceptions are intended to be rare events, and it is assumed that the cost of handling them gracefully is worth the performance hit. When monitoring application performance, some people are tempted to hunt for the most expensive exceptions. But why tune an application for the case that isn't supposed to happen? An application that disposes of exceptions quickly is still just blazing through exceptions instead of doing real work. Therefore, we recommend that you work to identify the areas where exceptions most often occur, and let them take the time they need so that your application can continue running gracefully.

.NET Performance Counters

Now that you have been introduced to those aspects of the .NET Framework that have a direct impact on the performance of your Web application, we will discuss some of the new .NET performance counters that allow you to measure the performance of the .NET Framework and your managed code. This section is not intended to discuss all of the counters; doing so would require far more than a chapter of material. Instead, we set out to present those counters that would give you the most bang for your buck. The counters presented below, in our opinion, are the ones that can tell the most about your application in the shortest amount of time. Note that this subset of counters does not represent all of the requirements for monitoring the performance of your .NET Web application. Depending on your system architecture, you may find it necessary to monitor other .NET related counters along with counters not specific to .NET.

> **Tip**   If you are interested in capturing performance counter data as part of an application that you are developing, you can reference under managed languages in the *System.Diagnostics.Performance-Counter* namespace.

.NET CLR Memory Object

All of the counters found under this object relate memory usage by the .NET framework. No matter whether you are running a .NET Web application or .NET desktop application, these counters will help you understand how the framework is using the system's memory resources. It is important to note that if your application consists of both managed and unmanaged code, these counters will only draw a partial picture of memory usage, since they do not track memory use by unmanaged code even though it may be running as part of the same application.

GC Handles Performance Counter

The *# GC Handles* performance counter displays the current number of garbage collection handles in use. Garbage collection handles are handles to resources outside of CLR and the managed environment. A single handle may only occupy a tiny amount of memory in the managed heap; however, the unmanaged resource it represents could actually be very expensive. You may encounter a large amount of activity with GC handles if multiple objects were created through the use of your Web application. For instance, if a particular user scenario required the allocation of an unmanaged resource such as a network socket each time a user executed that scenario an object consisting of this array would be created along with a corresponding GC handle. When under heavy load—specifically when this scenario is called—your Web site would create a large number of GC handles, possibly causing your application to become unstable.

Gen 0 Collections

This and the following two counters are important for understanding how efficiently memory is being cleaned up. The *# Gen 0 Collections* counter displays the number of times generation 0 objects have been garbage collected since the start of your application. Each time an object that is still in use is garbage collected at generation 0, it is promoted from generation 0 to generation 1. As we described earlier, one scenario in which generation 0 promotions occur is if your Web application needs to create a new object whose required memory resources exceed the resources available at generation 0. In that case an object remaining in use at the generation 0 level would be promoted, freeing the resources needed for the newest object. The rate of Gen 0 collections will usually correspond with rate at which the application allocates memory.

Gen 1 Collections

This counter displays the number of times the Gen 1 heap has been collected since the start of the application. You should monitor this counter in the same fashion as the *# Gen 0 Collections* counter. If you see numerous collections at generation 1, it is an indication that there are not sufficient resources to allocate for objects being promoted from generation 0 to generation 1. Thus, objects will be promoted from generation 1 to generation 2, leading to high resource utilization at the generation 2 level.

Gen 2 Collections

This counter displays the number of times generation 2 objects have been garbage collected since the start of the application. Of the three counters discussing generation-level collection information (*# Gen 0 Collections*, *# Gen 1 Collections* and *# Gen 2 Collections*) the *# Gen 2 Collections* is the most important to monitor. With Web applications if you are seeing a high activity for this counter, the *aspnet_wp* process could be forced to restart. The restart will occur if the amount of global memory has been fully allocated to resources at the generation 2 level. The restart of the *aspnet_wp* process forces additional memory to be allocated to the global memory.

Total Committed Bytes

This counter displays the amount of virtual memory committed by your application. It is obviously ideal for an application to require as little memory as possible, thereby reducing the amount of work required for the garbage collector to manage it.

% Time in GC

This counter indicates the amount of time spent by the garbage collector on behalf of an application to collect and compact memory. If your application is not optimized, you will see the garbage collector working constantly, promoting and deleting objects. This time spent by the garbage collector reflects its use of critical processor and memory resources.

Gen 0 heap size

The *Gen 0 heap size* counter displays the maximum bytes that can be allocated in generation 0. The generation 0 size is dynamically tuned by the garbage collector; therefore, the size will change during the execution of an application. A reduced heap size reflects that the application is economizing on memory resources, thereby allowing the GC to reduce the size of the application's working set.

Gen 0 Promoted Bytes/sec

This counter displays the amount of bytes promoted per second from generation 0 to generation 1. Even though your application may exhibit a high number of promotions, you may not see a high number of promoted bytes per second if the objects being promoted are extremely small in size. You should monitor the *# Gen 1 heap size* counter along with this counter in order to verify whether promotions are resulting in poor resource allocation at the generation 1 level.

Gen 1 heap size

This counter displays the current number of bytes in generation 1. Unlike its *Gen 0 heap size* counterpart, the *Gen 1 heap size* counter does not display the maximum size of generation 1. Instead, it displays the current amount of memory allocated to objects at the generation 1 level. When monitoring this counter, you will want to monitor the *# Gen 0 Collections* counter simultaneously. If you find a high number of generation 0 collections occurring, you will find the generation 1 heap size increasing along with them. Eventually, objects will need to be promoted to generation 2, leading to inefficient memory utilization.

Gen 1 Promoted Bytes/sec

Gen 1 Promoted Bytes/sec displays the number of bytes promoted per second from generation 1 to generation 2. Similar to the approach for the *Gen 0 Promoted Bytes/sec* counter, you should monitor the *Gen 2 heap size* counter when monitoring the *Gen 1 Promoted Bytes/sec* counter. The two counters will provide you with a good indication of how much memory is being allocated for objects being promoted from generation 1 to generation 2.

Gen 2 heap size

This counter displays the current number of bytes in generation 2. When monitoring an application that is experiencing a high number of promotions from generation 1 to generation 2, the generation 2 heap size will increase since objects cannot be further promoted.

.NET CLR Loading

The following counters found under the *.NET CLR Loading* performance object, when used alongside other counters such as *% Processor Time*, allow you to gain a more detailed understanding of the effects on system resources through the loading of .NET applications, AppDomains, classes and assemblies.

Total AppDomains

This counter displays the peak number of AppDomains (application domains) loaded since the start of the application. As mentioned earlier, AppDomains are a secure and versatile unit of processing that CLR can use to provide isolation between applications running in the same process. AppDomains are particularly useful when you need to run multiple applications within the same process. In the case of a Web application, you may find yourself having to run multiple applications within the *aspnet_wp* process. From a performance standpoint, understanding the number of AppDomains currently running on the server is critical because each time you create or destroy an AppDomain system resources are taxed. Just as important is the need to understand the type of activity occurring between AppDomains. For example, if your applications must cross AppDomain boundaries during execution, this will result in context switches. Context switches (as discussed in Chapter 4) are expensive, particularly when a server is experiencing 15,000 context switches per second or more.

Total Assemblies

This counter displays the total number of assemblies loaded since the start of the application. Assemblies can be loaded as domain-neutral when their code can be shared by all AppDomains, or they can be loaded as domain-specific when their code is private to the AppDomain. If the assembly is loaded as domain-neutral from multiple AppDomains, then this counter is incremented once only. You should be aware of the total number of assemblies loaded on the server because of the resources needed to create and destroy them. Sometimes developers will load assemblies that aren't really required by the application. Alternatively, developers may not be aware of how many assemblies they are truly loading because they are making an indirect reference.

Total Classes Loaded

This counter displays the total number of classes loaded in all of the assemblies since the start of the application. Each class loaded is not a static class, so it has a constructor. When calling the class the developer will have to instantiate the class, which is more resource intensive than creating the object once and calling the object's method.

.NET CLR LocksAndThreads

When tracking down a bottleneck that could be related to thread or process contention, the *.NET CLR LocksAndThreads* performance object is the best place to start. Here, we describe those counters under the *.NET CLR LocksAndThreads* performance object that can help rule out possible contention issues quickly and efficiently.

Contention Rate/sec

This counter displays the number of times per second that threads in the run time attempt to acquire a managed lock unsuccessfully. It should be noted that under conditions of heavy contention, threads are not guaranteed to obtain locks in the order they've requested them.

Total # of Contentions

This counter displays the total number of times threads in CLR have attempted to acquire a managed lock unsuccessfully.

Current Queue Length

This counter displays the total number of threads currently waiting to acquire some managed lock. If you see that the queue length continues to grow under constant application load, you may be dealing with an irresolvable lock rather than a resolvable lock. The difference between irresolvable and resolvable locks is that irresolvable locks are caused when an error within the application code's logic makes it impossible for the application to release a lock on an object.

.NET CLR Exceptions

Applications that throw excessive amounts of exceptions can be extremely resource intensive. Ideally, an application should not throw any exceptions. However, many times developers will intentionally throw exceptions as part of the error checking process. This exception generating code should be cleaned up before taking an application into production. Here we have listed two counters found under the *.NET CLR Exceptions* object. If you choose to monitor only one of these, you should pay most attention to the *# of Exceps Thrown/sec* counter. If you see this counter exceed 100 exceptions per second, your application code warrants further investigation.

of Exceps Thrown

This counter displays the total number of exceptions thrown since the start of the application. These include both .NET exceptions and unmanaged exceptions that are converted into .NET exceptions (for example, a null pointer reference exception in unmanaged code would get rethrown in managed code as a *.NET System.NullReferenceException*), but excludes exceptions which were thrown and caught entirely within unmanaged code. This counter includes both handled and unhandled exceptions. Exceptions that are rethrown will be counted again. This counter is an excellent resource when you are attempting to determine what portion of the code may be generating a high number of exceptions. You could do this by walking through the application while simultaneously monitoring this counter. When you find a sudden jump in the exception count, you can go back and review the code that was executed during that portion of the walkthrough in order to pin down where an excessive number of exceptions are thrown.

of Exceps Thrown /sec

This counter displays the number of exceptions thrown per second. These include both .NET exceptions and unmanaged exceptions that get converted into .NET exceptions but excludes exceptions that were thrown and caught entirely within unmanaged code. This counter includes both handled and unhandled exceptions. As mentioned earlier, if you monitor a consistently high number of exceptions per second thrown (100 or more), you will need to review the source code in order to determine why and where these exceptions are being thrown.

.NET CLR Security

Depending on how much emphasis you place on the security of your Web application, you will find the following set of counters to be either extremely active or hardly used. These counters should be kept active when truly necessary. Conducting security checks of your application is critical even if there is an effect upon application performance. However, using the security features of the .NET Framework unwisely will not only create security holes in your application, but performance issues will emerge due to poor application design.

Link Time Checks

Many times you will monitor a counter and see excessive activity for that counter. This activity can be deceiving unless you truly understand what is going on with the counter. The *# Link Time Checks* counter is just one example. The count displayed is not indicative of serious performance issues, but it is indicative of the security system activity. This counter displays the total number of linktime Code Access Security (CAS) checks since the start of the application. An example of when a linktime CAS check would occur is when a caller makes a call to a callee demanding execution of an operation. The linktime check is performed once per caller and at only one level, thus making it less resource expensive than a stack walk.

% Time in RT checks

This counter displays the percentage of elapsed time spent in performing runtime Code Access Security (CAS) checks since the last such check. CAS allows code to be trusted to varying degrees and enforces these varying levels of trust depending on code identity. This counter is updated at the end of a runtime security check;

it represents the last observed value and is not an average. If this counter contains in a high percentage, you will want to revisit what is being checked and how often. Your application may be executing unnecessary stack walk depths (the *Stack Walk Depth* counter is discussed next). Another cause for a high percentage of time spent in runtime checks could be numerous linktime checks.

Stack Walk Depth

This counter displays the depth of the stack during that last runtime CAS check. Runtime CAS check is performed by walking the stack. An example of when the stack is walked would be when your application calls an object that has four methods (method A–D). If your code calls method A, a stack walk depth of 1 would occur. However, if you were to call method D, which in turn calls methods C, B and A, a stalk walk of depth of 4 would occur.

Total Runtime Checks

This counter displays the total number of runtime CAS checks performed since the start of the application. Runtime CAS checks are performed when a caller makes a call to a callee demanding a particular permission. The runtime check is made on every call by the caller, and the check is done by examining the current thread stack of the caller. Utilizing information from this counter and that of the *Stack Walk Depth* counter, you can gain a good idea of the performance penalty you are paying for executing security checks. A high number for the total runtime checks along with a high stack walk depth indicates performance overhead.

Profiling Managed Code

In this next section we'll be discussing how to instrument and profile your managed (and your unmanaged) code using Compuware's DevPartner Studio 7.0. There are many good profilers available on the market, but we are using DevPartner Studio as an example because it is the profiler of choice used by the ACE Team at Microsoft.

Using Compuware DevPartner Studio

Compuware Corporation's DevPartner Studio Professional Edition can assist you in creating reliable, high-performance applications. The performance analysis component makes it easy to pinpoint performance bottlenecks anywhere in your code, third party components, or operating system, even when source code is not available. An evaluation version of DevPartner Studio 7.0 Professional Edition can be obtained at *http://www.compuware.com/products/devpartner/*.

Profiling with DevPartner Studio

In many applications, a relatively small portion of the code is responsible for much of the application's performance. The challenge is to quickly identify which parts of the code are the most likely candidates for changes that can improve performance, so developers can focus their limited time on tuning efforts that have a high probability of improving overall performance.

The performance analysis capability in DevPartner Studio measures the frequency of execution and execution time down to the line of code for a wide variety of components: Visual Basic, Visual C++, Visual Basic .NET, C#, Visual C, native C/C++, as well as Web applications using ASP.NET, JScript and VBScript when using IE or IIS.

Collecting performance data is straightforward with DevPartner Studio. For managed code, simply run your application with Performance Analysis enabled. For unmanaged code, enable the Instrumentation Manager and rebuild. While you are exercising your application, you can optionally use the session controls (start, stop, and clear) to focus your data collection on areas of specific interest.

One possible methodology is to collect performance data at the method level only (rather than the line level), avoiding the instrumentation step for the moment, assessing which methods are most expensive, and then running line-level data collection on the methods of most interest. This technique points you very quickly in the direction of which subset of methods are the most likely candidates for improvement.

> **Note**   To avoid collecting data for all system (nonsource) files, check Exclude System Images on the DevPartner Performance and Coverage Exclude Images options page. Once you optimize your source code, turn off this option so you can examine how your application uses system code, especially if you are using the .NET Framework.

Profiling Session Window

Once you are done executing your application, performance data is displayed in a Session window, as shown in Figure 7-1. The filter pane on the left lists the source files and system images used during the session, along with the percentage of time spent in each file during execution. You can quickly browse to any file and view the methods contained within that file. In this example, note that we have an application with a mixture of native C++ and C# code. You can also select useful collections of files or methods (such as the Top 20 methods) in order to focus attention on which code is using the most execution time or is called most frequently. The Session data pane on the right provides the detailed method list and associated source code, along with overall summary information.

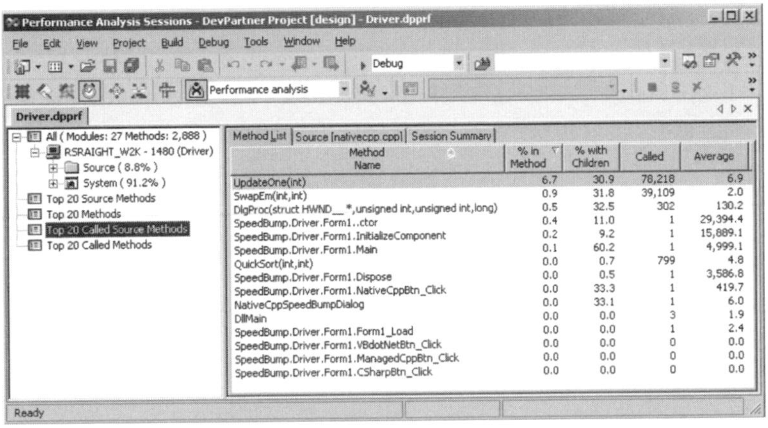

Figure 7-1   DevPartner Studio Performance Analysis Session Window

One way to proceed is to sort the session data by the average time spent in each method, and then to begin to examine the most expensive methods for possible improvements. By selecting a method in the Session data pane, you can examine the source code in more detail. Figure 7-2 provides example source code, which is annotated with the number of times each line of code has executed, the percentage of time spent in called (children) functions, and the total time spent executing the line of code. The most expensive line is also highlighted, which could be your starting point for candidate code to further tune.

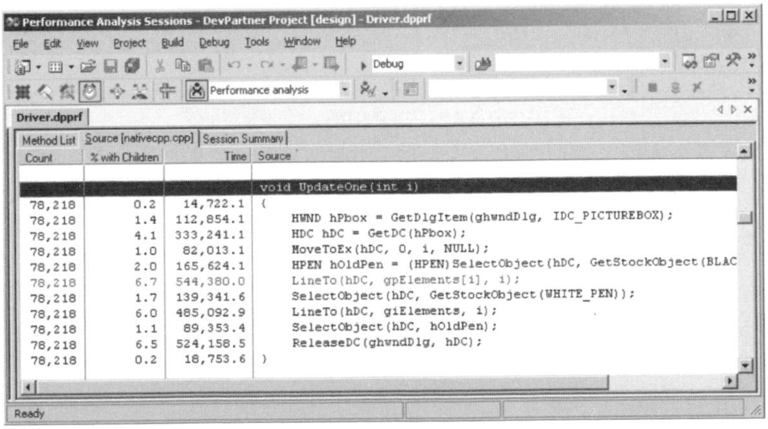

Figure 7-2   DevPartner Studio Performance Analysis Source Code Window

Profiling Method Details

Another approach to improving performance is to explore the relationships between the functions called in your application. By selecting a method, the details of that method—including what other methods it calls and what methods call it—are displayed as shown in Figure 7-3. The top section of the display identifies the selected method and contains performance data for the method. The Parents section lists all methods that called the selected method, and the Children section lists all methods called by the selected method. Using the Method Details view allows you to quickly understand the method calling relationships and costs, traverse the calling sequence to help you better understand both how your own code is working, and understand the impact of calls to the supporting infrastructure.

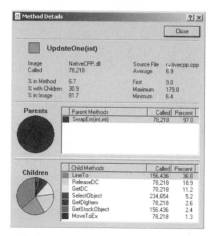

Figure 7-3 DevPartner Studio Performance Analysis Method Details Window

Working with Distributed Applications

DevPartner Studio provides performance data gathering and reporting capabilities for the distributed application environment, including Web-based applications. It provides end-to-end profiling for distributed, component-based applications. For distributed Web-based applications, DevPartner collects data for Web applications created in Visual Studio .NET, as well as applications that use the scripting languages supported by IE and IIS.

When you run a distributed application, DevPartner can collect data for each separate local or remote process, including server session data, and correlate the session data. Data correlation combines session data from multiple processes into a single session file that you can view to analyze results for the entire application. DevPartner automatically correlates the session data between different processes when there are

■   DCOM-based calls between methods in different processes

■   HTTP requests between IE as client and IIS as server

To preserve the relationship between the methods of DCOM objects or the relationship between HTTP client and server (IE and IIS), DevPartner automatically correlates the data from those sessions. It then combines the correlated data with the client session data into a single session file. You can view the session file with the correlated data and navigate between calling and called methods in the Method Details view. You can use the Correlate Performance Files command by choosing DevPartner from the Tools menu to manually combine data from different session files when there is no COM-based relationship or client/server relationship between IE and IIS.

Effective Performance Analysis for .NET

The .NET Framework is particularly rich and complex, and you can accomplish a lot with a few lines of code. This offers great opportunities to developers, but can make it difficult to tune application performance. For example, you may discover that 95 percent of your application's execution time is spent in the .NET Framework. How do you improve performance in that case? Here are some basics to make the performance analysis process using DevPartner Studio more productive.

Understand What You Want to Measure   Consider how your application behaves before you begin collecting performance data. For example, if you are profiling a Web services or ASP.NET application, think about how Web caching will affect your results. If your test run inputs the same data repeatedly, your application will fetch pages from the cache, skewing the performance data. In such a case, you could take pains to ensure variable input data, or more simply, edit the machine.config file to turn off caching while you test. Comment out the line that reads:

```
<add name="OutputCache" type="System.Web.Caching.OutputCacheModule"/>
```

Understand Start-up Costs   The .NET Framework performs many one-time initializations. To prevent these from skewing performance results, warm up the application by exercising all the features you want to profile, and then clear the data using the Clear button on the Session Control toolbar. Next, run a test that exercises the same features to get a more accurate performance picture.

Understand .NET Framework Costs   Use *% with Children* on the Method List or Source tab to see how much time you are spending in the .NET Framework. Use the Child Methods window in Method Details to drill into the .NET Framework to understand which calls are expensive and why. Rework the application to do less work or to call the .NET Framework less often.

Collect Complete Data for Distributed Applications   When you analyze performance for a Web application, a multi-tier client/server application, or an application that uses Web services, include all remote application components in the analysis. Use DevPartner Performance and Coverage Remote Agent to configure performance data collection on remote systems. If your application uses native C/C++ components, instrument the components for performance analysis before collecting data. Of course, the recommendations regarding awareness of application behavior, start-up costs, and .NET Framework costs apply equally to collecting data for server-side components.

Using AppMetrics to Monitor .NET Enterprise Services Components

COM+ provides COM (unmanaged code) components with services to let applications easily achieve higher scalability and throughput. For .NET Framework (managed code) components, these same services are also available through Enterprise Services. These services include transaction coordination across distributed resources, object pooling, role-based security, etc. You can set up your managed and unmanaged code components to use these services.

AppMetrics for Transactions (AppMetrics) is a monitoring system for Enterprise Services applications that we use internally to profile the performance of heavily used COM+ components. Many of the application groups we deal with find themselves having to wrap their managed code in COM+ components in order to communicate with legacy systems. Capturing performance data produced by AppMetrics enables us to easily determine whether or not the COM+ application may be the cause of poor application performance.

You can use AppMetrics to monitor managed and unmanaged Enterprise Services components. It is designed to monitor applications running in either pre-production or production environments. AppMetrics monitors applications without any code instrumentation.

AppMetrics Manager and Agent Monitors

To reduce the effects of monitoring on system and application performance, AppMetrics uses a Manager and Agent setup. In this arrangement, AppMetrics runs its Agent on the application server. The Agent collects data about the Enterprise Services components while using a minimal amount of system resources. This lets AppMetrics capture more precise data about the applications, whether they run under simulated or real load.

The Agent sends its data to a Manager, which resides on a separate machine. Based on this data, the Manager generates metrics about the applications and their components. These metrics include the total number of activations for component instances, the rates at which the instances finish, and the actual durations of individual instances. You can use these metrics to find any bottlenecks that may occur in your applications during runtime.

The Manager machine stores the metrics in a database. From here, you can generate reports about the application processes and their component instances.

Setting Up AppMetrics Manager and Agent

To evaluate your managed and unmanaged code components while they run under Enterprise Services, set up AppMetrics within your application system with the following tasks:

1.   On the AppMetrics Manager machine, add a Manager monitor.

2.   Add an Agent monitor to the Manager monitor. In effect, this creates the Agent monitor on the application server.

3.   Select the application(s) to be monitored on the application server.

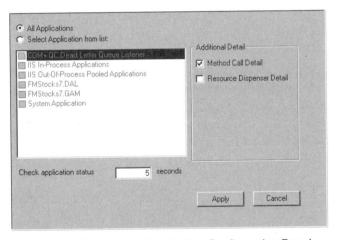

Figure 7-4   Diagnostics Application Configuration Panel

4.   Within the selected applications, you can set up specific components for monitoring.

Pre-Production Monitoring in AppMetrics

For pre-production monitoring, AppMetrics offers a type of analysis that it calls the Diagnostics Monitor. The Diagnostics Monitor records details about individual component and transaction activity in a running application.

The Diagnostics Monitor displays the metrics in a drill-down report. This report shows durations for each active component in the application. It also shows the logical chain of method calls between the components. This is important because merely viewing the metrics for each component in isolation from other components does not tell the whole story. It says nothing about how a component may make calls to other components.

With the information about the method call chains between components in the drill-down report, you can begin to see the relationships between components during runtime. It lets you analyze the overall response time of a component based on its constituent parts.

From this analysis, you can determine if the bottleneck occurs either in the root component object or somewhere further down the method call chain in a subordinate component.

Figure 7-5 shows a snippet from an AppMetrics for Transactions report, which illustrates the following:

- The logical chain of method activity.

- An FMStock7.DAL.Broker component that invokes a subordinate FMStocks7.GAM.7 component instance.

- The *CreditAccountBalance* method, which was invoked on the subordinate component.

- The unique naming convention for cross-application calls. When the code makes such calls, they are preceded with the other application name plus a colon. In this case, the FMStocks7.GAM.7 component resides in a different application from the FMStocks7.DAL.Broker component.

Transaction	Method	Rel Start (ms)	Rel End (ms)	Duration (ms)
FMStocks7.DAL.Broker		0	9960.599609	9960.599609
	FMStocks7.DAL.Broker->GetComponentInfo	2.712890625	2.78125	0.068359375
	FMStocks7.DAL.Broker->GetObjectIdentity	4.42578125	4.443359375	0.017578125
	FMStocks7.GAM : FMStocks7.GAM.7->CreditAccountBalance	72.74416063	7354.029297	7281.285156

Figure 7-5   Diagnostics drill-down report

> **Note**   In addition to the information shown here, the Diagnostics drill-down report also provides actual start times, end times, and error codes for each item.

With the information about cross-application calls in these reports, you can evaluate whether the subordinate component deserves to be in the other application. Cross-application calls can be expensive in terms of CPU utilization. They can also prolong the duration of the method call itself.

If one component makes several cross-application calls during a single transaction into a subordinate component, it may be advisable to make the subordinate component run in the same application process with the first component. You can accomplish this in several ways. For example, you can move the subordinate component into the same application with the first component. Alternatively, you can move the subordinate component into a library application.

Additional Diagnostics Information

Before an application goes to production, you will want to know its limitations. Figure 7-6 shows a snippet from an AppMetrics report that details method activity on the FMStocks7.GAM.7 component instances during a 10-minute period of intense load.

Observe that the average duration for the monitored methods is quite long and not all method calls succeeded during the period.

Name	Duration (ms)			Completed		
	Average	Minimum	Maximum	Total	Successful	Exceptions
FMStocks7.GAM.7->CreditAccountBalance	1599.90436	2.66625	11454.443	417	85	332
FMStocks7.GAM.7->DebitAccountBalance	2147.85472	3.33789063	13554.584	421	227	194

Figure 7-6 Diagnostics report on methods

Observing the performance of a component over time can be quite revealing. Figure 7-7 shows a snippet from an AppMetrics for Transactions report, which illustrates component activity over a four-hour period of intense load.

Components	Active			Total (selected period)			Duration (ms)			Rate (per second)		
	Average	Min	Max	Started	Completed	Aborted	Average	Min	Max	Started	Completed	Aborted
FMStocks7.DAL.Account	0.529411	0	6	4256	4256	0	7.411654	2	382	0.595	0.595	0
FMStocks7.DAL.Broker	10.924369	0	30	8481	2312	6144	6178.4827	11	24641	1.187	0.323	0.86
FMStocks7.DAL.Position	12.352941	0	33	22174	22173	0	3407.7646	43	97448	3.105	3.105	0
FMStocks7.DAL.Ticker	10.991596	0	30	12733	12708	0	4193.5482	2	37170	1.783	1.779	0
FMStocks7.DAL.Tx	10.941176	0	30	8481	8456	0	6285.3292	17	37166	1.187	1.183	0
FMStocks7.GAM.7	22.521008	0	91	8478	2312	6132	18242.212	21	176628	1.187	0.323	0.858

Figure 7-7 Diagnostics report on components

Production Monitoring

To monitor Enterprise Services applications running in full production environments, AppMetrics offers the Production Monitor. This monitor generates metrics about the activity in Enterprise Services applications on an interval basis, but with lower overhead and information granularity than is available in the Diagnostics Monitor. More specifically, the Production Monitor calculates totals and rates of activity about components and their instances, as shown in Figures 7-8, 7-9, and 7-10.

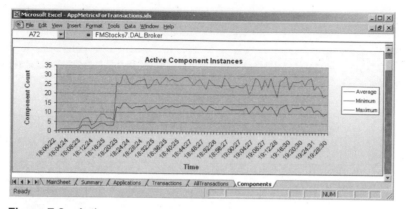

Figure 7-8 Active components chart

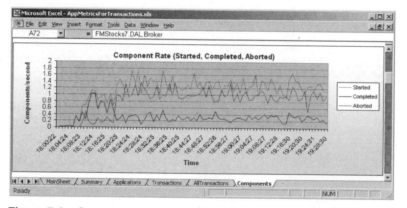

Figure 7-9 Component rate chart

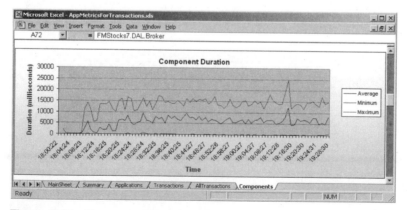

Figure 7-10 Component duration chart

The Production Monitor can also generate application-process metrics, such as application starts, stops, and crashes. The AppMetrics runtime UI shows process metrics for each Enterprise Services application process. The following example shows resource utilization by the process corresponding to FMStocks7.GAM.

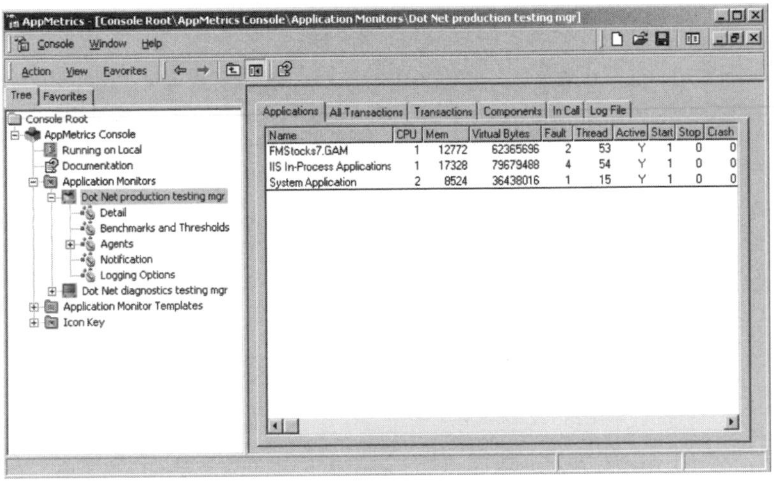

Figure 7-11   Application Process Runtime view

The Production Monitor also offers proactive monitoring through alerts. This means that you can set up thresholds of activity for a specific component metric, such as its average duration. If AppMetrics detects activity above these levels in your system, it can send alerts by email or SNMP. AppMetrics can also respond to alert conditions by invoking a custom COM component, where you can program an automated response to the condition.

The AppMetrics runtime UI shows metrics for each monitored Enterprise Services component. Figure 7-12 shows that the FMStocks7.DAL.Broker component instances are taking an average of over ten-seconds from creation to completion. Since such numbers fall outside the specified thresholds, an alert will be triggered.

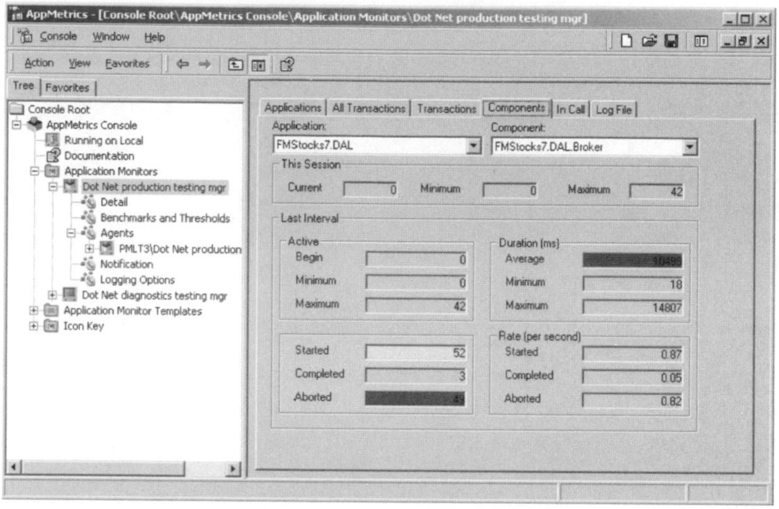

Figure 7-12   Application Process Runtime view

Conclusion

Understanding how to profile and interpret the performance of managed code is key to building scalable and robust .NET Web applications. Profiling of managed code can be done using System Monitor and the .NET performance counters. This counter information can then be used in conjunction with any code instrumentation that you may be doing. If you want to read more about writing high-performing scalable code, look for the upcoming Microsoft Press book, *Writing Scalable Code* by Simon Meacham and Mike Parkes.

8

Analyzing the SQL Tier

Among the most important uses of any business application are getting, saving, and displaying data. .NET applications are no exception to this rule, and having a properly analyzed and tuned SQL tier is critical to achieving high scalability. For applications with bottlenecks at the SQL tier, purchasing more or better hardware generally does not fix the problem. Before getting new hardware, you should first identify the bottlenecks affecting the scalability. The performance issues, for example, could be excessive I/O or processor utilization resulting from poorly chosen indexes or poorly written queries.

In this chapter, we will focus on how to detect SQL bottlenecks, and discuss some of the typical index problems that our team encounters frequently. The primary goal of this chapter is to share our experience as a performance analysis team at Microsoft. It is beyond the scope of this chapter to list every possible performance problem that you might encounter with the SQL tier. By sharing the methods we use to identify bottlenecks, we hope that you will be able to pinpoint your own problems. After you've identified the problem, it is much easier to research the issue or seek help. For the purpose of demonstration, we will use examples based on the IBuySpy sample site; and if necessary, we will intentionally introduce problems. The results of examples in this chapter were obtained using a dual 1-GHZ Pentium III processor server with a 1-GB RAM system, running Microsoft SQL Server 2000 Enterprise Edition with Service Pack 2 and Windows 2000 Advanced Server with Service Pack 2.

Getting Started

To troubleshoot performance and scalability problems, you first need to understand the application's database design. Assuming you are using SQL Server 2000, you should also have a good understanding of Transact-SQL (T-SQL); SQL Server internals, such as how the Query Optimizer chooses an execution plan; how data and indexes are stored; and how SQL Server utilizes the data and execution plan caches. To focus on identifying the bottlenecks, we will assume that you have already worked with SQL Server 2000 and are somewhat familiar with the built-in tools such as SQL Query Analyzer and SQL Profiler. Fortunately, there are many great books available that treat the necessary topics in depth. We have found the following to be good reference sources:

- *SQL Server Books Online* (installed as part of SQL Server 2000)

- *Inside Microsoft SQL Server 2000* by Kalen Delaney (Microsoft Press, 2000).

- *The Guru's Guide to Transact-SQL* by Ken Henderson (Addison Wesley Longman, 2000).

- *Microsoft SQL Server 2000 Performance Tuning Technical Reference* (Microsoft Press, 2001).

In addition to learning as much as you can about SQL Server, you also need to be able to stress the SQL server at a production equivalent load level or anticipated load level. Often, load generated by a single user is insufficient to reveal scalability problems at the SQL tier. This is where Chapter 3, in which we introduced Microsoft Application Center Test as a Web stressing tool, is useful. By creating accurate stress scripts that reflect real-world scenarios in a testing environment, you can find the bottlenecks before they occur in production. If you determine that the solution to the problem requires index or query tweaks, you can then test your solution in the test environment for confirmation before applying the changes to the production environment.

Identifying Bottlenecks

In many cases, you can use simple logic to detect whether the SQL tier is a bottleneck. For example, when you have multiple Web servers accessing data from a single SQL server, reducing the number of Web servers should decrease the overall application throughput. If changing the number of Web servers does not vary the throughput, the SQL tier is probably the source of the bottleneck.

> **Note**   Frequently, the stress clients may reach a bottleneck before enough stress has been applied on the Web servers or the SQL servers. Therefore, it is important to periodically check the stress clients' resource utilization during each stress test.

Finding out whether the SQL tier has a problem isn't a terribly difficult task. You can reduce the number of Web servers as mentioned earlier, or monitor the processor utilization at each tier. In contrast, pinpointing the problems and producing valid solutions is not easy, and this chapter will not give you such skills instantly. Instead, we'll show you how we discover the SQL tier bottlenecks and hope that you will learn from our experience. We will start by discussing the tools included with SQL Server 2000.

Tools We Use

We troubleshoot most SQL related problems using only the tools included in SQL Server 2000. Slow queries can be identified using SQL Profiler; blocking can be detected using SQL Profiler and SQL Query Analyzer; and other causes of bottlenecks, such as disk or memory, can be identified using System Monitor. Let's look at each tool and discuss how we use them.

SQL Profiler

SQL Profiler, if installed in the default location, can be found under Start\Programs\Microsoft SQL Server\Profiler.

> **Note**   To run a trace, the user must have administrator rights on the SQL server being monitored.

After launching SQL Profiler, select the server that you want to monitor and then enter your login information. After a connection has been established, the Trace properties dialog box will open. This dialog box has four tabs: General, Events, Data Columns, and Filters, which are used to specify the trace properties.

On the General tab, you can specify the name of a trace, specify a trace template, and choose to save the data to a trace file or a SQL table. If you choose to save to a file, you have to specify a directory and filename; if you choose to save the data to a SQL server, you need to specify the server, database, and table.

On the Events tab, you can select the events to monitor. The events are grouped into collections under which individual events are listed. Selecting an event should display a description on the bottom of the tab. Monitoring all the events might be overkill and can put a burden on the server. Some of the events that we typically capture are:

- **Stored Procedures: SP:StmtCompleted, SP:Completed, RPC:Completed and TSQL: SQL:StmtCompleted, SQL:BatchCompleted** These events are triggered whenever a statement, stored procedure, RPC or batch is completed. By including the text, reads, CPU, and duration data columns in the trace, you can identify the slow running code and the cost in terms of CPU resources used. It is valuable to know the reads incurred for establishing a baseline against which you can compare optimization efforts.

- **Stored Procedures: SP:Starting, SP:StmtStarting and TSQL: SQL:StmtStarting** By including these events with the completed events, you can profile a stored procedure down to the line of code. This is useful for long-running stored procedures because it lets you identify the problematic statement before the completion. Additionally, if errors occur while running the stored procedures, you can pinpoint the statement at which an error is occurring.

- **Sessions: Existing Connection** With this event you can verify the SQL Server options set for database connections. Session options can affect the way queries are processed. For example, to use indexed views, the *ARITHABORT* option must be set to ON, otherwise the underlying table will be used to retrieve data instead of the clustered index on the view.

- **Stored Procedures: SP:Recompile** The steps involved in running a stored procedure are parsing, compiling, and executing. Each of these steps takes a finite amount of time. Ideally, code should be parsed and compiled only once, utilizing only the server resources to execute the query. Improperly coded stored procedures can cause a recompile every time they are called, which has an adverse effect on the duration and even can cause blocking. By including this event in your trace, you can gauge the amount of recompiling and identify the code that needs to be optimized by including the *SP: Starting* event in the same trace.

- **Lock: Timeout and Lock: Deadlock**   You must track this event because it directly affects scalability of the application. A lock time-out or a deadlock can equate to incomplete transactions and result in errors on the client side.

- **Errors and Warnings: Attention**   This event is generated any time there is a disconnect by a client or a timeout. For applications that typically require a significant amount of time to process, you may need to increase the timeout value to reduce the number of timeouts. For example, in ADO.NET you may need to increase the value of the *CommandTimeOut* property to more than 30 seconds (default) for queries that have long durations.

- **Errors and Warnings: Missing Column Statistics**   SQL Server can automatically create and maintain statistics on tables and indexes. This information is merely a distribution of the values in particular data columns of the tables or indexes and is used by the query processor to select an execution plan. Missing or outdated statistics could cause the query processor to pick an inefficient execution plan, which can have an impact on the overall throughput of the application.

- **Errors and Warnings: Missing Join Predicate**   This event is triggered whenever a cross join is run. Cross joins are very rarely used and could be a potential oversight in a developer's code. Tracking this event will let you confirm whether queries reference tables in such a manner.

- **Errors and Warnings: Exception and Error Log**   These events are useful for determining if any unusual errors are occurring as a result of stressing the application. By monitoring this event you can establish whether these errors are a result of load. You can, for example, set the trace flag 1204 and 3605 for all connections made to a server, and SQL Profiler can capture information relating to deadlocks. Deadlocking is a serious problem that will result in a poor client experience and significantly affect your application throughput.

For more information, search under "event classes" in SQL Server Books Online.

On the Data Columns tab, you can specify the data columns that you want to capture. There are 43 columns, of which Event Class and SPID are required. Depending on the level of activity a given application might generate on the SQL server and how many users are in the environment, you might end up with a huge amount of data. Keep in mind that not all data columns will be populated, because every column is not meaningful for every event. For example, duration is only meaningful for complete events such as *SP:Completed*; this column will be blank for *SP:Starting*. Some of the data columns that we collect are listed in Table 8-1:

Table 8-1   Typical Data Columns

Data Column	Description
Event	The name of the event. For example, the start of a stored procedure, a connection established, and so on.
Text	The text of the SQL command being run. This column can be blank if it is irrelevant for a particular event.
CPU	CPU resources used in milliseconds.
Reads	Number of logical reads performed to execute a query.
Writes	Number of physical writes performed by a SQL command.
Duration	The duration of an event, such as the time to execute a stored procedure.
StartTime	Time the event was triggered.
EndTime	Time the event completed. This applies to end events.
NestLevel	The depth within a nesting operation. For example, if a stored procedure calls another stored procedure, the nest level of the calling procedure is 1 and that of the called procedure is 2. This is equal to the *@@NestValue* global variable.
Application Name	The name of the application that has a connection to the server.
HostName	The machine name on which the application that submits a SQL command is running.
NTUserName	The Windows user that the connecting application is running under.
LoginName	Either the Windows user name or the SQL server login, depending on the authentication method used to connect.

For more information, search under "data columns" in SQL Server Books Online.

On the Filters tab, you can specify filters to further limit the data collected. For example, if you are only interested in the SQL activity generated by one particular application, you can set a filter on the application name. By default, events triggered by SQL Profiler are excluded. You can familiarize yourself with all the filters available by examining the Filters tab in the Trace Properties dialog box. Selecting a filter should display an explanation of the filter at the bottom of the tab.

Now that you know what to track, you may be wondering how to analyze the trace you have captured. SQL Profiler gives you two choices for saving the data: a trace file or a SQL table. In fact, if you save the data to a file, you can always open the trace file and still choose to save the data to a SQL table. The choice is yours and depends on your preference.

> **Tip**   You can also directly query a trace file by using a system function called *fn_trace_gettable*. For example, the following query returns all events with greater than 1000 milliseconds duration from trace.trc file in a table format:
>
> SELECT * FROM ::fn_trace_gettable('c:\trace.trc', default) WHERE Duration > 1000
>
> For more information, see "fn_trace_gettable" in *SQL Server Books Online*.

We find that for large amounts of data, it is easier to analyze a trace by saving the data to a table and writing queries against this table to retrieve information such as the top few stored procedures that had the longest duration or to get the average duration across all instances of a stored procedure. Before you decide that some code is slow, you need to define criteria for a slow running query.

> **Tip**   We consider any code that has a duration of a second or more while the application is under minimal load to be an area for further investigation and potential improvement. The logic behind this criterion is that under load these durations will simply increase and hence reduce application throughput.

As you run more and more traces, you will find that you always track certain events and data columns or specify certain filters. SQL Profiler makes this task easy by letting you create a template containing the trace properties that you most often use. This will save you from having to define your trace properties every time you need to run a trace. The steps to create a template are very simple: Choose New Trace Template from the File menu to display the Trace

Properties dialog box, in which you can specify events, data columns, and filters. You can then click Save As on the General tab. Alternatively, you can choose Open Trace Template from the File menu to open an existing template. You can then customize the template and save it under a different name.

System Monitor

SQL Server exposes a number of performance objects that can be monitored with System Monitor. Chapter 4 covers this tool in great detail and focuses on counters such as Processor, Memory, Disk, and Network that relate to system level resources. This section will only cover the SQL Server–specific counters that we tend to look at most often. The reference books listed at the start of this chapter cover the other counters in more detail. Depending on your specific needs, you may want to look at other counters. The SQL Server–specific counters that we use most often are:

- *SQLServer:Buffer Manager*
  - ❑ *Buffer cache hit ratio*   The percentage of pages that were found in the buffer pool without having to incur a read from disk (physical I/O). Low values might be a symptom of low memory conditions or poor indexing.

- *SQLServer:General Statistics Object*
  - ❑ *User Connections*   The number of active SQL connections to the system. This counter is informational and can be used in reporting results to quantify the level of concurrency on the system.

- *SQLServer:Locks*
  - ❑ *Lock Requests/sec*   The number of lock requested per second. Optimizing queries to reduce the number of reads can reduce this counter.

  - ❑ *Lock Timeouts/sec*   Number of lock requests that time out while waiting for a lock to be granted. Ideally this counter should be zero.

  - ❑ *Lock Waits/sec*   Number of lock requests that could not be granted immediately. Ideally this counter should be as close to zero as possible.

❑ *Number of Deadlocks/sec*   Number of requests that resulted in a deadlock condition. Deadlocks are detrimental to the scalability of applications and result in a poor user experience. This counter must be zero.

By monitoring the instances available for these counters, you can find out what types of locks were involved and their contribution to total values of these counters. Good indexing and possibly lock hints should alleviate any adverse lock conditions.

■ *SQLServer:Memory Manager*

❑ *Memory Grants Pending*   Number of processes waiting for a workspace memory grant. This counter should be as close to zero as possible; otherwise it may indicate a memory bottleneck.

■ *SQLServer:SQL Statistics*

❑ *Batch Requests/sec*   Number of batch requests submitted to the server per second. This counter is used to quantify the amount of load on a system.

❑ *SQL Compilations/sec*   Number of compilations per second. Ideally this counter should be low. If the number of *Batch requests/sec* counter is close to this counter, there might be a lot of ad-hoc SQL calls being made.

❑ *SQL Re-Compilations/sec*   Number of recompilations per second. This counter should be low as well. Stored procedures should ideally be compiled once and their execution plans reused. A high value for this counter might require alternative coding for the stored procedures to minimize recompilation.

SQL Query Analyzer

SQL Query Analyzer can be used in various ways, for example, to execute SQL scripts to deploy new code, to count the number of records inserted or updated, to analyze query execution plans, or to execute various system stored procedures. Among the tools included with SQL Server 2000, Query Analyzer is by far the most frequently used tool in our team. Rather than describe Query Analyzer in detail, we will show you specific examples of how the tool can be used to analyze blocking and analyze execution plans in the later part of this chapter.

Quick Row Count

For a scenario that inserts records into tables, counting the number of rows before and after the stress test is useful for calculating the transaction throughput. Counting all the rows in a very large table can be time-consuming. Instead, the *sysindexes* system table in the application database can be queried to get the total row count for each table with the following query:

```
SELECT o.name, rows
FROM sysobjects o INNER JOIN sysindexes i on o.id = i.id
WHERE  i.indid < 2
ORDER BY o.name
```

Reading the *sysindexes* table requires less I/O compared to counting a large table with thousands or millions of records. Therefore, the more records you have to count, the greater will be the benefit of querying the *sysindexes* table. Note that it is generally not recommended to query system tables directly. Only if the query duration of counting records from the table is unacceptable should you consider the *sysindexes* table.

Blocking Problems

A *blocking condition* occurs whenever a connection cannot acquire a lock on a resource because that resource is already locked by another connection. Blocking only occurs if the requested locks from each connection are incompatible. This causes one connection to wait until the other connection releases the locks. For instance, if Connection A requests an exclusive lock on Table A, no other connections can place another exclusive lock on the same table. Other connections that require an exclusive lock on Table A must wait until the existing lock is released by Connection A.

Depending on the type of application, blocking can occur even in a highly tuned application; however, if the blocking occurs often enough that there are long wait times, it will lead to a performance problem. Knowing how to troubleshoot the blocking problem can have a terrific pay off, and anyone interested in SQL Server tuning should acquire this skill. Again, discussing every available method is beyond the scope of this book. However, we will show you a few methods that we use in performance testing to identify blocking issues.

Identifying Blocking Connections

Typical symptoms of blocking bottlenecks are low system resource (CPU and disks) utilizations while the SQL tier throughput is maxed out. If you suspect blocking is the bottleneck, the first step towards identifying the cause is to query the *sysprocesses* table in the master database. Listing 8-1 shows a script that returns information on the blocked connections and the last statement sent by the root blocker:

Listing 8-1

```
-- Script returns blocking information from the sysprocesses table
SELECT spid, blocked, status, waittime,
    waittype, waitresource, db_name(dbid) DatabaseName, cmd,
    hostname, loginame
FROM master..sysprocesses
WHERE blocked != 0

DECLARE @spid int

-- Get the root blocker's spid id
SELECT @spid =  A.spid
FROM master..sysprocesses A
    INNER JOIN master..sysprocesses B
    ON A.spid = B.blocked
WHERE A.blocked = 0

IF NOT @spid IS NULL
BEGIN
    -- Returns last statement sent from the connection
    DBCC INPUTBUFFER(@spid)
END
```

The IBuySpy sample site included with this book does not inherently have blocking issues on the SQL tier. For the purpose of demonstration, we will add a new stored procedure that recompiles each time it is executed to simulate a compile blocking. The following script will add such a stored procedure:

```
CREATE  PROCEDURE ProductCategoryList_Recompile
WITH RECOMPILE
AS

SELECT
    CategoryID,
    CategoryName
FROM
    dbo.Categories
```

(continued)

```
ORDER BY
    CategoryName ASC
GO
```

To observe the compile blocking behavior, we will have to run several instances of the recompiling stored procedure simultaneously. As discussed in Chapter 3, we can use ACT to simulate load on the SQL server. The ACT script in Listing 8-2 can be used to apply the required load:

Listing 8-2

```
-- The ACT script that can simulate simultaneous
execution of the stored procedure.
Dim oConn

On Error Resume Next

Set oConn = CreateObject("ADODB.Connection")

oConn.Open "driver={SQL Server};Server=SQLServer;" & _
"Database=Store;uid=user;pwd=user"

If err.Number <> 0 Then
    Test.Trace("Error Opening connection: " & _
err.number & ", " & err.description)
ELSE
    oConn.Execute("EXEC ProductCategoryList_Recompile")
    If err.Number <> 0 Then
        Test.Trace("Error Executing: " & _
err.number & ", " & err.description)
    End If
End IF
```

You can set the simultaneous browser connections to 10 and run a test for five minutes. While stressing the SQL server, executing the script in Listing 8-1 will give you information regarding the blocked connections and the last statement sent by the root blocker. In this example, the blocked connection's waitresource column should indicate compile blocking with the following information:

```
TAB: 7:1173579219 [[COMPILE]]
```

> **Note**   The "7" after "TAB:" indicates the Store database, and "1173579219" indicates the object being compiled. In our case, "1173579219" represents *ProductCategoryList_Recompile*. You can get this information by running *SELECT Object_Name(1173579219)* in the Store database. Note that the format of the waitresource field may change in the next version or the next service pack, and the current method of retrieving the database and stored procedure name may not be valid.

The last statement sent by the root blocker should be displayed as *ProductCategoryList_Recompile*. Although we purposefully created the problem on *ProductCategoryList_Recompile*, querying the *sysprocesses* table revealed the recompile issue on the same stored procedure.

The occurrence of excessive compiles is just one of the numerous causes of blocking. Long running transactions, improper Transaction Isolation Level, and inappropriate indexes can also cause blocking. Regardless of the cause, the approach in this section can be used to identify the blocking stored procedures or ad-hoc queries. After they are identified, you can analyze the query further to pinpoint the problem.

Locks

In-depth knowledge of lock types used in SQL Server is essential for troubleshooting blocking problems. We strongly recommend that you thoroughly review the lock topics in the aforementioned reference materials. Understanding the topics will help you troubleshoot lock timeouts as well as deadlocks.

For applications that experience SQL blocking, we typically execute *sp_lock* to look at the granted or waiting locks. It's a snapshot of locks at the time of execution of the *sp_lock* system store procedure; therefore, we execute it multiple times during the stress test to see a pattern of locking behavior. The output of *sp_lock* is cryptic and needs to be cross-referenced to get the table names or index names. Thus, we run a custom stored procedure that is similar to *sp_lock_verbose*, included in *The Guru's Guide to Transact-SQL*, to eliminate the repetitive cross-referencing task.

Again, for demonstration purposes, we will introduce a lock problem in one of the stored procedures. The following script will add such a stored procedure:

```
CREATE PROCEDURE ProductCategoryList_XLOCK
AS

-- Use transaction to hold the exclusive lock
BEGIN TRANSACTION

SELECT
    CategoryID,
    CategoryName
FROM
    dbo.Categories (XLOCK)
ORDER BY
    CategoryName ASC

WAITFOR DELAY '00:00:01' -- Hold the lock for 1 second

COMMIT TRANSACTION
GO
```

Executing *sp_lock* while stressing the SQL server with this new stored procedure will produce an output similar to the following:

```
spid   dbid   ObjId        IndId  Type Resource          Mode     Status
-----  -----  -----------  -----  ---- ---------------   -------- ------
51     7      0            0      DB                      S        GRANT
53     7      0            0      DB                      S        GRANT
53     7      1977058079   0      RID  1:89:0            X        WAIT
53     7      1977058079   0      PAG  1:89             IX       GRANT
53     7      1977058079   0      TAB                   IX       GRANT
54     7      1977058079   0      TAB                   IX       GRANT
54     7      1977058079   0      RID  1:89:2           X        GRANT
54     7      1977058079   0      RID  1:89:6           X        GRANT
...
(Result abbreviated)
```

The interesting parts of the *sp_lock* output are the ObjId, Type, Mode, and Status columns. For example, the output shows exclusive mode, row identifier (RID) type locks granted on the ObjId of "1977058079". The RID lock type is shown instead of the KEY lock type due to the lack of a clustered index on the *Categories* table. In addition, an exclusive lock is waiting to be granted, as indicated by the WAIT status. You can execute *SELECT Object_Name(<ObjId>)* to get the object name, and in this case, "1977058079" represents the *Categories* table. Combining the results obtained by querying the *sysprocesses* table to get the blocking connection and the output of the *sp_lock* stored procedure to get the lock information will make it easier to narrow the problem down to a statement.

Deadlocks

A *deadlock* occurs when two or more connections block each other and each are waiting on some resources that the other connection has locked. For instance, Connection A holds a lock on Row A and is waiting to get a lock on Row B. Connection B holds a lock a Row B and is waiting to get a lock on Row A. Each connection is waiting on the other, and neither can proceed to commit or roll back the transactions. This type of deadlock is referred as *cyclical*. Another possible deadlock type is a *conversion deadlock*. A conversion deadlock occurs when two or more connections have shared locks on some resources and they both want to convert their shared locks to exclusive locks. Regardless of deadlock type, we use trace flags to troubleshoot the deadlock problems. The following statement will write the deadlock trace report (1204) to the SQL Server error log (3605) and set the trace flag for all connections (-1):

```
DBCC TRACEON(-1, 1204, 3605)
```

After the trace flags are turned on, you can capture the ErrorLog event using SQL Profiler or view the error log using Enterprise Manager. For demonstration purposes, we created the following script to add a stored procedure that forces a conversion deadlock:

```
CREATE CLUSTERED INDEX IXC_ModelName
    ON dbo.Products (ModelName)
GO

CREATE PROCEDURE ProductsUnitCostUpdate_DeadLock
AS
BEGIN TRANSACTION

SELECT *
FROM
    dbo.Products (HOLDLOCK)
WHERE ModelName = N'Bullet Proof Facial Tissue'

WAITFOR DELAY '00:00:05'

UPDATE dbo.Products
    SET UnitCost = UnitCost * 0.90
WHERE ModelName = N'Bullet Proof Facial Tissue'

COMMIT TRANSACTION
GO
```

You must run the deadlock stored procedure in the two separate SQL Query Analyzer windows within a few seconds apart to produce a deadlock. The following report is a sample produced by enabling trace flag 1204:

```
Deadlock encountered .... Printing deadlock information
Wait-for graph
Node:1
KEY: 7:2041058307:1 (a60421ba9ed3) CleanCnt:2 Mode: Range-S-S Flags: 0x0
Grant List::
Owner:0x42be1340 Mode: Range-S-S Flg:0x0 Ref:0 Life:02000000 SPID:52 ECID:0
SPID: 52 ECID: 0 Statement Type: UPDATE Line #: 12
Input Buf: Language Event: ProductsPriceUpdate_DeadLock
Requested By:
ResType:LockOwner Stype:'OR' Mode: X SPID:51 ECID:0 Ec:(0x42f77568) _
    Value:0x42be1360 Cost:(0/0)
Node:2
KEY: 7:2041058307:1 (a60421ba9ed3) CleanCnt:2 Mode: Range-S-S Flags: 0x0
Grant List::
Owner:0x42be5240 Mode: Range-S-S Flg:0x0 Ref:0 Life:02000000 SPID:51 ECID:0
SPID: 51 ECID: 0 Statement Type: UPDATE Line #: 12
Input Buf: Language Event: ProductsPriceUpdate_DeadLock
Requested By:
ResType:LockOwner Stype:'OR' Mode: X SPID:52 ECID:0 Ec:(0x430b5568) _
    Value:0x42be1260 Cost:(0/0)
Victim Resource Owner:
ResType:LockOwner Stype:'OR' Mode: X SPID:52 ECID:0 Ec:(0x430b5568) _
    Value:0x42be1260 Cost:(0/0)
```

Detailed information is produced by the trace flag 1204 for each deadlock occurrence and we usually focus our attention on a few sections. We look for the lock resource in "Key:"; check the lock mode in "Mode:"; and search for the stored procedure name or the ad-hoc query in "Input Buf:". With this information, we can narrow our troubleshooting to a few stored procedures or queries. More detailed information on troubleshooting deadlocks and the trace flag 1204 report can be found in *SQL Server Books Online* and *Inside Microsoft SQL Server 2000*.

Additional Resources

So far we discussed manual methods of troubleshooting blocking problems. Several articles have published the blocking scripts. Using those scripts can reduce the human error factor, and we highly recommend the following article:

- "INF: How to Monitor SQL Server 2000 Blocking (Q271509)" at *http:/ /support.microsoft.com/default.aspx?scid=kb;en-us;q271509*

In addition, the following articles are recommended:

- "INF: SQL Blocking Due to [[COMPILE]] Locks (Q263889)" at *http:// support.microsoft.com/default.aspx?scid=kb;en-us;Q263889*

- "INF: Troubleshooting Application Performance with SQL Server (Q224587)" at *http://support.microsoft.com/default.aspx?scid=kb;en-us;Q224587*

Index Tuning

Using the methods discussed in the previous section, you should be able to narrow your troubleshooting efforts to problematic queries or stored procedures. Identifying which SQL calls are causing the problem is a big step towards finding a solution. Unfortunately, it is almost impossible to list every problem that could occur using SQL Server 2000. Our team discovers new and difficult problems every day and the more we work on SQL Server, the more we realize books or whitepapers alone aren't enough to help us to become expert in SQL Server performance tuning. So if you can't come up with solutions to your current performance problem right after reading this chapter, don't be discouraged; you should understand that you can't learn to tune your application's SQL Server issues overnight.

Another issue that we frequently encounter is the lack of proper indexes. We usually take a similar approach for index tuning each problematic SQL call. In the next section, we will discuss the methods that we use to tune indexes.

Analyzing the Execution Plan

One approach to identifying the cause of long durations is to analyze the query execution plan and check the data retrieval method chosen by the SQL Server 2000 query optimizer. You can do this by using Query Analyzer to get a graphical view of the execution plan.

Populating Data

Before we begin, we will add 100,000 rows to the *Orders* table and 1,000,000 rows to the *OrderDetails* table in the IBuySpy sample site database. Actual numbers of rows used for analyzing the SQL tier will vary depending on the business requirements and the projected database growth. We chose an arbitrary number of rows to demonstrate how to analyze with large data sets. SQL Server behaves differently depending on the number of rows and the uniqueness of column data; therefore, it is crucial to tune queries on the correctly sized database. Listing 8-3 shows the T-SQL used to generate the additional records.

Listing 8-3

```
-- The T-SQL used to load additional data
SET NOCOUNT ON   -- Stop the number of rows effected messages

DECLARE @Count int
DECLARE @OrderID int
DECLARE @CustomerID int
DECLARE @DateAdd int
```

(continued)

```
DECLARE @DateAdd2 int
DECLARE @Today DateTime
DECLARE @SQL nvarchar(4000)

-- Count the records before the inserts
SELECT Count(*) Orders FROM Orders
SELECT Count(*) OrderDetails FROM OrderDetails
SELECT Count(*) Customers FROM Customers

SET @Today = GetDate()

SET @Count = 1

-- Add 100000 Orders and 10000 Customer
WHILE @Count <= 100000
BEGIN

    --Insert a new customer every 10 records
    IF @Count % 10 = 0 OR @Count = 1
    BEGIN
        INSERT INTO Customers
        (
            FullName,
            EMailAddress,
            Password
        )
        VALUES
        (
            'TestUser_' + Cast(@Count as varchar(10)),
            'TestUser_' + Cast(@Count as varchar(10)) + '@test.com',
            'password'
        )

        SET @CustomerID = @@Identity
    END

    -- Vary the OrderDate and ShipDate
    SET @DateAdd = (-1 * (@Count % 365))
    SET @DateAdd2 = (-1 * (@Count % 365)) + 1

    INSERT INTO Orders
    (
        CustomerID,
        OrderDate,
        ShipDate
    )
```

```
VALUES
(
    @CustomerID,
    DateAdd(d, @DateAdd, @Today),
    DateAdd(d, @DateAdd2, @Today)
)
SET @OrderID = @@Identity

SET @SQL = N'INSERT INTO OrderDetails
    (
        OrderID,
        ProductID,
        Quantity,
        UnitCost
    )
    SELECT TOP 10
        @OrderID, ProductID, 1, UnitCost
    FROM Products '


-- Use 4 different sorts to add different products
IF @Count % 4 = 1
    SET @SQL = @SQL + N'ORDER BY CategoryID'

IF @Count % 4 = 2
    SET @SQL = @SQL + N'ORDER BY ModelNumber'

IF @Count % 4 = 3
    SET @SQL = @SQL + N'ORDER BY ModelName'

IF @Count % 4 = 0
    SET @SQL = @SQL + N'ORDER BY UnitCost'

EXEC sp_executesql @SQL, N'@OrderID int', @OrderID = @OrderID

SET @Count = @Count + 1

END

-- Count after the inserts
SELECT Count(*) Orders FROM Orders
SELECT Count(*) OrderDetails FROM OrderDetails
SELECT Count(*) Customers FROM Customers
```

Viewing the Execution Plan

Now that we have loaded the data successfully, we will execute *ProductsMost-Popular*, one of the stored procedures that is affected adversely by an increase in the database size. To get the execution plan, the Show Execution Plan option must be on in Query Analyzer (press CTRL+K). Figure 8-1 shows the output of the *ProductsMostPopular*'s execution plan.

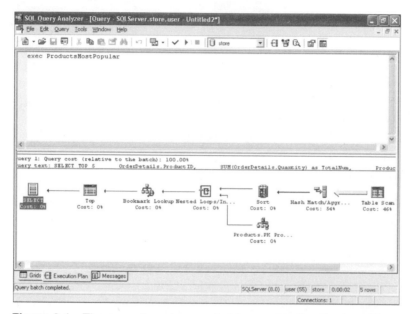

Figure 8-1 The execution plan created by running the *ProductsMost-Popular* stored procedure

In this relatively simple example, *ProductsMostPopular* contains the following code:

```
CREATE Procedure ProductsMostPopular
AS

SELECT TOP 5
    OrderDetails.ProductID,
    SUM(OrderDetails.Quantity) as TotalNum,
    Products.ModelName
FROM
    OrderDetails
INNER JOIN Products ON OrderDetails.ProductID = Products.ProductID
```

```
GROUP BY
    OrderDetails.ProductID,
    Products.ModelName
ORDER BY
    TotalNum DESC
GO
```

All icons representing physical operators used to execute statements are too numerous to list here. They are well documented in SQL Server Books Online. In addition, the SQL Server Books Online provides details on how to interpret the graphical output. In this section, we will focus on the things to look for that can cause long call durations.

Among the various physical operators, look for the operators that are showing a high percentage of cost. For example, in Figure 8-1, the Hash Match/ Aggregate and Table Scan operators indicate high costs, 54 percent and 46 percent respectively. When you pause the pointer on top of each icon in the execution plan, you will see a ToolTip appear with detailed information. Figure 8-2 shows the ToolTip information on the Table Scan icon.

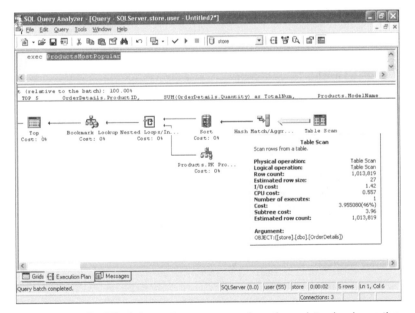

Figure 8-2   ToolTip information appears when the pointer is above the Table Scan icon

The ToolTip shows that Query Optimizer picked a Table Scan operator to retrieve data from the object, [store].[dbo].[OrderDetails]. In a typical execution plan, Table Scans and Index Scans can cause longer duration compared to an execution plan that uses Index Seeks. In our case, however, reading the entire *OrderDetails* table is required to determine which top five products are the most popular. Table Scans and Index Scans on small tables are not unusual and in such cases may be more efficient. You should not be automatically alerted when you find such operators in the execution plan; adding more indexes to a small table may not make any difference in terms of the query execution duration. Therefore, you will need additional information to the physical operators to perform an effective index tuning.

Note Table scan operator is used on tables without clustered indexes. The lack of clustered indexes may cause poor performance. For more details about the problem, see "PRB: Poor Performance on a Heap (Q297861)" at *http://support.microsoft.com/default.aspx?scid=kb;en-us;Q297861*

Additional Tuning Information

SQL Server has useful statistic options with which you can measure the resource utilizations, such as *STATISTICS IO*. A combined analysis of the query execution plan and the I/O utilization statistics can help you discover the tables that are the source of the performance problem. Ultimately, the goal is to reduce the execution duration of the queries, and this is where the *STATISTICS TIME* option can help you measure the durations. Turning on the *STATISTICS TIME* option displays the parse and compile time for the query execution, letting you can measure how long it takes to generate the query's execution plan.

Tip The query's durations can be captured by SQL Profiler; however, with the *STATISTICS TIME* option you can view the duration from the same window that executed the query.

In addition to the *STATISTICS* options, there are two DBCC commands that clear the data buffer and procedure cache. With *DBCC DROPCLEANBUFFERS* you can test queries with a cold buffer cache without restarting SQL Server, and is useful for measuring consistent query statistics. Another helpful command is *DBCC FREEPROCCACHE*. With this command you can compare the query performance with or without the procedure cache.

> **Caution**   You should avoid the *DBCC DROPCLEANBUFFERS* or *DBCC FREEPROCCACHE* commands in the production environment.

Now, let's take a look at the performance metrics obtained by executing the stored procedure *ProductsMostPopular* via the following script in Query Analyzer:

```
DBCC DROPCLEANBUFFERS
DBCC FREEPROCCACHE

SET STATISTICS IO ON
SET STATISTICS TIME ON
GO

EXEC ProductsMostPopular
```

Depending on the complexity of the stored procedure, the amount of extra information generated by the *DBCC* commands and the *STATISTICS* options will vary. In the case of *ProductsMostPopular*, the following output is what we are interested in:

```
...
SQL Server parse and compile time:
   CPU time = 32 ms, elapsed time = 187 ms.

(5 row(s) affected)

Table 'Products'. Scan count 5, logical reads 10, _
    physical reads 4, read-ahead reads 0.
Table 'OrderDetails'. Scan count 1, logical reads 3800, _
    physical reads 0, read-ahead reads 3801.

SQL Server Execution Times:
   CPU time = 1813 ms,  elapsed time = 1826 ms.
...
(Result abbreviated)
```

The resulting statistics will vary depending on the database size, the SQL Server version, and the server hardware capability. The output that we obtained shows that it took 187 milliseconds to parse and compile the stored procedure *ProductsMostPopular*, and 1826 milliseconds to execute it. This timing information is what you obtain by enabling the *STATISTICS TIME* option. The most interesting part of the output is the logical reads on the table *OrderDetails*. The logical reads indicates the number of pages that were read from the buffer; the value of "3800" that we obtained confirms that the Table Scan operator used to retrieve the data is expensive compared to the reads on the *Products* table. The scan count measure can also be useful from time to time. It represents how many times the object was accessed. It is directly correlated with the type of join used. For example, a query that uses a loop join and returns 100 rows may show a scan count value of 100, while the same query using uses a merge join instead may show a scan count value of 1. In our case, scan counts are negligible due to their low values. The physical and read-ahead reads varies depending on whether the required data was already in the buffer. For query tuning purposes, the two reads counters can be ignored.

After the execution plan of a poorly performing query has been analyzed, you can decide whether to add, drop, or modify indexes, modify queries, or make database schema changes. The best scenario would be to pick a modification that gives the most gain, and our team has seen the most performance gains from index tuning. Also, index optimizations typically minimize the risk of introducing new functional bugs. In the next section, we will show you how we go about index tuning.

Understanding Indexes

If you worked on SQL servers before reading this chapter, you probably have heard of clustered and nonclustered indexes. Learning as much as you can about how the indexes are stored and retrieved is critical for proper index tuning. Again, a detailed discussion of the indexes in SQL Server is beyond the scope of this book. Instead, we will introduce you briefly to each index type in Table 8-2.

Table 8-2 **Available Indexes in SQL Server**

Index Types	Description
Clustered Index	Physically sorts a table based on the order of indexed column(s). This type of index contains all the table data. Unless specified, a clustered index will be created by default when a primary key constraint is added.
Nonclustered Index	Index does not contain table data; instead it contains pointers to the location of the table data. If a column, not included in the index, needs to be queried, a Bookmark Lookup will be performed on a heap or on a clustered index.

Choosing Right Indexes

In real world situations, choosing the right indexes can be a complex task. You cannot just focus on one poorly performing query, because modifying indexes could potentially affect other queries that rely on existing indexes. For example, if creating new indexes decreases query duration in a *SELECT* query, it may increase the duration in an *INSERT, DELETE*, or *UPDATE* query. A worse scenario would be to add an index on frequently changing columns. Changing values will force re-positions to keep the index values in order, and in a large table, this may cause additional delay for each transaction modifying the indexed columns. The longer transaction durations will hold the exclusive locks longer, and might cause blocking to occur to a point where it becomes the bottleneck.

Fortunately, as mentioned in Chapter 3, real-world user scenarios can be scripted and stress tested. After the scenarios are scripted, you can easily execute multiple stress tests to compare the results between each modification. Running the stress tests will allow you to find the bottlenecks and will minimize the risk of creating additional problems by verifying the validity of the index changes. Also, using the script to test each modification allows you to measure the overall improvement for each change. For the purpose of demonstration, all of our index tuning examples will focus on one query.

Nonclustered Index

A nonclustered index does not contain the entire table data. Instead, it contains duplicates of chosen column data and pointers to the location of the rest of the table data. The location may be a clustered index key or a row identifier if the table lacks a clustered index. Such characteristics can make the nonclustered index compact, and as a result, scanning the entire index tree will takes fewer pages to read compared to a clustered index scan. Therefore, when you are looking for a range of data, as long as all required columns are contained in the nonclustered index, a nonclustered index is typically faster than a clustered index.

Our team frequently sees significant performance gains by applying appropriate nonclustered indexes. Although we can't discuss every possible nonclustered index usage case in this chapter, we will discuss the covering index that we encounter often.

A covering index can be created by choosing all columns that are referenced by a query to be part of the index. Given the right situation, a covering index can greatly improve a query's performance by eliminating bookmark lookups. Because a nonclustered index does not contain table data other than the selected column(s), any need for column data that is not part of the index will have to be retrieved from either a clustered index or a heap. By adding extra column(s) not specified in the Searchable Arguments (SARG) or join conditions, all data can be resolved from the nonclustered index and this extra lookup can be eliminated.

Covering Index Example 1   From the earlier analysis of the execution plan generated by the *ProductsMostPopular* stored procedure, we discovered that most of the logical reads occurred on the *OrderDetails* table. Let's first look at the index information on *OrderDetails* by executing following statement:

```
sp_helpindex OrderDetails
```

The output shows one nonclustered index on the OrderID and ProductID columns. Moreover, the index_description field indicated Primary Key constraint. Based on the index information and the query used in *ProductsMostPopular*, we can build Table 8-3 to help us determine which columns should be used and in what order.

Table 8-3   Column Choice and Order

OrderDetails Table	Columns
Searchable Argument (SARG)	None
GROUP BY or ORDER BY	ProductID
JOIN	ProductID
All other columns used in the query	Sum(Quantity)
Existing Index	Primary Key, Nonclustered Index on (OrderID, ProductID)

Query Shortcuts

Stored procedures or SQL statements can be saved in the Customize window under the Tools menu. Once configured, the stored procedure will be executed every time the shortcut key is pressed. For example, *sp_helpindex* can be mapped to CTRL+F1 as shown in Figure 8-3.

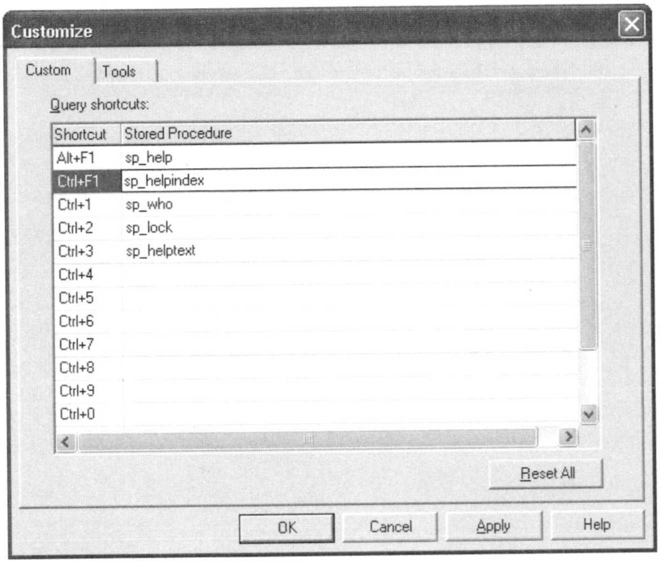

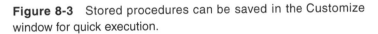

Figure 8-3   Stored procedures can be saved in the Customize window for quick execution.

Next time you need to execute *sp_helpindex*, simply highly the table name you are interested in and press CTRL+F1. *sp_helpindex* and *sp_helptext* are good ones to customize.

As indicated in Table 8-2, creating a nonclustered index on the ProductID and Quantity columns will cover all columns. In addition, ProductID is used in *GROUP BY* clause; therefore, an index that is first sorted by ProductID should be more efficient than sorted by Quantity. Regardless, let's create two indexes with different column orders and see which one is more efficient. The following script creates the two indexes:

```
CREATE INDEX IX_OrderDetails_ProductID_Quantity
    ON OrderDetails (ProductID, Quantity)

CREATE INDEX IX_OrderDetails_Quantity_ProductID
    ON OrderDetails (Quantity, ProductID)
```

When we execute *ProductsMostPopular* again, different operators and the covering index on ProductID and Quantity were chosen by Query Optimizer. Again, the same dual1-GHZ Pentium processor server was used for this example. Figure 8-4 shows new execution plan.

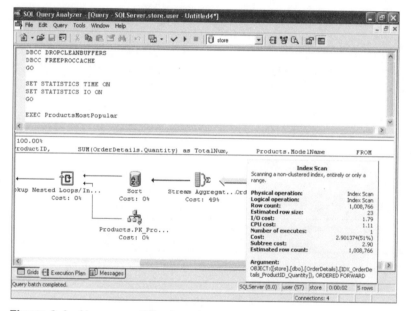

Figure 8-4 New execution plan after creating covering indexes on the OrderDetails table

The Table Scan operator was replaced with the Index Scan operator, and the Stream Aggregate was chosen instead of Hash Match/Aggregate. For the second covering index comparison, an *INDEX* hint was used, and the following code shows the hint usage in bold:

```
SELECT TOP 5
    OrderDetails.ProductID,
    SUM(OrderDetails.Quantity) as TotalNum,
    Products.ModelName
```

```
FROM
    OrderDetails (INDEX=IX_OrderDetails_Quantity_ProductID)
    INNER JOIN Products ON OrderDetails.ProductID = Products.ProductID

GROUP BY
    OrderDetails.ProductID,
    Products.ModelName

ORDER BY
    TotalNum DESC
```

Note   Most of the time, Query Optimizer chooses the most efficient indexes and operators to retrieve data. However, it is good practice to validate the chosen plan by forcing alternate plans and measuring the differences.

In this example, three execution plans were observed. For comparison purposes, statistics from each plan are listed in Table 8-4.

Table 8-4   Comparing Execution Plan Queries

	Original Query	**Covering index on ProductID and Quantity**	**Covering index on Quantity and ProductID**
Operator used and cost percentage	Table Scan (46 percent) and Hash Match/Aggregate (54 percent)	Index Scan (51 percent) and Stream Aggregate (49 percent)	Index Scan and Hash (38 percent) Match/ Aggregate (61 percent)
Logical Reads on OrderDetails	3800	2184	2370
Query Duration in milliseconds	1826	1021	2095

As predicted earlier, the first covering index on ProductID and Quantity column results in the most improvement. In fact, when order of the columns used in the covering index was reversed, the query duration took longer than without the index. Therefore, each index modification should be tested and validated. Without thorough testing, your index tuning attempts may hurt the application's performance.

In this example, approximately 800 milliseconds were reduced by implementing a covering index. Typically we would analyze the query further to see if an indexed view can help reduce the duration even more. We will discuss indexed views in the clustered index section.

Covering Index Example 2   In this example, we will examine the *OrdersList* stored procedure. The query retrieves an order history for a customer and requires the CustomerID as a parameter. The following code was used to execute the stored procedure:

```
DBCC DROPCLEANBUFFERS
DBCC FREEPROCCACHE
GO

SET STATISTICS IO ON
SET STATISTICS TIME ON
GO

EXEC OrdersList @CustomerID = 10704
```

Following the same method used in example 1, we first capture the query statistics by turning on *STATISTICS IO* and *STATISTICS TIME* and review the execution plan. By enabling the *STATISTICS TIME* setting, we determine that the query takes approximately 640 milliseconds. The duration is not as severe as *ProductsMostPopular*; however, the query's execution plan does reveal a Table Scan and Bookmark Lookup being performed, which usually means that an index tuning is necessary. For demonstration purposes, we will assume that *OrdersList* gets executed frequently and that it needs tuning. We should therefore analyze the columns used in *OrdersList*. Running the system store procedure *sp_helptext* with *OrdersList* as a parameter displays the following code:

```
CREATE Procedure OrdersList
(
    @CustomerID int
)
As

SELECT
    Orders.OrderID,
    Cast(sum(orderdetails.quantity*orderdetails.unitcost) as money) _
    as OrderTotal,
    Orders.OrderDate,
    Orders.ShipDate
```

```
FROM
    Orders
    INNER JOIN OrderDetails ON Orders.OrderID = OrderDetails.OrderID

GROUP BY
    CustomerID,
    Orders.OrderID,
    Orders.OrderDate,
    Orders.ShipDate
HAVING
    Orders.CustomerID = @CustomerID
```

Based on the T-SQL used in *OrdersList*, we can build the following tables similar to Table 8-5:

Table 8-5   Orders Table Columns Used in OrdersList

Orders Table	Columns
Searchable Argument (SARG)	CustomerID
GROUP BY or ORDER BY	CustomerID, OrderID, OrderDate, ShipDate
JOIN	OrderID
All other columns used in the query	None
Existing Index	None

Table 8-6   Order Details Table Columns in OrdersList

OrderDetails Table	Columns
Searchable Argument (SARG)	None
GROUP BY or ORDER BY	None
JOIN	OrderID
All other columns used in the query	SUM(Quantity*Unitcost)
Existing Index	Primary Key, Nonclustered Index on (OrderID, ProductID)

> **Tip**   Writing out the columns used in each table as shown in Table 8-6 is highly recommended, especially for more complex queries.

Similar to the covering index example 1 shown earlier, we can use the following script to create the two covering indexes based on Table 8-5 and Table 8-6:

```
CREATE INDEX IX_Orders_CustomerID_Covered
    ON OrderDetails (CustomerID,OrderID, OrderDate, ShipDate)
CREATE INDEX IX_OrderDetails_OrderID_Quantity_UnitCost
    ON OrderDetails (OrderID, Quantity, Unitcost)
```

For the purpose of comparison, statistics obtained before and after adding the covering indexes are listed in Table 8-7.

Table 8-7 Statistical Comparison of Each Execution Plan

	Original Query	After Adding Covering Indexes
Operator used and cost percentage	Table Scan on Orders (22 percent)	Index Seek on Orders (42 percent)
	Bookmark Lookup on OrderDetails (75 percent)	Index Seek on OrderDetails (51 percent)
Logical reads	Orders = 520	Orders = 3
	OrderDetails = 160	OrderDetails = 30
Query duration in milliseconds	644	6

As indicated in Table 8-7, *OrdersList* is executing almost a hundred times faster with the new covering indexes. In our experience, it's not rare to see such dramatic improvements by adding the appropriate covering indexes. Again, the improvement is just for one stored procedure running in isolation. The remaining frequently used scenarios should be thoroughly tested before implementing any new indexes to a production system to confirm that the overall performance is improved.

Clustered Index

Since a clustered index physically sorts the table data, you can only have one clustered index per table. Such characteristics can be beneficial in many cases. For instance, having a clustered index on a table allows you to defragment the table. Unless there is a good reason not to use clustered indexes, one should be created for each table. In addition, you should consider choosing narrow columns as clustered index column since all nonclustered indexes will contain the clustered index key. Using a wide clustered index key will cost you in terms of extra space used by the nonclustered indexes and it will also cause additional I/O.

SQL Server makes it easy to create a clustered index on each table by making it the default index that is created when defining a primary key constraint. The difficult part of clustered index tuning is to pick the proper column(s) to use in the index. It is beyond the scope of this chapter to go over every possible clustered index usage. Instead, we will discuss the following typically neglected areas that our team faces frequently:

- The *FILLFACTOR* option
- Clustered index on a view

Let's look at each scenario with examples.

FILLFACTOR   The *FILLFACTOR* option determines how much extra space to reserve on each page. For example, a *FILLFACTOR* option of 80 will reserve 20 percent of free space, which is approximately 1.6 KB. It is useful on tables or indexes that are used in many inserts or updates. The reserved extra space helps reduce page reorganizations (page splits) caused by insert or update operations on a full page. For instance, let's say a customer information table has an address field, and initial customer record created had an empty address field. If the page containing the customer record is full or nearly full, an update to the address information may require additional space and cause a page split.

Frequent page splits can lead to fragmentation and reduce the overall data density. If pages were only 50 percent full due to the heavy page splits, it will require twice as much I/O to get the data compared to pages that are 100 percent full. Applications that experience heavy inserts and updates can benefit from having the free space on each page by reducing page splits and the resulting data fragmentation. Since fillfactors guarantee free space at creation time only, table or index fragmentation and page densities should be monitored periodically.

The *DBCC SHOWCONTIG* command allows you to view the fragmentation and data density in tables or indexes. To demonstrate fragmentation, we will slightly modify the *Orders* table in the IBuySpy sample site database. The following code will add a nullable description field and add a clustered index on the OrderID column:

```
ALTER TABLE Orders
    ADD OrderDesc Varchar(500) NULL
GO

CREATE CLUSTERED INDEX IXC_Orders_OrderID
    ON Orders (OrderID)
GO
```

Using the code in Listing 8-4 we can measure query performance at different fragmentation levels:

Listing 8-4

```
-- Gathers query performance based on varying fragmentation
-- Clears cached data buffer and execution plans
DBCC DROPCLEANBUFFERS
DBCC FREEPROCCACHE
GO
-- Displays IO and TIME related statistics
SET STATISTICS IO ON
SET STATISTICS TIME ON
GO
-- A query on the Orders table.
SELECT TOP 10 WITH TIES CustomerID, _
    MAX(DateDiff(hh, OrderDate, ShipDate)) MaxShippingDelay
FROM Orders (INDEX=IXC_Orders_OrderID)
GROUP BY CustomerID
ORDER BY MaxShippingDelay DESC, CustomerID
GO
-- Displays Fragmentation information on the Orders table
DBCC SHOWCONTIG('Orders')
GO
```

The following text is an excerpt of the output generated by executing the code in Listing 8-4 script:

```
DBCC SHOWCONTIG scanning 'Orders' table...
Table: 'Orders' (2025058250); index ID: 1, database ID: 7
TABLE level scan performed.
- Pages Scanned...............................: 418
- Extents Scanned............................: 54
- Extent Switches............................: 53
- Avg. Pages per Extent......................: 7.7
- Scan Density [Best Count:Actual Count].....: 98.15% [53:54]
- Logical Scan Fragmentation .................: 0.24%
- Extent Scan Fragmentation ..................: 1.85%
- Avg. Bytes Free per Page...................: 25.2
- Avg. Page Density (full)...................: 99.69%
DBCC execution completed. If DBCC printed error messages, _
    contact your system administrator.
...
Table 'Orders'. Scan count 1, logical reads 419, _
    physical reads 0, read-ahead reads 0.

SQL Server Execution Times:
   CPU time = 297 ms,  elapsed time = 302 ms.
...
(Result abbreviated)
```

The output of the *DBCC SHOWCONTIG* execution that we are most interested in are the scan density and avg. page density. The scan density checks the contiguousness of extent links; a table with more fragmentation will have a scan density less than that of a table with less fragmentation. Fewer extent switches will be required to retrieve the data from less fragmented tables.

An average page density closer to 100 percent will require less I/O for retrieving data from tables. This is due to the way SQL Server retrieves data from a page; regardless of how full the page is, an entire 8-KB page will be read. In our case, both density values are optimal. Now, let's see what happens when we modify the OrderDesc column for every tenth row in the *Orders* table. We can accomplish this by executing the following statements:

```
-- REPLICATE function isn't necessary here, but it can be
-- useful when you want to generate test data.
UPDATE Orders
    SET OrderDesc = 'Some description ' + REPLICATE('X', OrderID % 10)
    WHERE OrderID % 10 = 0
```

We can execute Listing 8-4 again to see the query performance and the Orders table's fragmentation level. Output from this execution is

```
Table: 'Orders' (2025058250); index ID: 1, database ID: 7
TABLE level scan performed.
- Pages Scanned................................: 834
- Extents Scanned.............................: 110
- Extent Switches.............................: 833
- Avg. Pages per Extent........................: 7.6
- Scan Density [Best Count:Actual Count].......: 12.59% [105:834]
- Logical Scan Fragmentation ..................: 50.00%
- Extent Scan Fragmentation ...................: 36.36%
- Avg. Bytes Free per Page.....................: 3768.9
- Avg. Page Density (full).....................: 53.44%
DBCC execution completed. If DBCC printed error messages, _
    contact your system administrator.
...
Table 'Orders'. Scan count 1, logical reads 836, _
    physical reads 0, read-ahead reads 0.

SQL Server Execution Times:
   CPU time = 307 ms,  elapsed time = 307 ms.
...
(Result abbreviated)
```

After forcing the fragmentation with the sample code, the query's duration did not change significantly; however, the logical reads almost doubled, 836 compared to 419. This is most mostly due to the reduced avg. page density, which went from 99 percent to 53 percent. The duration in this example is based on a single user executing the query. As more user load is put on the server, the impact of the additional reads will be manifested by a further increase in the duration.

The fragmentation could have been prevented if the *Orders* table clustered index's *FILLFACTOR* was set at 90 percent. You can modified the *FILLFACTOR* in a few ways. You can drop and recreate the clustered index while specifying the *FILLFACTOR* to be 90, or you can execute *DBCC REINDEX* to change the *FILLFACTOR*. For more information, see "DBCC DBREINDEX" and "CREATE INDEX" in SQL Books Online.

Indexed View Indexed views are a new feature in SQL Server 2000 Enterprise Edition. In previous SQL Server versions, the server had to retrieve data from the base tables each time a query used a view. With an indexed view, however, the results are built before a query uses the view. Depending on a view's overhead of retrieving data from the base table, you may find that the materialized result set can make a dramatic difference in a query's performance. In this section, we will continue with the example used in the nonclustered index example 1 section to demonstrate the use of an indexed view.

It has been our experience to see significant improvements with indexed views in queries that uses aggregation functions such as *SUM* or *COUNT*. Incidentally, the *ProductsMostPopular* stored procedure in the IBuySpy application uses the *SUM* function. The following query is part of the stored procedure:

```
SELECT TOP 5
    OrderDetails.ProductID,
    SUM(OrderDetails.Quantity) as TotalNum,
    Products.ModelName

FROM
    OrderDetails
  INNER JOIN Products ON OrderDetails.ProductID = Products.ProductID

GROUP BY
    OrderDetails.ProductID,
    Products.ModelName

ORDER BY
    TotalNum DESC
```

Based on the query used in *ProductsMostPopular*, a view and a unique clustered index can be created with the T-SQL statements in Listing 8-5:

Listing 8-5

```
-- User option requirements for creating an indexed view
SET QUOTED_IDENTIFIER ON
SET ARITHABORT ON
SET CONCAT_NULL_YIELDS_NULL ON
SET ANSI_NULLS ON
SET ANSI_PADDING ON
SET ANSI_WARNINGS ON
SET NUMERIC_ROUNDABORT OFF
GO


if exists (select * from dbo.sysobjects
    where id = object_id(N'[dbo].[ProductOrderCount]') and _
        OBJECTPROPERTY(id, N'IsView') = 1)
drop view [dbo].[ProductOrderCount]
GO


CREATE VIEW dbo.ProductOrderCount
WITH SCHEMABINDING
AS
SELECT  od.productid,  p.modelname,  SUM(od.Quantity) OrderSum
    , COUNT_BIG(*) RecordCount
-- COUNT_BIG aggregate function is required
FROM  dbo.orderdetails od
    INNER JOIN dbo.products p
        ON od.productid = p.productid
GROUP BY  od.productid,  p.modelname
GO


-- The first index on the indexed view must be clustered and unique
CREATE UNIQUE CLUSTERED INDEX IXUC_ProductOrderCount
    ON dbo.ProductOrderCount (ProductID)
```

When you are creating an indexed view, make sure that the all of the required user options are set correctly. The required user options are shown at the top of Listing 8-5. In addition, the view must be created with the schema binding view attribute. Lastly, the first index on the view must be a unique clustered index. Once the clustered index is created, additional nonclustered indexes can be created as necessary. More information on indexed views can be obtained from SQL Server Books Online, especially the section outlining the requirements that have to be met. Now that the indexed view is created, we can execute the *ProductsMostPopular* stored procedure again to observe the effect on performance. Table 8-8 compares the query using the indexed view.

Table 8-8 Query Comparison of the Indexed View

	Original Query	Covering index on ProductID and Quantity	Indexed View
Operator used and cost percentage	Table Scan (46 percent) and Hash Match/Aggregate (54 percent)	Index Scan (51 percent) and Stream Aggregate (49 percent)	Clustered Index Scan (77 percent) and Sort (23 percent)
Logical reads on OrderDetails	3800	2184	2
Query duration in milliseconds	1826	1021	20

As indicated in Table 8-8, using the ProductOrderCount indexed view significantly reduces the query duration and logical reads. In fact, the logical reads no longer occur on the *OrderDetails* table but now occur on the ProductOrderCount view. The following output shows the *STATISTICS IO* results generated by running *ProductsMostPopular*:

```
...
(5 row(s) affected)

Table 'ProductOrderCount'. Scan count 1, logical reads 2, _
    physical reads 0, read-ahead reads 0.
...
(Result abbreviated)
```

If *ProductsMostPopular* was the only stored procedure that was executed by the application, you can conclude that the indexed view is the best solution. Real-world applications would typically execute more than just one stored procedure. Indexed views can drastically improve the read performance, however, they can also degrade the performance of queries that modify or update data. Therefore, before deciding to use an indexed view, further stress testing is required to verify that the indexed view does in fact improve overall application throughput.

SQL Server includes an Index Tuning Wizard, which can sometimes help you come up with efficient indexes to implement. An interesting exercise would be to allow the Index Tuning Wizard to analyze the execution of *ProductsMostPopular*. You can do this by running the Index Tuning Wizard from Query Analyzer. (Press CTRL+I.) In the case of *ProductsMostPopular*, the Index Tuning Wizard recommended an almost identical indexed view. In many cases, the Index Tuning Wizard can be a time saver and give you useful insight on indexes. If you have never used the Index Tuning Wizard before, we highly recommend that you read the related articles in SQL Server Books Online for more information. Microsoft TechNet also has an excellent article on the Index Tuning Wizard.

By no means do the examples in this section cover all index tuning situations; however, you should have a good idea on the importance of proper index tuning. A simple indexing mistake or a lack of proper indexing in a high transaction volume server can bring performance to its knees. Evaluating each index in a database with many objects can be a daunting task but is worth the pain. In most cases, a properly indexed database will give you fewer headaches in the long run. We highly recommend that you investigate indexes in your efforts to identify and solve SQL bottlenecks before attempting to modify the underlying queries or deciding to upgrade hardware.

Conclusion

This chapter highlights the ways to identify bottlenecks at the SQL layer. The tools used to monitor the server and identify bottlenecks as well as ways to analyze and improve common bottlenecks have been discussed. Learning everything there is to know about SQL Server will certainly take time and experience. This chapter will not make you an expert overnight but will certainly give you insight into identifying bottleneck and coming up with quick fixes to common performance issues encountered at the SQL tier.

Estimating IIS Tier Capacity with Transaction Cost Analysis

Jonathan Swift said, "Necessity is the mother of invention;" but when you're performing capacity planning, Mark Twain's words are more applicable: "Necessity is the mother of taking chances." Why? Because capacity planning is the art of reducing the probability that a Web application's performance will degrade as a result of increasing or changing traffic patterns, while simultaneously avoiding unnecessary hardware purchases. Microsoft's Transaction Cost Analysis (TCA) is a science-based methodology to help you estimate Web application hardware needs. But you can never predict with 100-percent certainty what a user population actually ends up doing with your Web application. Prepare for surprises.

Capacity planning is not about absolutes; it is about intelligently preparing for probabilities. For example, if your company is planning to advertise their Internet address during the Superbowl, a TCA approach will help model hardware resource needs for the increased user traffic you'd expect from such a large marketing event, reducing the need to run performance tests for every possible traffic scenario. The TCA approach to capacity planning is nothing new. It has been around since the advent of client-server technology. However, the TCA methodology presented in this chapter is specifically adapted for Microsoft Web applications and services. It was developed in 1998/1999 by a team of Microsoft engineers including Hilal Al-Hilali, Morgan Oslake, David Guimbellot, Perry Clarke, and David Howell. There were a few business reasons for developing a TCA approach to capacity planning back then which are still relevant in today's .NET environment. Firstly, TCA is a scientific approach to estimating server hardware requirements. Secondly, as mentioned above, it enables Web application owners to model site capacity "what if" scenarios, greatly reducing the number of performance test iterations needed to define required hardware resources. For example, what happens to your Web application's performance if an additional 10,000 users are browsing in response to an e-mail marketing campaign? TCA enables you to answer that question without the need to set up and run additional performance tests. Lastly, TCA helps focus developers on optimizing the most costly code in terms of hardware resource consumption, to increase application scalability on existing hardware. Our team has successfully used the TCA methodology for Microsoft Web sites, including *http:// shop.microsoft.com.*

TCA defines hardware resource costs relative to user scenarios, and these costs are used to model required growth in hardware capacity. The ultimate end product of TCA is a set of user operation server resource costs that can be used to predict your Web application's maximum concurrent user levels. Since the TCA defines maximum concurrent user levels and the term *concurrent user* is often misunderstood, it merits a brief discussion before we proceed in describing the TCA methodology.

Concurrent Users: A Loosely Defined Term

How many concurrent users can my site support? This question is the one most often posed to our team in any performance planning discussion. Although the question is quite common, the term *concurrent user* is an often misunderstood, loosely defined industry-wide term. The answer to the question depends on how the word *concurrent* is defined and interpreted. The HTTP protocol is inherently stateless, getting and posting information as requested, but often remaining idle between user requests. For example, some people define a concurrent user through the Performance Monitor counter Current Anonymous Users. This can be misleading because one user could simply establish a connection by making one request and dropping off, where another user could make many requests that count as one connection.

In another scenario, imagine a thousand users browsing the IBuySpy .NET sample Web application. However, probably only a portion of the user requests are being concurrently processed on the Web server. The remaining user population is engaged in what is commonly called *think time*, meaning they are filling out a form or reading data before generating additional server activity by getting or posting data to the server. In this particular situation, there are a thousand IBuySpy users interacting with the site in the same general timeframe, but only a subset of one thousand client requests are concurrently processing on the server.

Concurrent Server Request Processing

When we use the term *concurrent users,* we assume that client requests are being processed on the server simultaneously. Effective capacity estimation requires a close analysis of the number of requests concurrently processed by the server relative to your user population, not just the finite number of people simultaneously using your Web application. The point is that you need to consider both concurrent server request processing and your user population, because users of your Web application are not necessarily making requests that concurrently generate server processing.

To further illustrate this important distinction, imagine 50 clients simultaneously requesting server data. The probability of those requests arriving at the server simultaneously in the real world can vary greatly. Variables affecting the arrival of those requests include client connection speeds, network latency, internet congestion, and the number of network segments the requests need to travel. If any of these variables change across those 50 client requests, the resulting activity at the server level can change significantly. Users requesting server data simultaneously do not necessarily produce a one-to-one relationship between the number of users and their requests concurrently being processed on the server. Understand the limitations of this term before committing to capital expenditures for capacity planning purposes.

TCA Concurrent Users

We felt it critical to discuss the term *concurrent users* because the TCA models site capacity by predicting the theoretical maximum level of concurrent users. TCA estimates hardware resource costs for *average users* concurrently utilizing your Web application. The user profile defines the average user for your site and is the first step in the five step TCA methodology. TCA concurrent users represent the level of average users consuming resources on your servers.

Benefits of Completing a TCA

Now that we have laid the groundwork for a clearer understanding of the concept of concurrent users, the next question is: "What level of server resources does your site require?" We find the TCA methodology provides a scientific approach to addressing this question.

Because TCA focuses on server resource costs relative to user operations, it can be used whether your Web application is based on the .NET architecture or Windows DNA. The methodology is virtually the same in both cases. The only difference we have found are some slight variations in Performance Monitor counters for Windows DNA versus .NET Web applications. Table 9-1 outlines the performance counters and performance objects in each case. Note that this is not a complete list of counters you will need to monitor. It is only a list of those that have changed locations from Windows DNA to .NET.

Table 9-1   TCA Performance Counters for Windows DNA and .Net

Performance Counter	Performance Object under Windows DNA	Performance Object under .NET
ASP Requests/Sec	Active Server Pages	ASP.NET Applications
ASP Execution Time	Active Server Pages	ASP.NET
ASP Wait Time	Active Server Pages	ASP.NET
Requests Queued	Active Server Pages	ASP.NET

TCA is an excellent approach for focusing development efforts on reducing hardware resource costs for your site's most expensive user operations, thereby increasing application scalability without increasing your hardware infrastructure.

Using TCA to reduce relatively high site operation costs will not only increase the scalability of your site but will also go a long way toward decreasing your site's total cost of ownership. This can be achieved by introducing a reliable method for modeling your site hardware capacity needs as your site traffic evolves and grows. A thorough TCA allows you to maximize site hardware resources already in place, to project when you will need to add more hardware, and to predict how much extra capacity, in terms of concurrent users, that extra hardware will adequately serve. In this manner, hardware costs can be more accurately associated with user population levels. The following real world example describes how a TCA approach assisted in increasing the scalability for Microsoft's *shop.microsoft.com* site.

Real World Example—*Shop.Microsoft.com*

In the spring of 1999, the ACE Team completed a TCA for Microsoft's eCommerce site *http://shop.microsoft.com* version 2.5. We found that the heavily trafficked Default homepage and Browse operations had relatively high CPU resource costs. This indicates that users requesting the homepage and product overview pages exacted a higher cost in terms of server resources when compared to other operations on the site. Identifying these high cost operations through a TCA allowed the developers to focus on reducing the site's CPU utilization. Subsequent to completing a TCA on the *http://shop.microsoft.com* version 4.5 code, we found that the shopper operational cost decreased by 25 percent between the versions, increasing the site's concurrent shopper capacity by the same percentage. This indicated that the shop site could adequately serve 25 percent more shoppers using the same hardware configuration and the version 4.5 code. The majority of the decrease in total cost could be attributed to cost reductions in the heavily trafficked Default homepage and Browse operations that were identified in our earlier version 2.5 TCA. These operations realized a lower cost in the version 4.5 code because they could achieve much higher ASP request per second throughput rates without significantly increasing the CPU utilization required to sustain those throughput rates. Additionally, our original version 2.5 TCA model allowed the developers to perform "what if" scenarios against subsequent versions by quickly calculating the impact of coding decisions on overall site capacity. The lesson learned in this TCA exercise was that if you understand your Web application's user traffic and subsequent hardware resource consumption, optimizing high resource cost application code will buy you more capacity without increasing your hardware budget.

TCA In Five Steps

There are five distinct steps to performing a TCA. The first critical step is to define your Web application's usage profile. Why is the usage profile so critical? Because the estimations that you assign to site operations in this step will ultimately weight your site's hardware resource costs, greatly influencing the final site capacity estimations. If you put garbage in you'll only get garbage out, so invest the time to do as thorough a user profile analysis as possible. The second step is to actually execute discrete stress tests on the scenarios defined in the user profile to identify server resource costs at maximum load. The third step is to make a set of calculations to quantify these costs. We have provided a Microsoft Excel spreadsheet that will help streamline these calculations. The TCA spreadsheet is included on this book's companion CD. The fourth step in this process is to make another set of calculations that will result in the actual number of estimated concurrent users. This calculation can also be made using the aforementioned spreadsheet. The fifth and final step is to run verification tests on your site to confirm the capacity numbers that you generated through the TCA model. Figure 9-1 illustrates the five step TCA methodology.

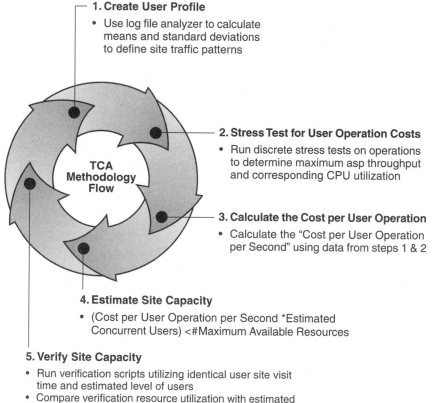

1. Create User Profile
- Use log file analyzer to calculate means and standard deviations to define site traffic patterns

TCA Methodology Flow

2. Stress Test for User Operation Costs
- Run discrete stress tests on operations to determine maximum asp throughput and corresponding CPU utilization

3. Calculate the Cost per User Operation
- Calculate the "Cost per User Operation per Second" using data from steps 1 & 2

4. Estimate Site Capacity
- (Cost per User Operation per Second *Estimated Concurrent Users) <#Maximum Available Resources

5. Verify Site Capacity
- Run verification scripts utilizing identical user site visit time and estimated level of users
- Compare verification resource utilization with estimated resource utilization

Figure 9-1 The Five Step TCA Methodology

Step 1—Create A User Profile

The first step is to create a user profile from existing production traffic data where available. This can be done by viewing historical data from your Web server log files (through various log parsers) or by analyzing database activity. If production traffic data does not exist, you can estimate user traffic loads by researching traffic patterns on similar sites. You will use the user profile to weight specific site transaction costs based on the ratio of specific operations to overall traffic. Our IBuySpy Web application browsing products transaction accounts for 61 percent of the traffic.

A good source for site traffic information is production IIS logs. However, analyzing gigabytes of IIS log data can be extremely time consuming, so automate this process wherever possible. There are many log file analyzers available, so find and use the one that suits your needs. In selecting the sampling of logs, it is better to use a set of logs covering as long a period of time as possible (at least a week's worth of IIS logs if they are available) to obtain realistic averages. The goal is to include as large a population of production traffic data as possible to generate more reliable usage profile weightings.

> **Tip**   When creating your profile, exclude traffic that extraordinarily inflates page view statistics. Ensure that page views are successful 200 code return requests and not just error pages represented as 200 code returns.

In some cases, to ensure that your Web application can meet the capacity needs regardless of seasonal peaks, you may have to use IIS logs for key peak traffic periods (for example, holiday shopping seasons). This will help your TCA estimates reflect your Web application's worst case traffic scenario. If historical production data is not available because your site is new, you can make an educated guess by reviewing publicly available statistics for similar sites including page views, unique users, and demographic data about their user base.

Identifying one profile that best represents your site traffic is just as critical as defining the probability of site usage distributions to be included in the "what if" scenarios. For example, after analyzing the IIS logs, we find that the browse operation has a normal distribution with a mean of 60 percent and a standard deviation of 10 percent. This means that determining the operational costs for 95 percent of the possible browse distributions would require you to calculate browse costs for two standard deviations or from a 40 percent browse weighting on the low end to an 80 percent browse weighting on the high end. Looking at the specific operational weightings as probability distributions rather than discrete data points provides a statistical basis for performing your site traffic "what if" scenarios mentioned in the beginning of this chapter. This allows you to easily model hardware capacity estimates across a range of probable traffic patterns.

Table 9-2 shows the user profile we created for our IBuySpy TCA:

Table 9-2   IBuySpy TCA User Profile

User Operations	Mean Hit Ratio (User Profile)	Standard Deviation
Basic Search	14.14 percent	2 percent
Browse for Product	61.49 percent	10 percent
Add to Basket	10.47 percent	1.5 percent
Login & Checkout	7 percent	.5 percent
Registration & Checkout	6.90 percent	.5 percent
Totals	**100 percent**	

Because this is only a sample site, we did not have production data from which to estimate our user profile. As an alternative, we based the ecommerce IBuySpy sample site user profile estimates on production data from the *shop.microsoft.com* e-commerce Web application. You will run into the same situation if you lack production data to base your user profile estimates on.

Another important aspect of setting up a user profile is determining the rate at which transactions occur. To illustrate, we estimated an average session length for our IBuySpy user to be 10 minutes. You use these transaction rates for stress script sleep times in the verification stress tests (Step 5) that verify the estimated capacity produced by the TCA model.

Step 2—Stress Test for User Operation Costs

After you have created the user profile, the next step is to create the transaction performance data needed to measure each user operation resource cost. You can do this by creating a stress script to exercise each of the identified shopper operations. The goal is to identify server resource costs such as CPU utilization at maximum throughput load. Microsoft ACT, a load generation/simulation tool discussed in Chapter 3, can be used for this task and is the one we used for this TCA. A set of sample ACT scripts that we utilized is included on this book's companion CD.

TCA Stress Test Goals and Parameters

Running a script exclusively for an individual operation loads the IIS server with as many requests as possible in order to achieve maximum ASP requests per second for that operation. Maximum ASP throughput occurs right before you observe a decline in ASP requests per second, as indicated in Performance Monitor at a higher load level. You also need to ensure that operational latency does not suddenly increase. We recommend keeping your average ASP latency under 2 seconds. You can calculate operational latency using the following formula:

```
Average ASP latency = (Avg. ASP execution time + Avg. ASP wait time)
```

Before each stress test, it's good practice to clear server level caches to restore the system to a consistent baseline for performance data collection. Each test should run for a duration sufficient to reach *steady-state*. This state is reached when resource consumption related to test start up are completed, network connections are established, server caches are appropriately populated, and periodic behavior such as batch jobs or production back up processes are occurring. For the IBuySpy TCA, we ran the stress tests for 10 minutes after allowing for a minute or two of test start up time. The resource measurements, such as CPU utilization and ASP requests per second, should be averaged over the length of the steady state test.

When you notice a decline in ASP request per second throughput as more load is applied, it could be due to context switching, excessive memory paging, disk I/O, network saturation or a stress client bottleneck. For example, in our IBuySpy TCA we monitored context switches per second to ensure they did not exceed 15,000. A context switch occurs when a thread no longer runs because it is blocked waiting for a logical or physical resource, or the thread puts itself to sleep. Symptoms of high context switching can include lower throughput coupled with high CPU utilization, which begins to occur at switching levels of 15,000 or higher. Record maximum ASP requests per second before your application demonstrates signs of performance degradation by closely observing these relevant performance counters and ensuring that your client is not bottlenecking overall throughput. More details on how to use Performance Monitor and important counters to monitor are presented in Chapter 4.

Identifying Maximum Throughput

A TCA approach to capacity planning can be used to measure any hardware resource costs, such as memory, disk I/O, or CPU utilization. For our IBuySpy TCA we are measuring CPU utilization as the limiting hardware resource. Transaction costs should be recorded, using Performance Monitor, at the point where maximum ASP requests per second is reached. See Table 9-1 for Windows DNA versus .NET counters. Increasing the number of users executing the script should increase the ASP requests per second throughput. When a site has been properly developed and tuned for performance, ASP requests per second and CPU utilization grow as the load increases. If adding more load results in lower ASP requests per second, you know that the load level needs to be decreased.

> **Tip**   Gradually increase the amount of load on your Web application while monitoring ASP requests per second. If you observe that an incremental increase in load applied does not subsequently result in higher ASP requests per second, ensure that your client isn't the throughput bottleneck. If your client is bottlenecking, reduce the load/client ratio and add more clients, to ensure your measuring the server resource cost at the true ASP request per second maximum. In addition, monitor ASP queuing on the server. If the queue exceeds a value of 1 then you have blocking. Reduce the load level.

If the number of ASP requests per second continues to grow until CPU utilization reaches 100 percent, the number of ASP requests per second at that point is the maximum. We do not recommend pushing CPU utilization to 100 percent, because this can introduce additional latency for your system and inaccuracies in TCA estimates. For IBuySpy, our maximum allowable CPU utilization was 90 percent.

Minimizing the Number of Pages Needed per Operation

When executing the operational cost stress tests it is important to reduce the number of pages required to successfully execute a particular operation. When you run a stress script to measure the Add to Cart costs including product browse pages, a portion of the cost you record from that test will be attributable to both Browse operations as well as the Add to Cart operations. The goal is to focus as narrowly as possible on the server resource cost produced by the operation in question. Narrowing the number of pages required to execute an operation down to the absolute minimum helps achieve that goal. This may require that you include parameters for dynamic pages such as shopper IDs or product IDs in your stress scripts to bypass pages that a user would normally be required to hit first.

Step 3—Calculate the Cost per User Operation

The stress tests you performed in Step 2 resulted in a set of resource costs measured in CPU cycles for each user operation. Our IBuySpy IIS server was configured with two processors with clock speeds of 1000 MHz per processor. The CPU utilization transaction costs were recorded when maximum ASP requests per second was achieved for the operation in question, while at the same time keeping the average operational latency (ASP execution time + ASP wait time) below 2 seconds, ASP queuing below 1, context switching per second below 15,000, and CPU utilization below a 90 percent average. The performance metrics we observed to verify that our test was achieving maximum ASP request per second are detailed in Table 9-3. These metrics are not used in the cost per operation calculations but are critical to monitor to ensure you're achieving the true maximum ASP requests per second. The results from our stress tests and subsequent cost per operations are detailed in Table 9-4.

Table 9-3   IBuySpy Cost per Operation Test Performance Monitor Metrics

User Ops	Execution Time (ms)	Wait Time (ms)	Avg. ASP Latency	Context Switches/Sec
Basic Search	62	56	118	8188
Browse for Product	1012	3.8	1015.8	4415
Add to Cart	350	5	355	3262
Login & Checkout	12.5	.88	13.38	5287
Register & Checkout	600	130	730	8355

Table 9-4 IBuySpy Cost/Operation

User Ops	CPU Util @ Max ASP Req/Sec	Max ASP Req/Sec	Cost (Mcycles)	Cost/Operation (Mcycles)
Browse for Product	58.20 percent	193.3	1164	6.02172
Basic Search	84 percent	349.8	1680	4.80722
Add to Cart	89.50 percent	98.3	1790	18.20956
Register & Checkout	76.20 percent	307.3	1524	4.95932
Login & Checkout	89.00 percent	279.9	1780	6.35941

The initial result of your TCA stress tests are the CPU costs per operation (last column in Table 9-4) calculated on the basis of megacycles (Mcycles) or 1 Mhz. For our IBuySpy TCA, we used a 1000-Mhz dual processor, which has a total capacity of 2000 Mcycles. Using the maximum number of ASP requests per second, you can calculate the costs per operation as follows:

```
Cost per Operation = CPU utilization * number of CPUs * speed of CPU (
in MHz) / ASP requests per second
```

To illustrate, when we stressed our IBuySpy browse operation, we achieved a maximum of 349.8 ASP requests per second with a CPU utilization of 84 percent, the cost per ASP page is then 84 percent * 2 * 1000 / 349.8 = 4.80274 Mcycles. Before you calculate the cost of an operation, you need to know the number of ASP pages involved in that operation. Checkout operations typically involve several ASP pages (personal information page, credit card page, shipping page, confirmation page, and so on). You calculate the cost of a shopper operation by normalizing the number of ASP pages involved.

> **Tip** Some ASP pages, such as redirects, are not visually seen by the clients since they contain server-side logic and redirect to a continuing page. You must also account for these types of redirect pages in your cost per operation calculations.

Cost Per User Operation/Sec Calculation

The behavior of user activity against a Web application can be random. But, over time Web usage statistically evens out to average behavior. The user profile you created in Step 1 should reflect your Web application's average user behavior. We calculated the hit ratio means as well as standard deviations to describe user activity for site traffic "what if" scenarios. In this fashion, you can model the effect that different site traffic distributions have on site capacity estimates, one of TCA's principle benefits. We calculated the number of shopper operations during the course of 10 minutes, and following that, the number of user operations per second. We need to know the number of operations per second because the total operation cost number is expressed in terms of clock speed per second (1000 MHz CPU speed is 1000 Mcycles per second). The cost per user operation per second for IBuySpy using the mean hit ratio distribution is detailed in Table 9-5:

Table 9-5   IBuySpy Cost Per User Operation/Sec (Mcycles)

Ops	Mean Hit Ratio (User Profile)	Min ASP Pages	Norm User Profile	User Profile Ops	User Profile Ops/Sec	Cost/Op	Cost/Sec
Browse for Products	61.49 percent	1	.61	2.18919	.00365	4.80	.01752
Basic Search	14.14 percent	2	.28	1.00684	.00168	6.02	.01010
Add to Basket	10.47 percent	3	.31	1.11827	.00186	18.21	.03394
Registration & Checkout	6.90 percent	13	.90	3.19353	.00532	6.36	.03385
Login & Checkout	7 percent	10	.70	2.49217	.00415	4.96	.02060
TOTAL	*100 percent*	*N/A*	*2.81*	*10.00*	*N/A*		*.11601*

Interpreting the Cost per User Operation Numbers

The key number in Table 9-5 is the Total Operational Cost/Sec number (.11601 Mcycles per user), which represents the total cost of the mean user profile. This number reflects the cost of an average user executing operations in the manner described by our mean user profile. This number will be used to estimate site capacity in Step 4 of the TCA methodology. Table 9-5 not only indicates the total cost of an average user but also provides clues regarding where to begin optimizing operations for better performance which will lead to improved site scalability. According to Table 9-5, the Add to Basket and Registration & Checkout operations have the highest cost per user, .03394 and .03385 respectively. In the case of the Add to Basket operation, the high cost per user operation per second partially results from a relatively high cost per operation of 18.21 Mcycles. This indicates that the development team should focus on reducing server CPU resource costs needed to complete this operation in order to increase overall site scalability.

In the case of the Registration & Checkout operation, the high cost per user operation per second results from a relatively high number of ASP pages (that is, 13) needed to complete this operation. The high number of pages means the operation's cost (6.36 Mcycles) needs to be weighted higher than the other operational costs. Development must focus on reducing the cost of this operation or reducing the number of pages needed to complete Registration & Checkout. Either approach will bring the cost per user per second for Registration & Checkout down, thereby increasing scalability.

Performing TCA "What If" Scenarios

At this stage in the methodology, we can perform the "what if" scenarios we discussed earlier. If you want to determine the impact of increasing the number of users performing the Add to Basket operation on your site's overall transaction cost per second and ultimately on your site's capacity, simply adjust your user profile by 2 standard deviations or more as needed.

In Step 1, we calculated the standard deviation for the Add to Basket operation at 1.5 percent. Therefore a 2 standard deviation increase in this operation's hit ratio means Add to Basket now represents 10.47 percent + (2*1.5 percent) = 13.47 percent of our Web application's traffic. When we increases the Add to Basket weighting, we must correspondingly decrease weightings in other operations. For the purpose of this example, we assumed that users increasing their Add to Basket activity were finding what they were looking for and subsequently browsing for fewer IBuySpy products. Hence, we reduced the browse hit ratio by 3 percent and correspondingly increased the Add to Basket operation hit ratio. The total effect on the cost for increasing the weight of our highest cost operation is detailed below in Table 9-6:

Table 9-6   IBuySpy Cost Per User Operation/Sec (Mcycles)

Ops	Mean Hit Ratio (User Profile)	Min ASP Pages	Norm User Profile	User Profile Ops	User Profile Ops/Sec	Cost/Op	Cost/ User/ Sec
Browse for Products	58.49 percent	1	.58	2.03883	.00340	4.80	.01632
Basic Search	14.14 percent	2	.28	1.00684	.00168	6.02	.0101
Add to Basket	13.47 percent	3	.31	1.40860	.00235	18.21	.04275
Registration & Checkout	6.90 percent	13	.90	3.19353	.00532	6.36	.03385
Login & Checkout	7 percent	10	.70	2.49217	.00415	4.96	.02060
TOTAL	100 percent	N/A	2.81	10	N/A		.12227

As detailed in Table 9-6, increasing the hit ratio for the Add to Basket scenario has resulted in a slight increase in our overall cost per user operation per second from .11601 Mcycles to .12227 Mcycles. At first glance this does not sound like much, but notice how much this seemingly small site traffic change affects our overall site capacity in Step 4.

Step 4—Estimate Site Capacity

Step 4 of the TCA process calculates hardware resource costs (in our case CPU utilization) relative to concurrent users levels. You can start by building a table similar to Table 9-7. In this table, we have taken the cost per user operation per second value that we calculated in Step 3 and multiplied it by the number of concurrent users we anticipate accessing our Web application.

Mean User Profile Capacity Estimates

When calculating maximum capacity, assign an allowable maximum server resource (i.e. CPU, Disk, or Memory) level. In this case we are using CPU utilization as the finite server resource. As we mentioned in Step 2, it is not a good idea to run your server at 100 percent CPU utilization. In order to estimate site capacity, we will assume an 85 percent CPU utilization as the maximum for a 2 processor IIS server. This leaves us with a maximum available CPU resource of

2000Mcycles * 85 percent = 1700 Mcycles. Table 9-7 illustrates the range of concurrent user capacity for our 2 processor 1000MHz IIS server in terms of concurrent users:

Table 9-7 shows us the maximum capacity of our IBuySpy IIS Server is 14,654 users, with a cost of 1700.01 Mcycles. This is the maximum limit, since the two processors with a theoretical maximum of 85 percent provide the site with a budget of 1700 Mcycles of capacity. In order to attain more capacity, given existing hardware, we will need to focus on reducing server CPU costs for those higher cost operations, which were Add to Basket and Register & Checkout.

Table 9-7   IBuySpy Capacity Estimates

Concurrent Users	Cost
14300	1658.94
14400	1670.54
14500	1682.15
14600	1693.75
14654	1700.01 (Maximum Available CPU Resources)
14700	1705.35
14800	1716.95

Increased Add to Basket Traffic "What If" Scenario Capacity Estimates

In Step 3 we illustrated how increasing the average users activity for the Add to Basket operation by two standard deviations affected our overall cost per user operation per second. The result was an increase in cost from .11601 Mcycles to .12227 Mcycles. How much does this small 3 percent change in traffic affect the overall concurrent user capacity for IBuySpy? Table 9-8 illustrates the capacity estimates with the higher average user cost:

Table 9-8   IBuySpy Site Capacity Estimates

Concurrent Users	Cost
13500	1650.65
13600	1662.87
13700	1675.10
13800	1687.33
13903	1700.04 (Maximum Available CPU Resources)
14000	1711.78
14100	1724.01

As illustrated above, increasing the average user's Add to Basket operation activity by two standard deviations or 3 percent has resulted in a drop in our IIS servers maximum concurrent user level from 14,654 to 13,903 users. This is a significant drop in our server's maximum concurrent user ability from only a small shift in the allocation of average user activity, and it only took a minor adjustment in our model to obtain this data.

The main point of this "what if" scenario is to illustrate the time saving value of TCA modeling. Now that we have completed our TCA model, we can reallocate site user traffic in an infinite number of distributions and immediately determine the probable effect on our overall site capacity. When you compare the time it takes to complete one TCA to the time it takes to run discrete stress tests to produce the same capacity data, you can appreciate the value of a TCA. The TCA provides the ability to predict site capacity for an infinite number of site traffic scenarios.

Step 5—Verify Site Capacity

The last step in the TCA process is to verify site capacity by running stress tests that reflect the user profile properties, including traffic distribution and session length. You then compare the resource utilization costs you obtain in these tests against those predicted by the TCA model. The actual values for tested resource utilizations and the TCA model resource predictions should fall within an acceptable margin of error. The goal in this step is to confirm the TCA model site capacity predictions. It is not necessary to run a verification test at every load level. After all, this would defeat the purpose of the TCA in predicting resource usage at various concurrent user levels. Rather, a single test will allow you to gain a desired level of confidence in the TCA model predictions.

To confirm our IBuySpy TCA model, we ran five verification tests across a wide range of concurrent user levels. The results for our IBuySpy verification tests were obtained using the same stress test scripts we created in Step 2. However, all scripts were run simultaneously and distributed as defined in our user profile. Additionally, since our model used a 10-minute user session length, our verification scripts all contained 10-minute sleep times. This means that each script takes 10 minutes to complete the IBuySpy operations, just as the average user would. Refer to Chapter 3 for details on sleep times in stress scripts. Figure 9-2 illustrates our IBuySpy verification test result.

When analyzing the verification test results we are checking to make sure that the percent difference in megacycles predicted and megacycles obtained does not exceed 10 percent. In addition, we also verify that our ASP scripts are executing within our 2 second maximum latency parameters. According to the results in Table 9-9, we see that for each of the test runs we fall well within our

10-percent margin of error. When running verification tests remember to keep an eye out for average ASP latency of greater than 2 seconds. As indicated in Table 9-9, ASP latency was not a limiting throughput factor during our verification tests.

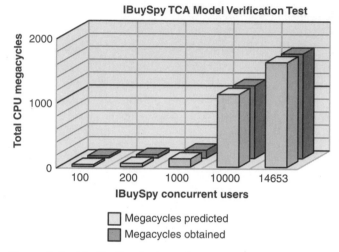

Figure 9-2 Verification test results

Our verification tests confirm the costs predicted by the TCA model and increase our confidence in the TCA estimate's accuracy. We can now use the TCA to predict hardware resource requirements for various traffic distribution scenarios.

Table 9-9 **IBuySpy Verification**

Concurrent Users	Mcycles Predicted	Mcycles obtained	ASP Wait Time (ms)	ASP Execution Time (ms)	ASP Latency (ms)
100	11.60	11.54	.238	4.063	4.301
200	23.2	23.8	.769	5.094	5.863
1000	116.01	120.19	1.9	6.09	7.99
10000	1160	1147	27.203	52.441	79.644
14653	1699	1661	39.98	72.47	111.45

Conclusion

Estimating a site's concurrent usage is part art and science. Careful analysis of server activity that different user populations create must be performed to appreciate the common misconceptions associated with the term *concurrent user*. Nevertheless, site owners need to estimate their maximum site capacity hardware needs to be better prepared for extraordinary traffic spikes. The TCA is a scientific methodology for estimating Web application hardware capacity needs. It consists of five steps:

1.   Creating a user profile

2.   Stress testing to define transaction hardware resource costs

3.   Calculating the hardware resource cost per user operation

4.   Using the transaction costs to model Web application hardware resource needs

5.   Verifying the TCA model is accurate

Using the TCA approach to better understand how varying Web application traffic affects hardware capacity needs allows you to make more informed hardware purchase decisions saving your company capital expenses.

10

Performance Modeling: Tools for Predicting Performance

TCA is the scientific method of determining server capacity—establish a hypothesis, and then run an experiment with live hardware and real or projected usage data to determine the validity of your expected result. Using this method, basic capacity planning and real-time evaluation of existing systems can be done with an acceptable degree of certainty. Provided the usage data, hardware, and network resources are available to test, TCA can also be used to anticipate changes in load and cost, and to determine where adjustments can be made in the name of either higher performance or lower financial impact.

When an established server's load grows to the point where performance is reduced, the most common solution is to add more resources, with the expectation that things like additional processor capacity or bandwidth will have a direct impact on the performance problem. Although this can be expensive, it is usually considered a good problem to have. A system that has reached its critical limit for performance is probably generating revenue, or at least experiencing high traffic. Additional hardware costs are justifiable on the surface, and hardware installation rarely involves a major reconfiguration of the server's software components. The expectation is that users will not experience an interruption in their service—just an improvement in its response time.

The attitude that more hardware solves the problem can get software engineers and network managers in trouble, however, because adding more physical resources does not always address the real issue.

For example, consider an e-commerce server that is taking too long to process order handling, and generating errors for some users who try to place an order. The IT staff may decide that because their processor load is often near maximum, the bottleneck is the result of a lack of hardware resources. However, this bottleneck in performance might be caused by the server application: perhaps the order processing application is only designed to handle a finite number of simultaneous open order input transactions. If this aspect of the application is not anticipated in TCA evaluations, the TCA results will not show that increasing processor speed will have no impact on the problem.

Predicting and Evaluating Performance Through TCA

TCA is greatly valuable for evaluating existing systems and gauging the improvement caused by changes in code or upgrades in hardware. By changing the parameters within an Excel spreadsheet, projections can easily be made. By running TCA evaluations against old and new versions of software, as illustrated in the Chapter 9 "Real World Example—Shop.Microsoft.com," changes are validated in a measurable way. TCA is a significant improvement over completing an entire system, including both hardware and software, and then attempting to make improvements to meet requirements after the fact. However, due to its dependence on the actual or projected data and system responses, it is a somewhat reactive method of evaluating performance.

When the overall architecture of a server system requires multiple changes to improve performance, a company's existing TCA criteria may not be designed to take all of these elements into consideration.

What about a new business launching a new Web service? In the last chapter, we discussed the need to have real user data in order to complete the TCA experiment. In addition, validating the impact of more bandwidth, processor capacity, or other physical improvements to the system can be expensive because those resources must be physically present. The cost of having hardware for testing purposes is often hard to justify, especially when the system being tested is not yet generating revenue.

Advanced Performance Modeling

To address this issue, a more advanced method of performance modeling is required. The purpose of this more advanced form is to facilitate testing of multiple hardware and network resource configurations without actually having all of the resources present. This allows an enterprise to run extensive tests, including what-if scenarios, in order to make informed decisions about their physical resource purchases. The difference between these two methods is most evident in their end results: TCA tests known data and existing resources to the point of failure, defining the physical limits of the system. Advanced performance modeling tests possible configuration scenarios with a greater number of variables, and can be used not only to predict the physical limits of the system, but also to suggest possible improvements prior to those limits being reached.

Performance modeling also allows software engineers to test models of their code before the code is complete. This can be achieved by defining the design of the software in a language like Universal Modeling Language (UML), which is an industry-standard design formalism. By creating code objects that encapsulate the performance characteristics of software in terms of expected resource utilization and workflow, performance engineering is accomplished through the creation and evaluation of performance models.

Another obvious benefit of this virtual model approach is the flexibility of testing during the design phase. Software engineers can establish the time and resource constraints of their system and test different architecture options before committing to writing finalized code. Doing this reduces the chance that code will have to be massaged or rewritten a second time to meet performance requirements—and therefore reduces both time to release and possible introduction of errors.

Performance Modeling Technology

One goal of performance modeling is to be truly proactive in performance engineering—to examine a proposed system in its entirety, from hardware and network resources to code optimization, before completely building any one component. In this section, we'll discuss the following:

- Scenarios in which performance modeling can replace other methods of performance assessment and engineering

- Different methods of modeling and when they are appropriate

- A brief look at currently available performance modeling tools

- A detailed look at the toolkit approach, represented by Microsoft's Indy project

Modeling Scenarios

How can performance modeling improve business practices and efficiency, as well as the overall performance of systems? Let's look at some of the common issues facing client-server systems.

Capacity Planning

Anticipating the need for more resources involves both business and engineering decisions. Once a company has determined an acceptable estimate for future growth, the process of improving available resources follows close behind. Simply adding more hardware, as discussed in our introductory example, can mean that the additional resources do not equal more capacity, and performance suffers, taking company profits along with it. Using TCA for capacity planning can be highly accurate, if the data in the TCA structure is accurate to begin with. However, it still requires verification and, possibly, unnecessary expenditures to verify the projected results. Through more detailed definition of the user load, hardware, and software components of a system, performance modeling can eliminate the verification step and suggest alternative ways to improve capacity before the need arises.

Bottleneck Analysis

Evaluating a system that suddenly reaches a plateau and does not respond to hardware upgrades can be a frustrating process. Using performance modeling to detail each transaction and the associated hardware requirements for those transactions can expose bottlenecks. In advance of an actual performance failure, it can also be used to test with higher potential system load and predict the occurrence of a bottleneck, simultaneously showing ways to alleviate the problem before it occurs.

Hardware Configuration

Detailed performance models can very accurately predict the behavior of proposed hardware upgrades, using performance counters and simulating transactions against the virtual hardware. The question of whether to spend money to upgrade from 2-CPU to 4-CPU servers can be answered in a performance model with a few clicks of a mouse, rather than through trial and error.

Architectural Assessment

One way to assess the performance quality of two radically different architectural structures is to build both and examine the actual results. This is hardly feasible in the real world of software engineering or multi-client services, however. Both cost and time would be prohibitive. TCA can be used to produce estimates regarding overall system performance based on hardware and network architecture, but it still requires verification. In this case, performance modeling can decrease both the time and money spent on architectural engineering by providing varying levels of detail, depending on the architecture questions to be answered.

User Scenarios

TCA is a simple and effective tool for examining what happens when the user load on a given system increases. It is more difficult, however, to use TCA to track the impact of changes in typical user behavior. Performance modeling adds the ability to test different user habits by relying on models of user actions instead of real or borrowed user data patterns.

Performance Modeling Methods

There are three main methods of modeling that can be used to predict, assess, and interpret performance during system construction. These methods are analytical, statistical, and simulation. Understanding the requirements and results of each method is critical for making decisions about which is best used for a given task.

Analytical Modeling

The process of analytical modeling involves the use of mathematical expressions to represent the interactions that take place on a system. In some cases mathematical notations such as queuing networks and Petri networks are employed to represent the architecture of a system.

Typically, each component in the model, whether it represents a hardware device, network transaction, section of software code, or user activity, is represented in the underlying system in mathematical terms. Complex equations, representing the relationships between these components, are developed and then solved to determine the projected value of a given variable in the model.

For example, if you have a Web server that only serves simple HTML pages to clients connecting over the Internet, you would need to gather information about the server's hardware configuration (CPU, disk speed, and memory usage), the content being served (including file sizes for HTML, image, and other elements of the Web pages), the network capacity at the server (the real bandwidth available to the server), and various scenarios for client activity (including low and high load situations, average number of page views, average amount of time between page requests, and various network connection speeds at the client level). Given this data, you can extrapolate a control equation that accurately relates all of the elements in terms of the time and resource utilization.

Once the control equation (which might be represented in a spreadsheet with embedded calculations) has been established, you can change the values of different elements in order to see how those changes impact other elements within the boundaries of the equation.

You will recognize this as the basic methodology behind TCA. Knowing the system's typical behavior, TCA can predict system performance based on possible changes in user behavior, or changes in hardware configuration (provided the data values are accurately modified to reflect the new hardware's capacity and response times).

Analytical approaches can provide an initial estimate of the performance of new systems, but typically can produce results for only a limited set of what-if scenarios. The use of a mathematical notation to describe the most challenging performance effects of a system, such as queuing delays and resource contention, requires substantial expertise on the part of the performance engineer.

Statistical Modeling

Statistical modeling in performance engineering relies on known performance metrics for existing systems. You can use this data as a basis to predict the behavior of a new, not yet built system. This is achieved by analyzing the measured data with techniques such as regression analysis. Then the resulting statistical models can be used to extrapolate the performance of the system in new configurations.

For example, a hosting company may have a number of existing e-commerce servers for its clients already in production. To recommend hardware and network capacity for a new client, aggregate statistical data about all of the production servers could be analyzed and a recommendation made, either to use similar hardware and bandwidth, or to use different elements in the new system in hopes of improving the current systems' performance.

As with any statistical analysis, the accuracy of the resulting projections increases with the sample size of existing data. For this reason, the hosting company in the example would want to measure performance on several systems before arriving at an average model. One barrier to using statistical analysis in performance engineering is the lack of either quantity or complexity of existing data. Reviewing the published site statistics for a comparable, competing e-commerce vendor might yield valuable statistical data about number of visitors and those visitors' traffic patterns, but probably would not include information about the site's hardware and network connection capacity, or the software used to provide the site's services. In this case, a combination of statistical and analytical models (again, similar to TCA when used to project behavior of a new service) would be required to accurately assess performance prior to launch.

Statistical models include assumptions about the way the performance extrapolates. For example, the performance engineer might assume that the CPU utilization is linearly increasing with load. Although this might be true for the observed performance measurements, the CPU utilization behavior changes when it approaches saturation. Experience is the only way to avoid these pitfalls.

Simulation

Simulation may be done in two ways. The first involves building a proposed system and subjecting it to simulated load patterns to assess its performance. The accuracy of simulation modeling in this manner is rivaled only by real-world experience, because the hardware and software in place are the real tools used to provide the service being tested. Load generation can be done through the creation and automation of use cases, or by using commercially available traffic generation tools such as ACT. Stress-testing a real system not only exposes the performance problems, but demonstrates the aftermath of a performance failure as well.

For example, consider a server application that processes telephone calls for an IP telephony system. Its performance requirements run the gamut from lightning-fast CPU response time to 100-percent bandwidth availability on the network connection, because it must complete all of its requests to the telephone network within a 200-millisecond time window. Such a system might perform flawlessly under minimal user load, but an increase in the load that results in either queuing on the CPU or congestion on the network would result in telephone service outages for its users. By simulating call-processing load on the actual system before deployment, you could determine the real limits of the system and avoid overuse by setting strict limits on the number of clients who use that server for the handling of their calls.

The trade-off for accurate results in this type of simulation modeling is the fact that improvements must be made to a complete, or nearly complete, system. In the preceding example, the only way to avoid service failures with the existing call processing server is to limit the potential number of simultaneous users. Alternately, the system engineers can test alternate hardware or software configurations, but must purchase the resources or rewrite the code to do so.

The second method of simulation modeling involves writing software that accurately represents the behavior of hardware devices, and using another software tool to process existing code or simulated software behavior (such as UML) through the hardware device simulations. This eliminates the hardware costs associated with simulating only the load on a system, but can be extremely time-consuming, if a performance engineer has to develop the constructs and applications for processing the simulation from scratch.

Advanced Performance Modeling

Each method of modeling has advantages and disadvantages. In the real world, it is necessary to balance the potential quality of test results with the time and money required to run those tests. Advanced performance modeling tools, such as the Indy example later in this chapter, combine these methods to provide flexibility and scalability with lower cost and a broader learning curve.

Performance Modeling Tools

A few tools are available today that use models to evaluate and predict performance. Most of them are customized solutions, which can be purchased either as an entire system, or built to specification by the vendor. They typically feature very large libraries of existing hardware models, graphical drag-and-drop interfaces, and the services of consultants to assist engineering staff in applying the techniques provided by the software.

The power and features of these tools come at a high price—often hundreds of thousands of dollars in licensing, and more in training for the engineer who will ultimately be responsible for the tool's use. More emphasis is typically placed on hardware than software.

The direction of most performance modeling tools on the market today is toward solving one or two specific problems, or addressing a single application's performance. For performance modeling to be more widely used, and accessible to a larger audience, it must be more modular and support a broader range of user skill levels.

Indy: A Performance Technology Infrastructure

In this chapter, we'll use examples from a Microsoft performance modeling project called Indy to compare the results available through TCA (from the previous chapter) and those available through more advanced forms of performance modeling. Indy is designed to tackle the problem of performance engineering by creating a *performance technology infrastructure.*

Performance modeling is a multidimensional space, with different modeling tools having different requirements for level of detail, modeling technique, and target audience. No one tool or static application can meet all these needs. However, a toolkit approach allows construction of specialized tools from a basic infrastructure combined with customized components. This approach also permits an infinite range of complexity in those tools and models. Thus, a simple question can be answered quickly, or a critical system component can be tested in great detail.

Indy Concepts

Indy uses a *simulation-based approach* to performance modeling with analytical shortcuts to improve its performance. That is, it uses internal models of each of the major devices of the system being modeled, and simulates how these devices behave and interact. After a simulated run, the performance of each device can be examined in detail.

Indy comes with a predefined library of device models. Each model can in turn have sub-models. Thus, the Indy model of a server farm might consist of various server models connected by a network model. The server models can in turn contain models of their CPUs, disks, and network interfaces. Instances of these *hardware models* can then be arranged in a *system topology* that matches the hardware configuration of the real server farm.

Given a model of the system configuration, we also need to model the input load that it will experience. The input load is referred to as its *workload*. For example, the Indy model of an e-commerce site might have a workload defined in terms of how often it receives requests for the various pages and actions on the site.

Finally, we must model how the various components in the system will react to the workload: that is, we must define the behavior of the system. Indy provides a range of ways to define this behavior, but here we will concentrate on an XML-based scripting language called Transaction Modeling Language (TML). A TML script defines the transactions that a Web site will support in terms of their component actions (such as computation, disk operations, or network traffic), and on what devices these actions will run.

Indy Architecture

Figure 10-1 illustrates the basic architecture of Indy and its components.

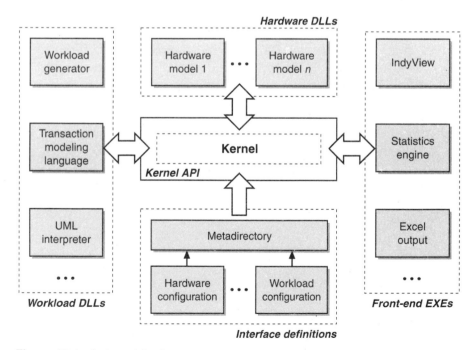

Figure 10-1 Indy architecture

Kernel

At the heart of Indy is the kernel, which interacts with and controls the other components via well-defined APIs. The kernel must be present in all tools produced with the Indy toolkit. It includes the central evaluation engine that is used to produce simulation results. As noted above, the current Indy kernel uses an *event-based* evaluation engine that combines direct simulation with some hybrid shortcut techniques to improve performance. However, for other purposes a different evaluation engine could be used: for example, one that uses analytical or statistical modeling techniques.

Hardware DLLs

The hardware DLLs implement the models of the individual system devices, such as CPUs and disks. A library of models is available to choose from, and additional models can be easily added. Multiple models might be available for a particular device, differing in the level of detail they go into to model performance. A more detailed model can give more accurate results and allow more performance effects to be considered, but may in turn require more information at run time and may take longer to simulate.

Workload DLLs

The workload DLLs are responsible for defining and injecting events into the kernel representing the workload for a particular simulated run. As shown, a variety of workload DLLs can be used. In this chapter we describe the use of a workload DLL that interprets TML scripts to create a workload. Alternate workload DLLs could be used to interpret UML diagrams or produce a customized workload for a specialized tool.

Interface Definitions

Information about the configuration of other components is stored by the kernel in a *metadirectory*. For example, different versions of the same basic disk can use the same hardware model, but with different performance characteristics. Similarly, performance characteristics of a workload, such as how often a transaction occurs or how much network traffic it causes, can be varied without having to recode the workload DLL or TML script.

Front-end EXEs

The front-end executable combines the kernel, hardware, and workload DLLs, and the metadirectory with an appropriate user interface for the final tool to use. In a production environment we might choose to export data about a simulated run to an Excel spreadsheet or a SQL database. However, in this chapter we will concentrate on a graphical interface called IndyView. It is intended to be used by performance engineers who require more detailed access to information about an Indy simulation. You will see samples of its output later this chapter.

IndyView

In this section we will see some elements of the IndyView interface used to examine a performance model of the IBuySpy sample Web site. We will also see the underlying XML code used to represent various aspects of the model.

System Topology

Consider a simple configuration of the IBuySpy sample Web site, as shown in Figure 10-2:

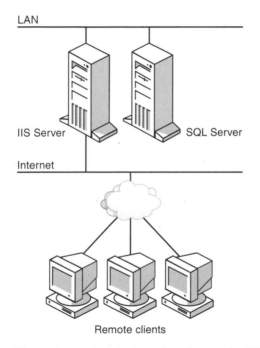

Figure 10-2   Physical topology for a typical IBuySpy sample Web site

The system consists of an IIS server and a SQL server (which together make up the IBuySpy sample Web site), connected to one another over the LAN. The IIS server is also connected to the Internet, and processes requests from remote clients via the Internet.

Figure 10-3 is an example of how this simple topology for the IBuySpy Web site can be represented using the IndyView interface.

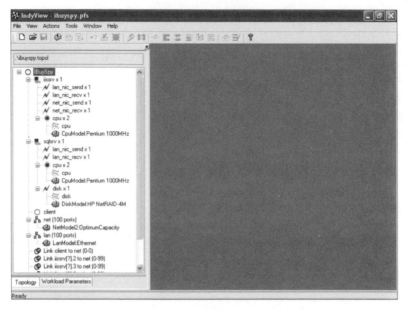

Figure 10-3 Indy topology for the IBuySpy sample Web site

Examining this in more detail, the IIS server (*iissrv*) includes Network Interface Card (NIC) devices and CPU devices. Devices that are functionally identical can be represented in multiples, as the CPUs are shown here. The SQL server (*sqlsrv*) includes NIC, CPU and disk devices. Although it is obvious that the real IIS server also has a disk, its performance is not relevant to the model being tested, and so it has not been included.

On the *sqlsrv* device, below the CPU x 2 heading, there are two more devices: a CPU performance counter, and the CpuModel:Pentium 1000MHz device, which defines the behavior of this particular type of CPU, including how quickly it can process calculations. Similarly, below the Disk x 1 heading, you find both a disk performance counter and a DiskModel: HP NetRAID-4M device, which has its access speed and other hardware performance factors predefined.

For the purposes of the performance being measured here, the client's hardware configuration does not need to be detailed. Therefore, the client device is just a black box, referenced in the transactions as the requester or recipient of data.

The *net* and *lan* devices, located at the same hierarchical level as the two servers, represent the properties of the network connections for the Internet and LAN segments respectively.

Finally, the links between each of the computer devices and the network devices are detailed, including which interface on each computer connects to which network device. This is so that the output of the test results will distinguish between the different devices' activities at any point in the transaction.

The following XML code underlies the diagram in Figure 10-3:

```xml
<?xml version="1.0" encoding="utf-8"?>
<system name="IBuySpy">
    <active_device type="computer" name="iissrv" count="1">
        <active_device type="generic" name="lan_nic_send" count="1"/>
        <active_device type="generic" name="lan_nic_recv" count="1"/>
        <active_device type="generic" name="net_nic_send" count="1"/>
        <active_device type="generic" name="net_nic_recv" count="1"/>
        <active_device type="cpu" name="cpu" count="2">
            <rct name="cpu"/>
            <use_template name="CpuModel:Pentium 1000MHz"/>
        </active_device>
    </active_device>
    <active_device type="computer" name="sqlsrv" count="1">
        <active_device type="generic" name="lan_nic_send" count="1"/>
        <active_device type="generic" name="lan_nic_recv" count="1"/>
        <active_device type="cpu" name="cpu" count="2">
            <rct name="cpu"/>
            <use_template name="CpuModel:Pentium 1000MHz"/>
        </active_device>
        <active_device type="generic" name="disk" count="1">
            <rct name="disk"/>
            <use_template name="DiskModel:HP NetRAID-4M"/>
        </active_device>
    </active_device>
    <open_device name="client"/>
    <passive_device type="network" name="net" ports="100">
        <use_template name="NetModel2:OptimumCapacity"/>
    </passive_device>
    <passive_device type="network" name="lan" ports="100">
        <use_template name="LanModel:Ethernet"/>
    </passive_device>
    <link active="client" passive="net" fromport="0" toport="0"/>
    <link active="iissrv[?].2" passive="net" fromport="0" toport="99"/>
    <link active="iissrv[?].3" passive="net" fromport="0" toport="99"/>
    <link active="iissrv[?].0" passive="lan" fromport="0" toport="99"/>
    <link active="iissrv[?].1" passive="lan" fromport="0" toport="99"/>
    <link active="sqlsrv[?].0" passive="lan" fromport="0" toport="99"/>
    <link active="sqlsrv[?].1" passive="lan" fromport="0" toport="99"/>
</system>
```

The devices referenced in the TML code are defined in the metadirectory of hardware configurations. By changing the underlying properties of one of the referenced devices, this same script could be used to test different architectural options. Similarly, the number of devices can be changed to examine the performance impact of factors such as number of CPUs in a server.

IBuySpy Search Transaction

Having constructed our topology, we can now define the transactions that it will support. Here we see a simple example of a transaction written in TML to simulate the request and processing of a search page on IBuySpy.

```
<tml>

    ...

  <!-- BasicSearch
    Request the .aspx and then the two gifs
  -->
  <transaction name="BasicSearch" frequency="BasicSearchFreq">
    <include name="ChooseClientSpeed" />
    <action name="net_msg_sync_async" connection="net" service="Client"
            saveschedule="clientstate">
      <param name="linkspeed" value="transaction.ClientSpeed" />
      <param name="msgsize" value="HttpRequestSize*3" />
      <peer name="target" service="IIS" saveschedule="iisstate" />
    </action>
    <action name="compute" service="IIS" useserver="iisstate">
      <param name="cpuops" value="BasicSearchCpu" />
    </action>
    <action name="net_msg_async_sync" connection="net" service="IIS"
            useserver="iisstate">
      <param name="linkspeed" value="transaction.ClientSpeed" />
      <param name="msgsize" value="BasicSearchSize" />
        <!-- just the .aspx page size -->
      <peer name="target" service="Client" useserver="clientstate" />
    </action>
    <fork>
      <branch>
        <action name="net_msg_sync_async" connection="net"
            service="Client" saveschedule="clientstate">
          <param name="linkspeed" value="transaction.ClientSpeed" />
          <param name="msgsize" value="HttpRequestSize" />
          <peer name="target" service="IIS" saveschedule="iisstate" />
        </action>
        <action name="net_msg_async_sync" connection="net" service="IIS"
            useserver="iisstate">
          <param name="linkspeed" value="transaction.ClientSpeed" />
          <param name="msgsize" value="0.04" /> <!-- 1x1.gif -->
          <peer name="target" service="Client" useserver="clientstate" />
```

```
          </action>
        </branch>
        <branch>
          <action name="net_msg_sync_async" connection="net" service="Client"
              saveschedule="clientstate">
            <param name="linkspeed" value="transaction.ClientSpeed" />
            <param name="msgsize" value="HttpRequestSize" />
            <peer name="target" service="IIS" saveschedule="iisstate" />
          </action>
          <action name="net_msg_async_sync" connection="net" service="IIS"
              useserver="iisstate">
            <param name="linkspeed" value="transaction.ClientSpeed" />
            <param name="msgsize" value="1.52" /> <!-- thumbs/image.gif -->
            <peer name="target" service="Client" useserver="clientstate" />
          </action>
        </branch>
      </fork>
    </transaction>

    ...
</tml>
```

The transaction definition begins with a name and a relative frequency with which the transaction occurs. Then the actions within the transaction are listed in the order in which they occur. In this example script, the individual actions (which each begin with action name and end with /action) are:

1. net_msg_sync_async: Send an HTTP request message from the client service (representing all of the possible client machines on the Internet) to the IIS service over the Internet, using variable parameters for the link speed and message size. This message is sent synchronously (that is, the client waits for a response), but is received asynchronously (the server can handle many simultaneous requests).

2. compute: Process the HTTP request on the IIS server with the variable parameter of how many CPU operations are required.

3. net_msg_async_sync: Send a message back from the IIS service to the client service over the Internet, using variable parameters of link speed and message size. In the comments, we see that the value *Basic-SearchSize* is just the ASPX page size, meaning that the variable *Basic-SearchSize* has been previously defined as a workload parameter that

contains the network size of the ASPX file. This variable can then be easily modified from within IndyView.

4. At this point, the script dictates a fork into two branches, which will be executed simultaneously:

The first branch, containing the actions `net_msg_sync_async` and `net_msg_async_sync`, make up the request and response for a GIF file (referred to in the comment as 1x1.gif) with a size of 0.04 KB.

The second branch, containing the actions `net_msg_sync_async` and `net_msg_async_sync`, make up the request and response for a GIF file (referred to in the comment as thumbs/image.gif) with a size of 1.52 KB.

Hard coding parameter values in this way results in a script that will require editing if any of the values changed. For parameters whose values a user might want to change frequently, it makes more sense to use a workload variable, as with the ASPX page size and CPU cost.

We can drill down to another level of detail to see what information is embedded in one of the service definitions in the script:

```
<service name="IIS">
    <serverlist>
        <server name="iissrv" />
    </serverlist>
    <actionscheduling>
        <schedule action="compute" policy="roundrobin">
            <target device="cpu" />
        </schedule>
        <schedule action="net_msg_async_sync" connection="net"
            policy="random">
            <target device="nic_send" />
        </schedule>
    </actionscheduling>
</service>
```

This tells us that for the service IIS, the device *iissrv* (defined in the system topology) is to be used. Actions can be scheduled on *iissrv*'s sub-devices. In this script, when the action compute is required by a transaction, the target sub-device is one of the two CPUs, chosen using a round-robin policy. When traffic must be sent out to the Internet (the net device in the system topology script), the target device is the NIC dedicated to sending.

When processed by the Indy kernel API using the device definitions in the system topology, IndyView can produce a number of different visual representations of the transaction as a whole, or can focus on specific devices and how they are affected throughout the flow of the transaction. Figures 10-4, 10-5, 10-6, and 10-7 were all produced using a sample model of the IBuySpy sample Web site.

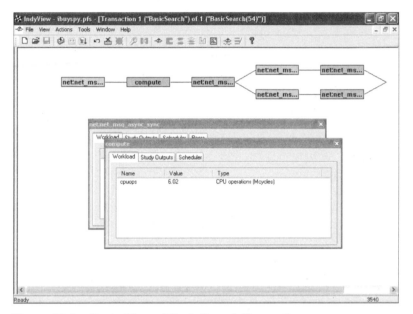

Figure 10-4   Control flow of Basic Search Transaction

After we have defined a transaction in TML, we can use IndyView to visualize it with a transaction flow diagram, as shown in Figure 10-4. This simple view can be used to inspect and debug the TML, and would typically be used by a performance engineer in the development stage of a model.

This search flow diagram shows the order and dependencies of each action in the transaction. The sequence of actions include: request from client to Web server, computation on the Web server, response from the Web server to the client, and then two image fetches in parallel being received by the client. Clicking on one of the actions in the flow diagram opens a window that provides more information. In this figure, one is a message from server to client (background) and the other is the computation on an iissrv CPU (foreground).

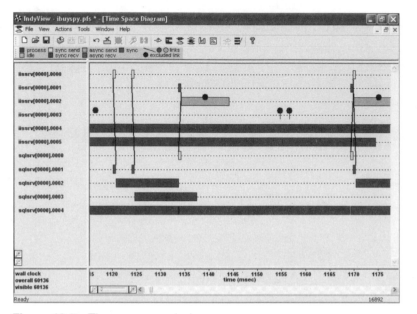

Figure 10-5   Time-space analysis

Figure 10-5 shows the time and resource requirements of events taking place on all system devices. This diagram can be used by a performance engineer to visualize the level of utilization of individual devices and determine possible performance problems by simple inspection of detailed events. Time goes left to right, and each line represents a device (identified in the device list on the left side of the screen), while boxes represent events. The color map, which corresponds to the type of event, is shown on the diagram below the toolbar. Lines in the window connect communication events where both partners in the communication are visible in the window. Black circles represent communication events in which one partner of the communication is not visible. Since clients are not shown in this view, communications with them are displayed this way. The device numbers on the left are derived from the topology script. The most utilized resources in the diagram are the IIS server CPUs (*iissrv[0000].0004-0005*) and the SQL disk (*sqlsrv[0000].0004*).

Rather than looking at all of the actions taking place on the entire system, we can use the Transaction Analysis view of IndyView to examine how long each of the individual actions in a particular instance of a transaction take, and what resources they require, as shown in Figure 10-6.

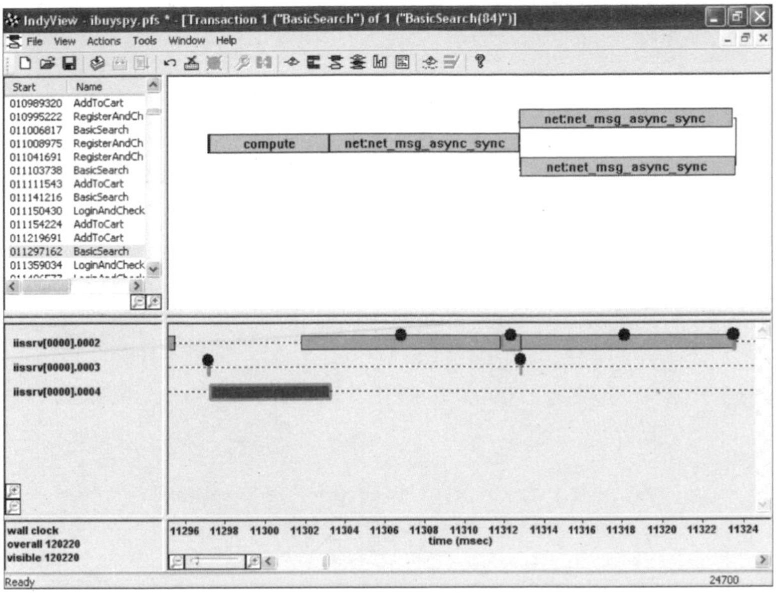

Figure 10-6   Search transaction analysis

The top half of the screen shows the control flow of a search transaction, stretched to represent the actual time of taken by each action. In addition, the panel to the left shows the start time and name of each transaction in the simulated run, allowing each of them to be examined individually.

In the lower half, the events that take place during the selected transaction are highlighted in green. The panel to the left of this section shows just the devices involved in this particular transaction: *iissrv[0000].0002* is the sending activity on the NIC that the first IIS server is connected to the Internet with; *iis-srv[0000].0003* is the receiving activity on the same; and *iissrv[0000].0004* is the first of the CPUs.

A performance engineer can use the previous views to construct and debug a performance model. Then, additional IndyView screens can be used to evaluate and analyze the performance impact of various scenarios. Figure 10-7 shows a diagram similar to that produced by the Windows monitoring tool System Monitor.

This screen shows the predicted CPU utilization for the SQL server (black line), displayed simultaneously with the utilization of the backbone network (highlighted blue line, averaging around 5 percent). For more information on performance counters, refer to Chapter 4.

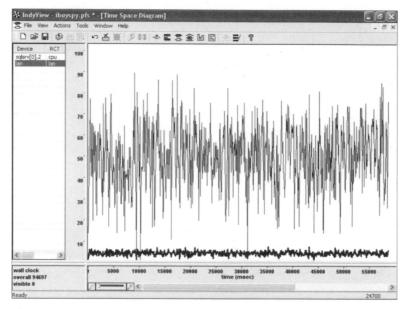

Figure 10-7 Performance counter prediction

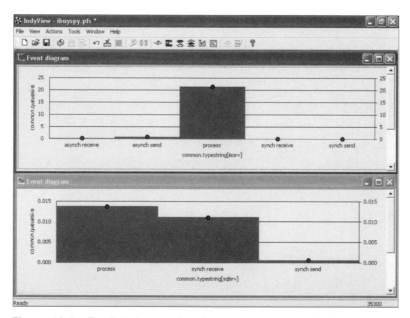

Figure 10-8 Predicted queue lengths

IndyView includes a statistics engine that allows users to examine any performance metric of the system being modeled, using either a built-in graphing tool or by exporting data to an Excel spreadsheet or a database. The two graphs in Figure 10-8 show the predicted average queue size for different event types during a sample run of IBuySpy on a particular system topology. The top graph shows event queues on the IIS server while the bottom graph shows event queues on the SQL server. Looking at the scales on the graphs, it is clear the system bottleneck of the system is the IIS processor since the average computation queue size is 21.4. By comparison, very little queuing is taking place on its NICs. The SQL server also has very small average queue sizes.

A performance engineer would typically use this view to predict possible methods of improving overall system performance. By changing the system topology script to include more processors or a set of load-balanced IIS servers, improvements in performance would immediately become visible. In addition, since the overall model takes into account the actual behavior of the other devices in the system, improving the CPU capacity of the IIS server in the model would then show the next possible bottleneck in the system's performance.

TCA vs. Performance Modeling Conclusions

In Chapter 9, we used verification tests to confirm the costs predicted by the TCA model (see Figure 9-9). For purposes of comparison, we used Indy to define a performance model of IBuySpy's concurrent user capacity, using the numbers we obtained from TCA as event costs. The results are shown here side by side:

Table 10-1   Comparing TCA and Indy Predictions

Concurrent Users	TCA Predicted Mcycles	Indy Predicted Mcycles	Measured Mcycles
1000	116.0	115.8	120.2
10000	1160.0	1166.0	1147.0
14653	1699.0	1694.0	1661.0

For this simple model, Indy accurately tracks the results of both TCA and the measurements. This shows that two completely different performance-modeling techniques, namely the analytical model of TCA, and the hybrid simulation approach of Indy, can accurately model the same system. We will now explore the areas in which Indy can extend upon the capabilities of TCA.

Building What-if Scenarios Using Indy

As we discussed earlier, one of the major advantages of performance modeling is the ability to configure each minute element of the overall client/server interaction, in order to test different scenarios before a particular configuration or code architecture is chosen. In the following examples, two key performance issues—bottleneck analysis and architectural evaluation—are evaluated using Indy.

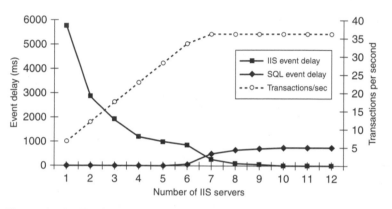

Figure 10-9   Bottleneck analysis

What-if Scenario 1: Bottleneck Analysis

Figure 10-9 shows an example of the type of bottleneck analysis possible with Indy. The graph shows the predicted performance of an e-commerce site as we change the number of Web servers. The site is being stress-tested to show the maximum achievable throughput for purchase transactions. As we would expect, increasing the number of Web servers increases the total throughput of the system in terms of purchase transactions per second. However, we reach a plateau at seven Web servers: beyond this point, adding extra Web servers does not increase the throughput of the system. When we use Indy to look at the simulated queuing delays in each of the active components, we see that the SQL server has reached saturation point. After this point the system throughput will remain the same until we increase the number of SQL servers or their performance.

Given this conclusion, further tests using this existing set of transactions could be performed to determine how much of an improvement hardware changes on the SQL servers might provide, or how many more SQL servers could feasibly be added before other elements like network performance were affected.

What-if Scenario 2: Architectural Improvements

Another feature of Indy is the ability to model how architectural changes will affect the performance of a system. For example, imagine we are running IBuySpy on an e-commerce site with only two old 450-MHz CPU Web servers with a static load-balancer. For the standard user mix we have used in this chapter, we can use Indy to determine a maximum throughput of 46.8 transactions per second. Christmas is coming, so we decide to add a third server to the mix. This is a more modern Web server with a 1-GHz CPU. Despite more than doubling the total CPU horsepower of our Web servers, Indy predicts that they will only support a maximum throughput of 53.5 transactions per second. The problem is that we are still using round-robin load balancing, so that only one-third of our transactions are benefiting from the faster CPU. If we change to using a dynamic load balancing technique that takes account of relative server load, Indy predicts our throughput will increase to 73.4 transactions per second. This type of modeling of dissimilar server types, combined with the dynamic runtime behavior of a load-balancing system, would be impossible in TCA.

Conclusion

The Indy system is just one example of an advanced performance-modeling tool. The toolkit approach, in which users can rely on an included library of hardware and network models, expands Indy's usability to include non-experts in the area of performance modeling. At the same time, the power of TML to infinitely customize objects related to one's own code and hardware makes Indy a valuable tool for very advanced software performance engineers.

In any engineering effort, the ability to predict success with certainty reduces the bottom line for both time and money, and improves the confidence of system architects and business managers alike. Using the principles discussed in this book, you should now be able to think about your own development and production processes with an eye toward how you can increase performance through careful consideration, rather than simply through trial and error.

Index

Send feedback about this index to *mspindex@microsoft.com*

Todd Kutzke

Todd Kutzke manages the Application Consulting and Engineering (ACE) Team at Microsoft. When Todd isn't writing about performance-testing Web applications, he can usually be found hanging from a rock or sailing somewhere in the Pacific Northwest. Before coming to Microsoft, Todd worked at Deloitte & Touche as a Senior Consultant and ABN-AMRO Bank as a financial analyst.

William Eric Morris

William Eric Morris performance-tests Web-based applications for the Microsoft ACE Team. Eric began his professional career in the telecommunications industry and has a passion for technology and gadgets, and a general curiosity about how things work. He has held many titles and performed many roles at various companies, from Fortune 500s to Internet start-ups, including network technical engineer, Web developer, server administrator, Webmaster, consultant, and performance analyst. Ultimately, he considers himself a creative problem solver. Eric holds a Bachelor of Science degree in Psychology from the College of William and Mary in Virginia. You can e-mail Eric at eric@07734.org.

Steve Lee

Steve Lee, MCDBA, MCSD, MCSE, and CCNA, is a database administrator for the Microsoft MSN group. He focuses on performance tuning and capacity modeling.

Brian D'Mello

Brian D'Mello is a member of the Microsoft ACE Team and does Web performance testing for Microsoft groups. He has held several positions in software testing and support at various companies, and is interested in Web programming and SQL development technologies.

Khiaw Meng (K.M.) Lee

Khiaw Meng (K.M.) Lee is a performance analyst for Microsoft. He holds a Master of Science degree in Information Systems and a Master of Business Administration degree in Marketing from Hawaii Pacific University. He enjoys swimming, kayaking, movies, and stamp collecting.

Nicolaas F. Jansen

Nicolaas F. Jansen is a performance analyst at Microsoft on the Microsoft ACE Team, and holds a Bachelor of Science degree in Computer Science. When not occupied with performance analysis, Nicolaas enjoys fly-fishing the abundant waters of the Pacific Northwest.

John Hopkins

John Hopkins is a senior performance analyst on the Microsoft ACE Team, and has several years of stress and performance testing experience. John enjoys camping and fishing with friends and family in the great outdoors of the Northwest.

Irfan A. Chaudhry

Irfan A. Chaudhry is a program manager on the Microsoft ACE Team. He is interested in performance analysis and application security. Irfan has been a contributing author to three other books: *MCSE Microsoft SQL Server 2000 Administration Readiness Review Exam 70-228* (Microsoft Press, 2001) *Microsoft Windows 2000 Performance Tuning Technical Reference* (Microsoft Press, 2000), and *Peter Norton's Complete Guide to Microsoft Windows 2000 Server* (Sams, 2000).

Tap and Die Set

You can cut and renew internal and external threads to exacting standards in metal bars or rods with a *tap and die set*. Use a tap—a round bar of hardened steel, ground square on one end and threaded on the other—to create threads inside a hole. Just fit the tap into a pilot hole in the metal piece and turn it with a special wrench. Cutting a thread on the outside of a round piece of metal is known as *die cutting*. Often made of tough carbon alloy tool steel, dies are turned around the piece to be fitted with threads with a double-handled die stock or, if none is available, even an adjustable wrench or socket. Performance testing your .NET applications lets you tap into all the power of the Web!

At Microsoft Press, we use tools to illustrate our books for software developers and IT professionals. Tools very simply and powerfully symbolize human inventiveness. They're a metaphor for people extending their capabilities, precision, and reach. From simple calipers and pliers to digital micrometers and lasers, these stylized illustrations give each book a visual identity, and a personality to the series. With tools and knowledge, there's no limit to creativity and innovation. Our tagline says it all: *the tools you need to put technology to work.*

The manuscript for this book was prepared and galleyed using Microsoft Word. Microsoft Press composed the pages using Adobe FrameMaker+SGML for Microsoft Windows, with text in Garamond and display type in Helvetica Condensed. Composed pages were delivered to the printer as electronic prepress files.

Cover Designer:	Methodologie, Inc.
Interior Graphic Designer:	James D. Kramer
Principal Compositor:	Elizabeth Hansford
Electronic Artist:	James D. Kramer
Principal Copy Editor:	Jan Bultmann
Indexer:	Hugh Maddocks

Learn how to
design, develop, and test international software *for the Windows 2000 and Windows XP platforms.*

**Developing International Software,
Second Edition**
U.S.A. $69.99
Canada $99.99
ISBN: 0-7356-1583-7

In today's global economy, there are clear advantages to developing applications that can meet the needs of users across a wide variety of languages, countries, and cultures. Discover how to develop for the whole world with the second edition of this classic guide—now revised and updated to cover the latest techniques and insights, and designed for anyone who wants to write world-ready code for the Microsoft® Windows® 2000 and Windows XP platforms. It explains how to localize applications easily and inexpensively, determine important culture-specific issues, avoid international pitfalls and legal issues, use the best technologies and coding practices, and more. DEVELOPING INTERNATIONAL SOFTWARE, SECOND EDITION covers all the essentials for developing international software—while revealing the hard-earned collective wisdom of the Microsoft international teams. A companion CD-ROM gives you an eBook containing the book's entire text, plus documentation, sample code, and tools.

microsoft.com/mspress

The complete guide to developing professional, reusable *ASP.NET* server controls and components— direct from the Microsoft ASP .NET team

Developing Microsoft® ASP.NET Server Controls and Components
U.S.A. **$59.99**
Canada $86.99
ISBN: 0-7356-1582-9

Web Forms—the page and control framework at the heart of Microsoft® ASP.NET—makes it easier to develop dynamic Web applications. But you can go beyond the controls that ship with ASP.NET—and power up your Web sites and applications—by creating your own server controls. You can also develop and distribute your own controls for commercial use. This comprehensive guide, direct from key insiders, combines conceptual and architectural details with practical, how-to information and real-world code samples to show exactly how to create custom, reusable, professional-quality server controls with rich design-time functionality. It also provides essential information about developing controls that incorporate XML Web services, configuration and the HTTP runtime, packaging, deployment, debugging, and other vital topics.

microsoft.com/mspress

Get a **Free**
e-mail newsletter, updates,
special offers, links to related books,
and more when you
register on line!

Register your Microsoft Press® title on our Web site and you'll get
a FREE subscription to our e-mail newsletter, *Microsoft Press Book
Connections*. You'll find out about newly released and upcoming books
and learning tools, online events, software downloads, special offers
and coupons for Microsoft Press customers, and information about
major Microsoft® product releases. You can also read useful additional
information about all the titles we publish, such as detailed book
descriptions, tables of contents and indexes, sample chapters, links to
related books and book series, author biographies, and reviews by other
customers.

Registration is easy. Just visit this Web page and fill in your information:

http://www.microsoft.com/mspress/register

Microsoft®

Proof of Purchase

Use this page as proof of purchase if participating in a promotion or rebate offer on
this title. Proof of purchase must be used in conjunction with other proof(s) of
payment such as your dated sales receipt—see offer details.

Performance Testing Microsoft® .NET Web Applications
0-7356-1538-1

CUSTOMER NAME

Microsoft Press, PO Box 97017, Redmond, WA 98073-9830

MICROSOFT LICENSE AGREEMENT

Book Companion CD

IMPORTANT—READ CAREFULLY: This Microsoft End-User License Agreement ("EULA") is a legal agreement between you (either an individual or an entity) and Microsoft Corporation for the Microsoft product identified above, which includes computer software and may include associated media, printed materials, and "online" or electronic documentation ("SOFTWARE PRODUCT"). Any component included within the SOFTWARE PRODUCT that is accompanied by a separate End-User License Agreement shall be governed by such agreement and not the terms set forth below. By installing, copying, or otherwise using the SOFTWARE PRODUCT, you agree to be bound by the terms of this EULA. If you do not agree to the terms of this EULA, you are not authorized to install, copy, or otherwise use the SOFTWARE PRODUCT; you may, however, return the SOFTWARE PRODUCT, along with all printed materials and other items that form a part of the Microsoft product that includes the SOFTWARE PRODUCT, to the place you obtained them for a full refund.

SOFTWARE PRODUCT LICENSE

The SOFTWARE PRODUCT is protected by United States copyright laws and international copyright treaties, as well as other intellectual property laws and treaties. The SOFTWARE PRODUCT is licensed, not sold.

1. **GRANT OF LICENSE.** This EULA grants you the following rights:

   a. **Software Product.** You may install and use one copy of the SOFTWARE PRODUCT on a single computer. The primary user of the computer on which the SOFTWARE PRODUCT is installed may make a second copy for his or her exclusive use on a portable computer.

   b. **Storage/Network Use.** You may also store or install a copy of the SOFTWARE PRODUCT on a storage device, such as a network server, used only to install or run the SOFTWARE PRODUCT on your other computers over an internal network; however, you must acquire and dedicate a license for each separate computer on which the SOFTWARE PRODUCT is installed or run from the storage device. A license for the SOFTWARE PRODUCT may not be shared or used concurrently on different computers.

   c. **License Pak.** If you have acquired this EULA in a Microsoft License Pak, you may make the number of additional copies of the computer software portion of the SOFTWARE PRODUCT authorized on the printed copy of this EULA, and you may use each copy in the manner specified above. You are also entitled to make a corresponding number of secondary copies for portable computer use as specified above.

   d. **Sample Code.** Solely with respect to portions, if any, of the SOFTWARE PRODUCT that are identified within the SOFTWARE PRODUCT as sample code (the "SAMPLE CODE"):

      i. **Use and Modification.** Microsoft grants you the right to use and modify the source code version of the SAMPLE CODE, *provided* you comply with subsection (d)(iii) below. You may not distribute the SAMPLE CODE, or any modified version of the SAMPLE CODE, in source code form.

      ii. **Redistributable Files.** Provided you comply with subsection (d)(iii) below, Microsoft grants you a nonexclusive, royalty-free right to reproduce and distribute the object code version of the SAMPLE CODE and of any modified SAMPLE CODE, other than SAMPLE CODE, or any modified version thereof, designated as not redistributable in the Readme file that forms a part of the SOFTWARE PRODUCT (the "Non-Redistributable Sample Code"). All SAMPLE CODE other than the Non-Redistributable Sample Code is collectively referred to as the "REDISTRIBUTABLES."

      iii. **Redistribution Requirements.** If you redistribute the REDISTRIBUTABLES, you agree to: (i) distribute the REDISTRIBUTABLES in object code form only in conjunction with and as a part of your software application product; (ii) not use Microsoft's name, logo, or trademarks to market your software application product; (iii) include a valid copyright notice on your software application product; (iv) indemnify, hold harmless, and defend Microsoft from and against any claims or lawsuits, including attorney's fees, that arise or result from the use or distribution of your software application product; and (v) not permit further distribution of the REDISTRIBUTABLES by your end user. Contact Microsoft for the applicable royalties due and other licensing terms for all other uses and/or distribution of the REDISTRIBUTABLES.

2. **DESCRIPTION OF OTHER RIGHTS AND LIMITATIONS.**

   - **Limitations on Reverse Engineering, Decompilation, and Disassembly.** You may not reverse engineer, decompile, or disassemble the SOFTWARE PRODUCT, except and only to the extent that such activity is expressly permitted by applicable law notwithstanding this limitation.

   - **Separation of Components.** The SOFTWARE PRODUCT is licensed as a single product. Its component parts may not be separated for use on more than one computer.

   - **Rental.** You may not rent, lease, or lend the SOFTWARE PRODUCT.

- **Support Services.** Microsoft may, but is not obligated to, provide you with support services related to the SOFTWARE PRODUCT ("Support Services"). Use of Support Services is governed by the Microsoft policies and programs described in the user manual, in "online" documentation, and/or in other Microsoft-provided materials. Any supplemental software code provided to you as part of the Support Services shall be considered part of the SOFTWARE PRODUCT and subject to the terms and conditions of this EULA. With respect to technical information you provide to Microsoft as part of the Support Services, Microsoft may use such information for its business purposes, including for product support and development. Microsoft will not utilize such technical information in a form that personally identifies you.

- **Software Transfer.** You may permanently transfer all of your rights under this EULA, provided you retain no copies, you transfer all of the SOFTWARE PRODUCT (including all component parts, the media and printed materials, any upgrades, this EULA, and, if applicable, the Certificate of Authenticity), **and** the recipient agrees to the terms of this EULA.

- **Termination.** Without prejudice to any other rights, Microsoft may terminate this EULA if you fail to comply with the terms and conditions of this EULA. In such event, you must destroy all copies of the SOFTWARE PRODUCT and all of its component parts.

3. **COPYRIGHT.** All title and copyrights in and to the SOFTWARE PRODUCT (including but not limited to any images, photographs, animations, video, audio, music, text, SAMPLE CODE, REDISTRIBUTABLES, and "applets" incorporated into the SOFTWARE PRODUCT) and any copies of the SOFTWARE PRODUCT are owned by Microsoft or its suppliers. The SOFTWARE PRODUCT is protected by copyright laws and international treaty provisions. Therefore, you must treat the SOFTWARE PRODUCT like any other copyrighted material **except** that you may install the SOFTWARE PRODUCT on a single computer provided you keep the original solely for backup or archival purposes. You may not copy the printed materials accompanying the SOFTWARE PRODUCT.

4. **U.S. GOVERNMENT RESTRICTED RIGHTS.** The SOFTWARE PRODUCT and documentation are provided with RESTRICTED RIGHTS. Use, duplication, or disclosure by the Government is subject to restrictions as set forth in subparagraph (c)(1)(ii) of the Rights in Technical Data and Computer Software clause at DFARS 252.227-7013 or subparagraphs (c)(1) and (2) of the Commercial Computer Software—Restricted Rights at 48 CFR 52.227-19, as applicable. Manufacturer is Microsoft Corporation/One Microsoft Way/Redmond, WA 98052-6399.

5. **EXPORT RESTRICTIONS.** You agree that you will not export or re-export the SOFTWARE PRODUCT, any part thereof, or any process or service that is the direct product of the SOFTWARE PRODUCT (the foregoing collectively referred to as the "Restricted Components"), to any country, person, entity, or end user subject to U.S. export restrictions. You specifically agree not to export or re-export any of the Restricted Components (i) to any country to which the U.S. has embargoed or restricted the export of goods or services, which currently include, but are not necessarily limited to, Cuba, Iran, Iraq, Libya, North Korea, Sudan, and Syria, or to any national of any such country, wherever located, who intends to transmit or transport the Restricted Components back to such country; (ii) to any end user who you know or have reason to know will utilize the Restricted Components in the design, development, or production of nuclear, chemical, or biological weapons; or (iii) to any end user who has been prohibited from participating in U.S. export transactions by any federal agency of the U.S. government. You warrant and represent that neither the BXA nor any other U.S. federal agency has suspended, revoked, or denied your export privileges.

DISCLAIMER OF WARRANTY

NO WARRANTIES OR CONDITIONS. MICROSOFT EXPRESSLY DISCLAIMS ANY WARRANTY OR CONDITION FOR THE SOFTWARE PRODUCT. THE SOFTWARE PRODUCT AND ANY RELATED DOCUMENTATION ARE PROVIDED "AS IS" WITHOUT WARRANTY OR CONDITION OF ANY KIND, EITHER EXPRESS OR IMPLIED, INCLUDING, WITHOUT LIMITA-TION, THE IMPLIED WARRANTIES OF MERCHANTABILITY, FITNESS FOR A PARTICULAR PURPOSE, OR NONINFRINGEMENT. THE ENTIRE RISK ARISING OUT OF USE OR PERFORMANCE OF THE SOFTWARE PRODUCT REMAINS WITH YOU.

LIMITATION OF LIABILITY. TO THE MAXIMUM EXTENT PERMITTED BY APPLICABLE LAW, IN NO EVENT SHALL MICROSOFT OR ITS SUPPLIERS BE LIABLE FOR ANY SPECIAL, INCIDENTAL, INDIRECT, OR CONSEQUENTIAL DAM-AGES WHATSOEVER (INCLUDING, WITHOUT LIMITATION, DAMAGES FOR LOSS OF BUSINESS PROFITS, BUSINESS INTERRUPTION, LOSS OF BUSINESS INFORMATION, OR ANY OTHER PECUNIARY LOSS) ARISING OUT OF THE USE OF OR INABILITY TO USE THE SOFTWARE PRODUCT OR THE PROVISION OF OR FAILURE TO PROVIDE SUPPORT SERVICES, EVEN IF MICROSOFT HAS BEEN ADVISED OF THE POSSIBILITY OF SUCH DAMAGES. IN ANY CASE, MICROSOFT'S ENTIRE LIABILITY UNDER ANY PROVISION OF THIS EULA SHALL BE LIMITED TO THE GREATER OF THE AMOUNT ACTUALLY PAID BY YOU FOR THE SOFTWARE PRODUCT OR US$5.00; PROVIDED, HOWEVER, IF YOU HAVE ENTERED INTO A MICROSOFT SUPPORT SERVICES AGREEMENT, MICROSOFT'S ENTIRE LIABILITY REGARDING SUPPORT SERVICES SHALL BE GOVERNED BY THE TERMS OF THAT AGREEMENT. BECAUSE SOME STATES AND JURISDICTIONS DO NOT ALLOW THE EXCLUSION OR LIMITATION OF LIABILITY, THE ABOVE LIMITATION MAY NOT APPLY TO YOU.

MISCELLANEOUS

This EULA is governed by the laws of the State of Washington USA, except and only to the extent that applicable law mandates governing law of a different jurisdiction.

Should you have any questions concerning this EULA, or if you desire to contact Microsoft for any reason, please contact the Microsoft subsidiary serving your country, or write: Microsoft Sales Information Center/One Microsoft Way/Redmond, WA 98052-6399.